Public Choice

Public Choice

Special Issue Editor

Franklin G. Mixon, Jr.

MDPI • Basel • Beijing • Wuhan • Barcelona • Belgrade

MDPI

Special Issue Editor
Franklin G. Mixon, Jr.
Columbus State University
USA

Editorial Office
MDPI
St. Alban-Anlage 66
4052 Basel, Switzerland

This is a reprint of articles from the Special Issue published online in the open access journal *Economies* (ISSN 2227-7099) from 2018 to 2019 (available at: https://www.mdpi.com/journal/economies/special_issues/Public_Choice?view=compact&listby=type)

For citation purposes, cite each article independently as indicated on the article page online and as indicated below:

LastName, A.A.; LastName, B.B.; LastName, C.C. Article Title. *Journal Name* **Year**, *Article Number*, Page Range.

ISBN 978-3-03921-271-2 (Pbk)
ISBN 978-3-03921-272-9 (PDF)

Contents

About the Special Issue Editor

Franklin G. Mixon, Jr. is a professor of economics and the director of the Center for Economic Education at Columbus State University. He is the author of more than 150 articles in academic journals and seven scholarly books, including his latest, *A Terrible Efficiency: Entrepreneurial Bureaucrats and the Nazi Holocaust*, published by Palgrave Macmillan in 2019. Prior to joining the faculty at Columbus State University, Mixon held academic posts at Auburn University and Mercer University.

economies

MDPI

Editorial
Editor's Introduction

Franklin G. Mixon Jr.

Center for Economic Education, Columbus State University, Columbus, GA 31907, USA;
mixon_franklin@columbusstate.edu

Received: 1 July 2019; Accepted: 4 July 2019; Published: 8 July 2019

Interest in politics and the political process—topics that economists consider to be the purview of the sub-field of study known as public choice—appears to be as high as ever. This edited volume, *Public Choice*, provides a collection of high-quality studies covering many of the varied topics traditionally investigated in the growing field of public choice economics. These include, but are not limited to, voting/voters, elections, constitutions, legislatures, executives, judiciaries, bureaucracy, special interest groups, parliamentary procedures, government failure, rent seeking, public finance, and international organizations. In bringing these topics together in one place, this volume offers a nice mix of conceptual/formal and empirical studies in public choice economics.

The study by J.R. Clark, of the University of Tennessee—Chattanooga, and Dwight Lee, of Southern Methodist University, re-considers the conclusions of a well-known test by Geoffrey Brennan and Loren Lomasky of instrumental voting (Brennan and Lomasky 1993), a concept indicating that as presidential elections become close, the probability of a tie, and of casting a decisive vote, increases "multi-billionfold", resulting in a large increase in voter turnout. As reported in their 25-year old study, Brennan and Lomasky failed to find a relationship between closeness and turnout in presidential elections since 1940, thus leading to their rejection of the instrumental voter hypothesis. Clark and Lee (2018) do not dispute the results of the Brennan-Lomasky test, only their arguments about the reason for the results.

Clark and Lee (2018) assert that expressive voting is the most reasonable explanation for why large-participation elections occur. As they argue, once an expressive voter has developed a political ideology that allows him or her to acquire a sense of moral virtue at little personal cost at the polls, that voter has little motivation to seek out information that might call his or her own political beliefs into question. In this regard, arguments hostile to one's political beliefs can be, and typically are, easily neutralized by confirmation bias, which is widely recognized as having a strong influence on voting decisions. According to Clark and Lee (2018), the prevalence of confirmation bias in voting runs counter to the concept of instrumental voting, given that instrumental voters should be more open to arguments indicating that their political beliefs are mistaken.

In his piece on constitutional constraints, Randall Holcombe of Florida State University points out that "the literature in constitutional economics has focused heavily on the design of effective rules to prevent the abuse of government power, and to facilitate government production that benefits the general population rather than concentrated special interests," while it "has focused less on the design of institutions that are able to effectively enforce those rules." Holcombe (2018) states that the question of enforcement begins with interpretation (e.g., laws are often intentionally vague), and includes selectivity (e.g., some laws are enforced to the benefit of enforcers) and oversight (e.g., rent-seeking and regulatory capture work to the detriment of oversight).

In describing the issues associated with interpretation, selectivity, and oversight in rules enforcement, Holcombe's study combines public choice theory with elite theory, which defines the "power elite" as those few at the top of a democratic society "who make the public policies to which everyone else is required to conform." As Holcombe (2018) points out, "[e]lite theory explains who designs and controls public policy, but it does not explain how they are able to exercise this control," while "[p]ublic choice theory explains how some are able to use the system for their benefit at the expense of others, but it does not identify who those some are . . . [Ultimately,] the elite make public policy, so one should expect that when they find themselves relatively unconstrained, public policy works to the advantage of the elite." While the power held by elites necessitates rules, problems surrounding interpretation, selectivity, and oversight lead Holcombe (2018) to conclude that checks and balances within government are essential to rules enforcement.

As Holcombe (2018) asserts, a necessary condition for checks and balances is a separation of powers, whereby the different branches of government should be designed so that they have conflicting interests, but must reach an agreement (i.e., they cannot act unilaterally) to take collective action. The system of checks and balances works, as Holcombe (2018) concludes, on "the principle that the individual branches of government guard their powers from being usurped by other branches," wherein "[t]he key feature here is that some elites check and balance the power of others."

The study by Miguel Martínez-Panero and Teresa Peña of Universidad de Valladolid, Verónica Arredondo of Universidad Autónoma de Zacatecas, and Victoriano Ramírez of Universidad de Granada takes a slightly more formal approach to the issue of electoral disproportionality, which exists when the notion of proportional representation is extended to a single legislative seat that cannot be divided between competing candidates. As a result of electoral disproportionality, some political parties are ultimately overrepresented, while others are underrepresented.

Researchers have attempted to address these distortions with disproportionality indexes, which, in many cases, are based on exact proportionality, something that is unaffordable in practice. Martínez-Panero et al. (2019) develop a new disproportionality index that entails a more realistic requirement, that "[n]o party's representation should deviate from its quota ([i.e.,] the number of seats that should be received by the parties in exact proportionality) by more than one unit." The new index measures only non-forced disproportionality (i.e., where the quota rule is not satisfied, which is usually the case), avoiding that portion of disproportionality inherent to the fact that exact proportionality is not feasible.

Another formal approach is presented by João Ricardo Faria of Florida Atlantic University and Daniel Arce of the University of Texas, Dallas in their study, motivated by the United States' recent opening of relations with Cuba under President Barack Obama's administration, on the relationship between foreign aid and freedom. More specifically, Faria and Arce (2018) present an extension of the two-period Samaritan's Dilemma game in order to analyze the potential for foreign aid to promote freedom, particularly in cases of dictatorships that might welcome economic growth but that are opposed to economic and political freedoms (i.e., the Samaritan's Dilemma).

Faria and Arce (2018) consider three different types of aid policies—one targeted on the recipient's economic performance, one coupling aid with freedom, and one targeted on the recipient's economic performance indirectly by way of pro-entrepreneurship reforms. These aid policies are combined with each of two policymaking environments—Stackelberg (leader-follower), which is most closely associated with the Samaritan's Dilemma within two-period settings, and Nash. In these contexts, Faria and Arce (2018) show that a Stackelberg policy environment that couples aid with freedom neither resolves the Samaritan's Dilemma nor fosters freedom, while a Nash policy environment that couples aid with freedom resolves the Samaritan's Dilemma but it does not commensurately increase freedoms within the recipient nation. Their final consideration—Nash play (representing donor commitment) and an explicitly freedom-based policy—succeeds at resolving both the Samaritan's Dilemma and increasing freedoms, provided that the donor tempers its altruistic motivation for supporting the recipient, especially in cases where the recipient is willing to test the donor's resolve.

The study by Raúl Pérez-Fernández and Bernard De Baets of Ghent University, and José Luis García-Lapresta of Universidad de Valladolid provides a bridge from the conceptual and more formal pieces in this volume to the empirical public choice studies included herein. These researchers analyze the 2017 Rector election at Ghent University, which covered 59 days between the first round of voting and the final round of voting. This study begins with a discussion of the differences between simple majority, the closely related concept of absolute majority, and other forms of qualified majority, such as unanimous majority. Among other regulatory features, the Ghent University Rector elections rely on a supermajority of two-thirds of the vote for a winner (or winning duo) to be declared. The Rector elections, described by Pérez-Fernández et al. (2019), are set to go no more than five rounds without declaring a winner, in which case the elections are restarted.

Pérez-Fernández et al. (2019) provide some solutions to the lengthy situation that occurred at Ghent University. One is a multi-stage process, wherein something slightly greater than a simple majority (e.g., 52%) determines the outcome in the first stage, and in the second stage the process implements the two-thirds supermajority. As they point out, such a procedure "will ... 'guarantee' ... a winner being selected after some voting rounds, while not electing a candidate that has just one more vote than its adversary." These researchers also suggest that "a more elegant solution would require ... totally reformulat[ing] the semantics of the election in an approval-voting fashion." Pérez-Pérez-Fernández et al. (2019) ultimately favor a process referred to as "majority judgment," which is based on what they state is "a common language of ... labels in a linearly ordered scale [that] needs to be agreed upon, [a]fter [which] each of the voters is required to evaluate each of the candidates independently according to this common language of [labels ... which] are ordered in an increasing manner." As they conclude, this process is easy for voters to understand and avoids other issues, such as irrelevant alternatives and voting cycles.

The empirical studies contained in this volume include my own piece on the stability of political ideology with Chandini Sankaran of Boston College and Kamal Upadhyaya of the University of New Haven. Our study extends the political science and political psychology literature on the political ideology of lawmakers by employing Nokken-Poole scores (Nokken and Poole 2004) of legislators' political ideology for members of the U.S. House of Representatives and the U.S. Senate who were elected prior to the 103rd Congress that began in early 1991 and who served consecutively through the 115th Congress, which ended in early 2019. These unidimensional policy scores assume that each Congress is entirely separate in terms of a legislator's political ideology, and they allow for movement of legislators along the unidimensional policy space from Congress to Congress.

As we indicate in the study (Mixon et al. 2019), our empirical investigation of the stability of political ideology of lawmakers is two-pronged. First, we investigate the political instability at the individual level by collecting both the largest and smallest Nokken-Poole scores over each U.S. Representative's legislative career. These are used to compute the absolute deviation in political ideology (over time) for each lawmaker, where smaller (larger) values represent greater stability (instability) of political ideology. An alternative approach to investigating the stability of political ideology of lawmakers relies on regression analysis, employing a legislator's Nokken-Poole scores. The results in Mixon et al. (2019) suggest that political ideology is unstable over time for a sizable portion of the long-serving members of both major political parties in the U.S. Congress. These results run somewhat counter to the finding in prior studies that the political ideologies of lawmakers and other political elites are stable over time.

An empirical study by Jessi Troyan of the Cardinal Institute for West Virginia Policy and Joshua Hall of West Virginia University explores the specific factors that determine federal spending on environmental goods, and whether severity of the hazard is the only metric of consideration, or if other factors play an important role in explaining spending. These issues are explored within the context of the Abandoned Mine Land Fund (AMLF) program in the U.S., a fund created as a feature of the *Surface Mining Control and Reclamation Act of 1977*. As they indicate, "this analytical setting is interesting because of the limited scope of program objectives and the rigidly defined funding source ... [, which] ... suggests that the execution of abandoned mine reclamation projects facilitated by the fund should be difficult to influence politically."

Troyan and Hall (2019) explore whether political factors, such as environmental interest group influence, legislator preferences and pressures to fund sites in their home states or districts, and environmental and health factors, play an explanatory role in disbursement of AMLF monies. Analysis of some relatively large data sets suggests that funding for abandoned mine reclamation is a mixture of the products of public and political interests, particularly regarding tenure on the Senate Appropriations Committee and state-ownership of lands, and whether the AMLF coffers are supported by the U.S. Treasury Department. They find that "after the allocations out of Treasury funds are capped to states, the political influence wanes and the hazard level of sites again becomes the primary influential factor in funding receipts—further bolstering a public interest view of the AML program in total." As Troyan and Hall (2019) conclude, this result supports the notion that political institutions can be changed to remove politics.

As Zachary Klingensmith of Pennsylvania State University—Erie explains in the introduction of his study, "targeted [government] expenditures, which are also called pork-barrel spending, allow incumbents to both *credit claim* and *advertise* simultaneously through three channels." Klingensmith (2019) is primarily concerned with the third of these channels, which is whether an incumbent can use pork-barrel spending to increase his or her ability to advertise through campaign contributions. His study extends the literature on on pork-barrel spending and campaign contributions, mainly by investigating whether the timing of the pork-barrel appropriations matter, and whether general federal appropriations have the same impact on fundraising as pork-barrel spending.

In order to investigate these issues, Klingensmith (2019) focuses on United States Senate elections from 2004 to 2018, rather than a single election. The results of his analyses indicate that (1) "pork-barrel spending can have a positive and significant impact on fundraising," (2) "the timing of the pork-barrel spending matters[, with] . . . only pork-barrel spending in the election year . . . hav[ing] an impact on campaign contributions," and (3) "the relationship between federal aid to states and incumbent fundraising is ambiguous[, although] . . . it is clear that the amount of fundraising per dollar of pork-barrel spending is far greater than the amount of fundraising per dollar of federal aid." The overall conclusion from Klingensmith's study is "that pork-barrel spending is used as a source of political capital for both politicians and political entrepreneurs."

Candon Johnson and Joshua Hall of West Virginia University point out that the sports economics literature has generally found that new professional sport facilities do not generate any new net economic activity. Their study "provide[s] context to this literature by exploring the public choice in the public financing of stadiums," with particular attention to the two 2016 ballot measures related to the San Diego Chargers (NFL franchise). More specifically, Johnson and Hall (2019) analyze voting on two ballot measures that would, respectively, allow officials to raise hotel taxes to pay for a new downtown stadium for the Chargers, and allow officials to raise hotel taxes, but would also explicitly prevent any money being spent on the Chargers. Neither of these ballot measures received 50% of the total votes cast.

The results of their empirical analyses indicate that populations in "zip codes with a higher voter turnout were more likely to vote against both measures, highlighting the importance of the timing of referenda in limiting the ability of clearly defined groups, such as Chargers fans, to have a large influence on the voting outcome," and that "areas with more Trump voters were more likely to support higher taxes for the purpose of building the Chargers a new stadium." With regard to this latter finding, Johnson and Hall (2019) state that the "results suggest that Trump voters were against tax increases for these public projects; but, if taxes were going to be raised, they wanted the Chargers to be part of the deal."

Finally, my study (Mixon 2018) on the 2017 U.S. Senate Special Election in Alabama extends the public choice literature on localism (i.e., "friends and neighbors") in voting, which occurs as a way of mitigating the agency costs of representative democracy, by investigating the impact on localism of political scandal. Prior literature in this genre places the home area advantage, or the advantage to local candidates, somewhere between 2.4 and 12.4 percentage points, with the most common estimate residing near five percentage points. The Republican candidate in this election, Roy Moore, gained notoriety during the 2017 campaign when a number of women alleged to national media that as

Economies **2019**, *7*, 69

teenagers they were subject to sexual advances by Moore, who was then in his early 30s and serving as a local assistant district attorney.

Econometric results presented in Mixon (2018) suggest that a candidate who is embroiled in political scandal suffers an erosion in the usual friends-and-neighbors effect on his or her local vote share in a general election. In this particular case, the scandal hanging over Moore, who lost the election contest to Democratic candidate Doug Jones, eroded all of the friends-and-neighbors effect that would have been expected (i.e., about five percentage points) in Moore's home county, as well as about 40% of the advantage Moore had at home over his opponent in terms of constituent political ideology. As the study concludes, "the exploration of the impact of political scandal on friends-and-neighbors voting undertaken in this study indicates that, this genre of the public choice literature is perhaps under-theorized, thus, opening up avenues for future research."

Funding: This research received no external funding.

Conflicts of Interest: The author declares no conflict of interest.

References

Brennan, Geoffrey, and Loren Lomasky. 1993. *Democracy & Decision: The Pure Theory of Electoral Preference.* Cambridge: Cambridge University Press.

Clark, Jeff R., and Dwight R. Lee. 2018. The Brennan-Lomasky Test of Expressive Voting: When Impressive Probability Differences are Meaningless. *Economies* 6: 51. [CrossRef]

Faria, Joao Ricardo, and Daniel Arce. 2018. On the Samaritan's Dilemma, Foreign Aid, and Freedom. *Economies* 6: 53. [CrossRef]

Holcombe, Randall G. 2018. Checks and Balances: Enforcing Constitutional Constraints. *Economies* 6: 57. [CrossRef]

Johnson, Candon, and Joshua Hall. 2019. The Public Choice of Public Stadium Financing: Evidence from San Diego Referenda. *Economies* 7: 22. [CrossRef]

Klingensmith, J. Zachary. 2019. Political Entrepreneurs and Pork-Barrel Spending. *Economies* 7: 16. [CrossRef]

Martínez-Panero, Miguel, Verónica Arredondo, Teresa Peña, and Victoriano Ramírez. 2019. A New Quota Approach to Electoral Disproportionality. *Economies* 7: 17. [CrossRef]

Mixon, Franklin G., Jr. 2018. Glass Houses and Friends-and-Neighbors Voting: An Exploratory Analysis of the Impact of Political Scandal on Localism. *Economies* 6: 48. [CrossRef]

Mixon, Franklin G., Jr., Chandini Sankaran, and Kamal P. Upadhyaya. 2019. Is Political Ideology Stable? Evidence from Long-Serving Members of the United States Congress. *Economies* 7: 36. [CrossRef]

Nokken, Timothy P., and Keith T. Poole. 2004. Congressional Party Defection in American History. *Legislative Studies Quarterly* 29: 545–69. [CrossRef]

Pérez-Fernández, Raúl, José Luis García-Lapresta, and Bernard De Baets. 2019. Chronicle of a Failure Foretold: 2017 Rector Election at Ghent University. *Economies* 7: 2. [CrossRef]

Troyan, Jessi, and Joshua Hall. 2019. The Political Economy of Abandoned Mine Land Fund Disbursements. *Economies* 7: 3. [CrossRef]

economies

MDPI

Article

The Brennan–Lomasky Test of Expressive Voting: When Impressive Probability Differences Are Meaningless

J. R. Clark [1,*] and Dwight R. Lee [2]

[1]   Probasco Distinguished Chair, The University of Tennessee at Chattanooga, Chattanooga, TN 37403, USA
[2]   O'Neil Center, Southern Methodist University, Dallas, TX 75275, USA; dwightl@uga.edu
*   Correspondence: probasco@utc.edu; Tel.: +1-423-425-4118

Received: 27 July 2018; Accepted: 13 September 2018; Published: 19 September 2018

Abstract: We consider a test of expressive voting developed by Brennan and Lomasky (1993). They point out that in presidential elections the probability of a tie, and casting a decisive vote, increases "multi-billionfold" as the election becomes increasingly close. They conjecture that if voters are instrumentally motivated there would be enormous increases in voter turnout for presidential elections as they became close. When they find no consistent relationship between closeness and turnout in presidential elections since 1940, they conclude their test justifies a "decisive rejection of the instrumental voter hypothesis." As dramatic as such a "multi-billionfold" increase is, we argue it would not motivate voting if an instrumental payoff was the only motivation for doing so. The Brennan–Lomasky test does give the correct result, but not for the reason they emphasize. They do see reasons why voting turnout would be moderated other than the dramatic probability of a decisive vote in close elections. Furthermore, they close their test by indicating that one reason turnout might be higher in close elections is that they are more interesting, which is congenial to an expressive account. We agree. We also argue that the observed tendency for voters to confirm their biases rather than change their minds provides additional support for expressive voting.

Keywords: expressive voting; instrumental voting; voter turnout; rational voter apathy; rational ignorance; confirmation bias

JEL Classification: D70; D72; H00

1. Introduction

Models based on expressive voting have yielded interesting results, implying support for such things as charitable policies by uncharitable voters (Tullock 1971) and brutal policies by decent voters (Lee and Murphy 2017). This represents a range of voter support difficult to imagine if voters were motivated solely by instrumental considerations, but intuitively plausible if voters are motivated by expressive considerations. The implications of expressive voting models not only are interesting, but also are consistent with common voting behavior that is both heartening and troubling. Yet, attempts to test whether voting decisions are influenced primarily by expressive motivations under conditions (very low probability of a tied election) which imply that those motivations would dominate instrumental motivations have been less than convincing.

The most popular approach for testing the explanatory power of expressive voting has been based on evidence provided by laboratory experiments. A paper by Tyran and Wagner (2016) indicates that the evidence favoring expressive voting is mixed. Of the nine papers they examine, two support the expressive voting theory, three provide weak support, and four provide no support at all. Tyran and Wagner (2016, p. 15) see the mixed findings to be "found in limitations of the experiment paradigms and techniques that have been used to identify expressive voting."

We believe that stronger support exists for expressive motivations being the overwhelming, indeed sole, impetus for going to the polls in which many millions are expected to turnout. That support can be highlighted by a critical examination of a test of expressive voting put forth by Brennan and Lomasky (1993, pp. 117–20) in their widely cited book. Their test is based on the logic of expressive voting coupled with observations on the connection between the closeness of U.S. presidential elections and voter turnout. Based on that test, Brennan and Lomasky reject the instrumental voter hypothesis. Our examination of their test leads us to conclude that it always yields the correct conclusion even though the central rationale for the test is flawed.

2. An Impressive but Meaningless Difference

Brennan and Lomasky (1993, pp. 117–20) test of the expressive voter model is grounded in an unquestionable mathematical result that leads to a testable conjecture. The unquestionable mathematical result is that the probability of a tied election rises dramatically ("multi-billionfold") as it becomes increasingly close. That result obviously implies that the instrumental payoff to voting increases by the same "multi-billion fold" amount as the election becomes increasingly close. Their conjecture is that "[i]f voting is *solely* instrumental, then one would expect enormous changes in turnout with quite small changes in expected closeness" (p. 118; emphasis in original). The conjecture is easily tested with evidence from presidential elections, and clearly found to be incorrect.[1] Thus, they state: "In our view, the fact that increases in expected closeness do not have a spectacular positive effect on voter turnout comes as close as one can in this muddy life to a decisive rejection of the instrumental voter hypothesis."[2] (p. 119)

Interestingly, Brennan and Lomasky did not expect enormous changes in turnout. Leading up to and after discussing their test, they point to other reasons why large turnout increases should not be expected in very close elections. For example, only those prospective voters "on the margin of participation" (p. 118) would be affected by an increase in the probability of a tied election. Yet they continue to emphasize that "even if the expected difference is one-tenth of the actual—the probability of being decisive in the close election would have been many billions of times greater than in the non-close ones, and the expected corresponding benefit correspondingly so" (pp. 119–20). We find their emphasis on the startling increase in the probability of a tie as elections become close to be a misleading distraction to their case for expressive voting despite the accuracy of the math.

The problem with the Brennan and Lomasky emphasis on the multi-billionfold increase in the instrumental payoff is that such an increase would create, at most, a miniscule incentive for an instrumentally motivated potential voter to become an actual voter. Before explaining why, it helps to consider the approximate sizes of the probabilities being discussed, assuming an election with 100 million voters, roughly the turnouts of recent U.S. presidential elections. Let P_T be the probability of a tied election by assuming that every voter is equally likely to vote for either one of two candidates.

---

[1]   We follow Brennan and Lomasky in assuming a presidential election with 100 million and one voters casting a vote for one of two candidates with the winner winning by one vote. So, the probability of a decisive vote (really 50 million and one decisive votes) is equal to the probability of a tied vote without one of the votes for the winner. Obviously, this ignores the complications created by the electoral college which creates the possibility of a higher probability of decisive votes being cast by one-half plus one of the voters in a small state in which the election is known to be extremely close and turns to be a swing state. This higher probability would have to be multiplied by the probability of the small state have more electoral college votes than the difference in those votes from the other states. Of course, a very large state, such as California is likely to be a swing state, but it is extremely unlikely that its presidential votes are decided by one vote. We would like to thank an unknown referee for mentioning the electoral college complication.

[2]   Brennan and Lomasky follow this comment by stating "[n]or does one need 'elaborate statistical technique" to make this point'" (p. 119). We agree that "elaborate statistical technique" is not needed since, as we are about to argue, potential voters motivated by instrumental interests would remain nonvoters in a presidential election no matter how close it is expected to be.

And let P_C be the probability of a tied election when every voter is slightly more likely to vote for the favored candidate than for the other candidate. In that case P_T is closely approximated by 0.00008 percent, or 8 one hundred thousandths of one percent. To approximate the value of P_C, we assume that each voter votes for the favored candidate with a probability of 51%, which means P_C effectively is $1/\infty$, or 0.[3]

The relative difference in these two probabilities, and in the instrumental payoffs in the two elections just described, are clearly as dramatic as Brennan and Lomasky claim, with the ratio P_T/P_C being effectively infinite. But dramatic relative differences can be completely irrelevant to practical decision making.[4] A more salient way to look at the differences in the two probabilities is as the ratio of the probabilities that an individual vote will be indecisive in the two elections just considered, or $(1 - P_T)/(1 - P_C)$. The ratio of these probabilities is (1–0.00008)/1, or 0.99992. As practical advice to a voter, rationally ignorant or otherwise, it would be more helpful to say that the probability of casting an indecisive vote is effectively 1 in both of the presidential elections than to say that the probability of casting a decisive vote is many billions of times greater in the former than in the latter election.

As far as the effect of the probability differences on the turnout of instrumental voters, the same advice—"it doesn't make any difference"—is still sound. Certainly, no instrumentally motivated voter who is not voting when the probability of casting a decisive vote is $1/\infty$ is going to rush to the polls to take advantage of a *marginal* increase in the probability of casting a decisive vote, even if the marginal increase is multi-billions of times larger than the probability $1/\infty$. This suggests that when Brennan and Lomasky tell us that only those "on the margin of participation" (p. 118) would be affected by the increase in the expected probability of a tied election, they are effectively referring to all would-be instrumentally motivated voters, since none of them will be voting before the expected closeness occurs, not just the few they lead us to believe they are talking about. And those voters will still be marginal, or inactive, instrumental voters after the multi-billionfold increase in the probability of a tie.

But wait. If you still have doubts about the instrumental impotence of the multi-billionfold probability increase from P_C to P_T, there is more. Even though Brennan and Lomasky concentrate on the influence of changing probabilities of tied elections, they do mention the costs of voting, which include things like the opportunity costs of registering to vote, going to polls, waiting in line and possibly, though unlikely, giving serious thought to the candidates and their policy positions. They do point out that these costs have more negative influence on voter turnout than the positive influence of dramatic relative increases in the probability of a tied election, at least in part because those costs affect the decisions of both instrumental and expressive voters. But they do not include them in their test. Yet, voting costs make it even more obvious that the dramatic increases in the probability of a tied election Brennan and Lomasky are considering are highly unlikely to turn dormant instrumental voters into active instrumental voters. For example, assume that the opportunity cost of voting in a presidential election is $20, a modest amount given that high-opportunity-cost people are more likely to vote than low-opportunity-cost people. If instrumental voters are aware that the probability of a tie has increased to 0.00008, then it would require an instrumental payoff of $250,000 from casting a decisive vote to expect to cover the cost of voting. Even if a voter overestimated the probability of casting a decisive vote by a factor of 100, it would require an instrumental payoff of $2500 from casting

---

[3]   The probabilities of a tied election with 100 million voters are derived from Brennan and Lomasky (1993, p. 57, Table 4.1). The table gives several differences in the probability that each voter will vote for one of two candidates or policies, with the first being 0, meaning a 0.5 probability for each, and the last being 0.01, meaning a 0.51 probability for the favorite and a 0.49 probability for the other. The column below each probability is the dollar payoff from casting a decisive vote that would be required to give the voter an expected return of one dollar, given the number of voters shown in the far-left hand column. Those numbers go from 101 to 100 million. We made use of the 0 and 0.01 columns and the 100 million voters row. At the 100 million, 0 coordinate is 12,500 which implies the probability of a tied election is 1/(12,500) or 0.00008. For the 100 million, 0.01 coordinate is ∞, which implies a probability of a tied election of effectively 0.

[4]   Consider space travel. The MACSO647-JD galaxy is about 13.3 billion light years from earth, but the instrumental payoff from sending a space probe there is indistinguishable from sending one to the Andromeda X1 galaxy, which is only 2.4 million light years from earth.

a decisive vote to cover the cost of voting.[5] On the other hand, it is easy to imagine an expressive voter receiving, with a probability of 1, enough expressive satisfaction from voting to comfortably exceed the $20 cost of voting.

Again, we see Brennan and Lomasky's focus on the effect of close elections or probabilities of tied elections as a misleading distraction in their case for expressive voting. In other words, the effect of large relative increases in miniscule probabilities of a tied election on voter turnout is miniscule.

We believe that if there is a tendency for increased voter turnout when elections are close, it is the result of expressive voters responding to the additional attention close elections receive, not of instrumental voters responding to the dramatic increases in the probability of a tied vote as elections become close. Brennan and Lomasky's test will always be correct by seeing small increase, or no increases at all, as justifying the rejection of the instrumental voter hypothesis, but for the wrong reason.

It is not even clear that Brennan and Lomasky will disagree with our criticism. As they say in concluding the discussion of their test:

> Close contests in the sporting arena are more engaging and induce more spectator interest than clear-cut contests. Given the analogy between voter and spectator behavior, it would surely not be implausible if closer contests induced more involvement in the electoral setting as well. In that sense, some small connection between closeness and turnout of the kind that empirical work seems to reveal (or at least does not reject) is quite congenial to the expressive account. (p. 120)

3. Conclusions

The concepts of rational voter apathy, rational voter ignorance and expressive voting are all based on the small probability that an individual's vote will be decisive, at least in large-participation elections. As far as we know, there has been little controversy about the influence of instrumental or expressive motivations of voters on the validity of rational voter apathy or ignorance.

Downs (1957, p. 48) clearly assumes instrumental voting when stating that "[a] rational voter first decides what party will benefit him the most . . . [but] even if he prefers party A, he is wasting his vote on A, if it has no chance of winning . . . the relevant choice in this case is between B and C. Since a vote for A is not useful in the actual process of selection, casting it is irrational." There is no indication of an expressive benefit here.[6] When considering voter apathy, or abstaining (p. 265) Downs points out that "voting is inherently costly . . . [and] since the returns to voting are often miniscule, even low voting cost may cause many partisan citizens to abstain." In considering rational apathy, or what they call "rational abstention," Brennan and Lomasky (1993, pp. 65–66) see "[t]he general thrust of the public choice literature on the turnout issue is to argue that the probability of being decisive is nothing like large enough to explain turnouts that are observed without appealing to something other than instrumental returns." (p. 66). They then consider Nash equilibrium models that attempt to show how "substantial voter turnout may occur in a totally instrumental, outcome-oriented polity" (p. 66). While Brennan and Lomasky "do not deny that some equilibria of this kind may exist in some cases—[they] believe the prospect unlikely. What [they] do deny is that the resulting equilibria much

---

[5] People commonly respond to the argument that a vote is unlikely to make any difference in the outcome of an election by pointing to close elections, such as the Florida presidential election in 2000. But the final official count had a 537-vote difference between Bush and Gore. So, one more vote for Bush would have made no difference. But this does not mean that people cannot convince themselves that their vote is far more likely to be decisive than it is. Findings by Kahneman and Tversky, and reported in Kahneman (2011, p. 315–16), indicate that voters tend to respond to probabilities less than 1 as if they were zero. Yet, if a highly improbably event becomes the focus of attention, like a terrorist attack, the probability of it occurring can be perceived as far greater than it is. Whether this means that some people really believe their vote in a presidential election is likely to be decisive seems to us to be pushing rational voter ignorance a little too far.

[6] Downs (1957, p. 46) does say "[t]hat to decide what impact each government act has upon his [the voter's] income, he appraises it as good or bad in light of his own view of 'the good society'." And it appears he is referring here to "hypothetical streams of utility income." Yet this "income" does not seem to help offset the cost of voting when deciding to vote or not to vote in Down's discussion.

resemble those we observe in electoral practice" (p. 69). What all this seems to say in a qualified way is that expressive voting is the most reasonable explanation for why voting turnouts in large-participation elections are anywhere near as high as they are.

The empirical evidence is overwhelming that a large percentage of voters in large-participation elections lack such basic information on the political process as who their political representatives are, the position of those representatives on important issues, or the pros and cons of the different positions.[7] None of this evidence on rational voter ignorance depends on whether voters are motivated by instrumental or expressive interests. One might argue, along the lines of Brennan and Lomasky, that if the dominant reason for voting is instrumental then a dramatic increase in the probability of a tied election, and therefore of a decisive vote, would not only motivate an increase in voter turnout, but also the average voter's being more informed politically to better evaluate the relative instrumental payoffs from alternative voting decisions. We know of no attempt to use this logic, along with possible reductions in voter ignorance as elections got close, to conduct a test of the instrumental voter hypothesis. There are two reasons why we would not expect such a test to be attempted. First, as we have argued in this paper, even the most dramatic increase in the probability of a tie in the large-participation elections being considered would have little, if any, effect on either voter turnout of instrumental voters, or on their desire to become more informed politically. Second, it is much easier to measure changes in voter turnout than to measure how the political ignorance of the average voter changes as the probability of tied elections increases.

Interestingly, if instrumental voters exist and could be identified, we would expect them to be more informed politically on average than voters motivated solely by expressive satisfaction for a reason having nothing to do with the probability of tied elections. The return received by an expressive voter depends entirely on how good he feels about voting for something or someone he believes to be worthy of the support of decent people like himself, such as those he identifies with as friends, associates, and role models. Such beliefs might result from serious study of complicated issues, but often they develop from the tendency to be in agreement with the views that prevail in one's social group, agreement which serves one's interest in becoming or remaining an accepted member of that group. The satisfaction one gets from such beliefs as a voter and a member of a like-minded group depends far more on retaining the prevailing beliefs of one's ideological tribe than it does on their accuracy.[8] So, once an expressive voter has developed a political ideology that allows him to acquire a sense of moral virtue at little personal cost at the polls, and to enjoy the political comradery of his ideological fellow travelers, he has little motivation to seek out information that might call his political beliefs into question. Of course, arguments hostile to one's political beliefs cannot be completely avoided, but they can be, and typically are, easily neutralized with confirmation bias. If most voters voted instrumentally because they believed their vote was likely to be decisive, they would be more open to arguments indicating that their political beliefs are mistaken. The fact that confirmation bias is recognized as a strong influence on voting decisions is further evidence that voting is primarily motivated by expressive instead of instrumental interests.[9]

This short paper should not be thought of as a criticism of Brennan and Lomasky's impressive book, *Democracy & Decision*. It is the seminal work on expressive voting, containing 225 pages of insights on the theory and applications of one of the key contributions of public choice to voting. Our paper considers only four of those pages to argue that the dramatic increase in the probability of a tie in a large-participation election is far less important to their rejection of the instrumental voter hypothesis than they seem to indicate. We believe that our argument adds insight into the theory of expressive voting and that Brennan and Lomasky will agree. We hope so.

---

[7] See Somin (2016, chp. 1).
[8] See Mason (2018). The entire book is relevant to this discussion, but particularly Chapter 1.
[9] See Nickerson (2016).

Economies **2018**, *6*, 51

Author Contributions: J.R.C. and D.R.L. collaborated on previous published research in expressive voting from which this application of the Brennan–Lomasky Test grows. D.R.L. wrote preliminary draft of the current article while J.R.C. edited drafts, submitted the article for review, and proofed final copy.

Funding: This research received no external funding.

Conflicts of Interest: The authors declare no conflict of interest.

References

Brennan, Geoffrey, and Loren Lomasky. 1993. *Democracy & Decision: The Pure Theory of Electoral Preference*. Cambridge: Cambridge University Press.

Downs, Anthony. 1957. *An Economic Theory of Democracy*. New York: Harper and Row.

Kahneman, Daniel. 2011. *Thinking, Fast and Slow*. New York: Farrar, Straus and Giroux.

Lee, Dwight R., and Ryan H. Murphy. 2017. An expressive voting model of anger, hatred, harm and shame. *Public Choice* 173: 307–23. [CrossRef]

Mason, Lilliana. 2018. *Uncivil Agreement: How Politics Becomes Our Identity*. Chicago: The University of Chicago Press.

Nickerson, Ray. 2016. Confirmation bias: A psychological phenomenon that helps explain why pundits got it wrong. *The Conversation*. November 21. Available online: http://theconversation.com/confirmation-bias-a-psychological-phenomenon-that-helps-explain-why-pundits-got-it-wrong-68781 (accessed on 17 September 2018).

Somin, Ilya. 2016. *Democracy and Political Ignorance: Why Smaller Government Is Smarter*. Stanford: Stanford University Press.

Tullock, Gordon. 1971. The charity of the uncharitable. *Western Economic Journal* 9: 379–92.

Tyran, Jean-Robert, and Alexander K. Wagner. 2016. Experimental evidence on expressive Voting. In *The Oxford Handbook of Public Choice*. Edited by Roger D. Congleton, Bernard N. Grofman and Stefan Voigt. Oxford: Oxford University Press, Available online: https://papers.ssrn.com/sol3/papers.cfm?abstract_id=2867954 (accessed on 17 September 2018).

economies   MDPI

Article

Checks and Balances: Enforcing Constitutional Constraints

Randall G. Holcombe

Department of Economics, Florida State University, Tallahassee, FL 32306, USA; holcombe@fsu.edu

Received: 28 August 2018; Accepted: 19 October 2018; Published: 24 October 2018

Abstract: Constitutional political economy has focused heavily on designing constitutional rules sufficient to constrain governmental power. More attention has been devoted to designing rules that are effective constraints than on the institutions that would be required to enforce them. One problem is that rules are interpreted and enforced by the political elite, who tend to interpret and enforce them in ways that favor their interests over those of the masses. Democratic oversight is ineffective because voters realize they have no influence over public policy, and are therefore rationally ignorant. A system of checks and balances within government is necessary for enforcing constitutional constraints because it divides power among elites with competing interests and enables one group of elites to check the power of others. Checks and balances within governmental institutions are necessary to constrain the government from abusing its power.

Keywords: constitutional constraints; checks and balances; political elite; democratic oversight

JEL Classification: H11

1. Introduction

Buchanan (1975, pp. 2–3, _italics in original_) discusses the distinguishing feature of constitutional economics. "In ordinary or orthodox economics, no matter how simple or how complex, analysis is concentrated on choices made _within_ constraints that are, themselves, imposed exogenously to the person or persons charged with making the choice. Constitutional economics directs analytical attention to the _choice among constraints_". North (1991, p. 97) says "Institutions are the humanly devised constraints that structure political, economic, and social interaction". Constitutional economics, following Buchanan and North, studies the choice among institutions—the choice among humanly devised constraints. The literature in constitutional economics has focused heavily on the design of effective rules to prevent the abuse of government power, and to facilitate government production that benefits the general population rather than concentrated special interests. It has focused less on the design of institutions that are able to effectively enforce those rules. This paper explains why checks and balances are essential as a constitutional enforcement mechanism.

2. Constitutional Rules

Much of the work in constitutional economics focuses on the process by which citizens choose constitutional rules, with a heavy emphasis on consensus among those who are governed by them. The literature draws a parallel between market exchange, in which all parties to transactions agree and thereby signal that they benefit from their exchanges, and political exchange, in which people cooperate to collectively produce goods and services that they would not be able to produce by themselves or through bilateral exchange. Maintaining that parallel construction, the political decision rule that signifies everyone agrees is unanimity. Just as all parties to market transactions voluntarily agree to them, unanimous agreement is the signal that all parties to political exchange are in agreement.

The constitutional framework pioneered by Buchanan and Tullock (1962) and Buchanan (1975) explains that for governmental activity to benefit everybody, agreement is required on the rules under which people interact, but not generally on every action government takes. For example, people might all agree that they benefit from paying taxes to finance roads, and might agree to delegate the decision of where to build those roads to some governmental authority. In some cases, citizens might be made worse off by the building (and financing) of some specific roads, but they would all agree they are better off with the government-financed roads than they would be without them. In keeping with the analogy to market exchange, optimal rules are rules to which everybody would agree.

Most of the literature in constitutional economics has dealt with the process by which constitutional rules are designed, and the types of rules that would result from those processes. There are many interesting and unresolved issues in this literature, which this paper bypasses. Assuming that a desirable set of constitutional rules has been put into place, how can those rules be enforced? The question of enforcement starts with interpretation. In a complex world, words can be interpreted in different ways. An easy way to see that is to note that slightly more than half of United States Supreme Court cases have been decided unanimously, which means that in nearly half of those cases, legal experts—the Justices themselves—were in disagreement about how the law applies to specific cases.

Schweizer (2013) says that laws are written to be deliberately ambiguous, for several reasons. One reason is that ambiguous laws can be selectively enforced. Those who exercise political power can use ambiguous laws to go after adversaries but to give allies a pass. Another is that those who write ambiguous laws become experts on their intent and interpretation, allowing them to sell their services to those who might be subject to enforcement.

Ambiguities in interpretation point to a second issue: Selective enforcement. Selective enforcement allows laws to be enforced for the benefit of the enforcers and to the detriment of others who are in an adversarial position to the enforcers, or are not being as cooperative as the enforcers would prefer.[1] Factors like these have not been addressed in the constitutional political economy literature, which has for the most part assumed that rules are unambiguous and objectively applied.[2]

To the extent that enforcement issues have been considered, the primary mechanism that appears in the public choice literature is democratic oversight of government actions. While voting models tend to point toward public policy being determined by the preferences of the electorate—in particular, models like the median voter model explained by Downs (1957)—the conclusion of much of the public choice literature is that democratic oversight is likely to be ineffective for a number of reasons. Rent-seeking (Tullock 1967; Krueger 1974), regulatory capture (Stigler 1971), and the undue influence of special interests (Olson 1965) all weigh against the idea that democratic oversight is an effective check on the abuse of government power. Meanwhile, checks and balances within government institutions have been underappreciated in the literature as an enforcement mechanism. To see why democratic oversight is likely to be ineffective, and why checks and balances within government are essential, the first step is to undertake a critical examination of the process by which public policy is made and carried out in democratic governments.

---

[1]   Allison (2013), CEO of BB&T bank during the 2008 financial crisis, recounts banking regulators pressuring him into participating in the government's bailout program, even though he said his bank was financially sound and did not need a bailout. They told him that new regulations were being written, and while they did not know what those regulations would be, if he did not join the program, his bank would be in danger of being out of compliance. Allison took that as a threat that unless he cooperated, regulations would be written and enforced to target his bank.

[2]   There is a literature on corruption that considers these issues. Aidt (2016) notes that there are commonalities between this literature and the public choice literature on rent-seeking that have been left relatively undeveloped.

3. The Public Policy Process

Democratic governments are, by necessity, representative democracies. Governments that rule over millions of people, or even thousands, cannot be governed by direct democracy because transaction costs are too high to allow that many people to negotiate public policy. Even if referendums on public policy were offered to voters, the choices given to voters would be determined by an elite few who have been delegated to exercise government power. Sometimes the political elite get their power through democratic elections and sometimes through political appointment. Applying the Coase (1960) theorem, a small group of people face low transaction costs and can bargain to design public policy. They are the political elite. Most people face high transaction costs and are unable to participate in the policy-making process. They are the masses.

The US House of Representatives, for example, has 435 members, a small enough group that they all know each other and are able to engage in logrolling to produce policies that they view as beneficial. Most readers of this paper will find themselves in the high transaction cost group, and will be unable to participate in the political bargaining process that produces legislation. Public policy is created by a small group of people, and the resulting policies apply to everyone.

The public choice literature offers well-established explanations for how the political process can be used to benefit some while imposing costs on others. Rent-seeking, following Tullock (1967) and Krueger (1974), describes how some are able have resources transferred to them from others using the political process. Stigler (1971) has explained how some are able to capture the regulatory process so that regulations nominally designed to constrain their actions benefit those who are being regulated at the expense of others. Olson (1965, 1982) has explained how concentrated and well-organized interests are able to use the political process for their benefit, at the expense of larger groups that are less well-organized. All of these theories explain how some people are able to use the political process to benefit themselves at the expense of others.

While the public choice literature offers many explanations for how some can use the political process for their own benefit, it has not followed up by explaining that there is a relatively small and stable group of individuals who are able to command rents, capture regulatory agencies, and organize influential interest groups. One reason is that the public choice literature tends to take an individualistic approach to analyzing political processes, which limits its vision in identifying the specific group of people who benefit from political processes. Buchanan and Tullock (1962, p. 12) "reject any theory or conception of the collectivity which embodies the exploitation of a ruled by a ruling class. This includes the Marxist vision, which incorporates the polity as one means through which the economically dominant group imposes its will on the downtrodden". When one analyzes the political process, though, public policy is made by a few—a ruling class—and imposed on everyone. Some people are consistently in the group that benefits, and most people are consistently in the group that bears the costs.

Elite theory, developed mainly in sociology and political science, paints a different picture, describing ruled and ruling classes along the lines that Buchanan and Tullock dismiss. Mills (1956, p. 3) says "The powers of ordinary men are circumscribed by the everyday worlds in which they live ... But not all men are in this sense ordinary. As the means of information and power are centralized, some men come to occupy positions in American society from which they can look down upon, so to speak, and by their decisions mightily affect, the everyday world of ordinary men and women". Those are the power elite—the few who make the public policies to which everyone else is required to conform. Elite theory explains who designs and controls public policy, but it does not explain how they are able to exercise this control. Public choice theory explains how some are able to use the system for their benefit at the expense of others, but it does not identify who those some are. Holcombe (2018) explains that when these two strands of academic literature are combined, they show that those who obtain the rents, capture regulatory agencies, and form powerful interest groups are a relatively stable group—the elite.

Elite control of the public policy process has not escaped observation by economists. Stiglitz (2012, pp. 39–40) says "We have a political system that gives inordinate power to those at the top, and they have used that power not only to limit the extent of redistribution but also to shape the rules of the game in their favor". Stiglitz (2012, p. 59) goes on to say, "It's one thing to win a 'fair' game. It's quite another to be able to write the rules of the game—and to write them in ways that enhance one's prospects of winning. And it's even worse when you can choose your own referees. It doesn't have to be this way, but powerful interests ensure that it is". Along these same lines, Acemoglu and Robinson (2008) develop a model in which democratic political institutions evolve to favor the elite.

Nor has elite control of the public policy process escaped observation by the general public. After the financial crisis that began in 2008, the Occupy Wall Street movement protested the government policies that bailed out the Wall Street financial firms that took losses on their mortgage-backed securities but did nothing to help people who found themselves under water on their mortgages and were unable to pay them because they had lost their jobs due to the recession. They were complaining about policies that they said favored the 1 percent over the 99 percent. In academic jargon, the 1 percent are the elite; the 99 percent are the masses.

To a certain extent, the actions of the 99 percent produced the very policies they were protesting. The twenty-first century view of the role of democratic government is to carry out the will of its citizens as revealed through a democratic political process.[3] When a crisis appeared in 2008, the 99 percent demanded that the government do something to mitigate the crisis. Looking at how the political process actually works, government is run by the 1 percent—the elite. Thus, the 99 percent were demanding that the 1 percent be given more power to take action in response to the financial crisis, which the 1 percent did. Understanding how the process works, one should not be surprised that when the 1 percent took action, the action they took furthered their own interests. The elite make public policy, so one should expect that when they find themselves relatively unconstrained, public policy works to the advantage of the elite.

This is, Brennan and Buchanan (1985) explain, the reason for rules. They explain that a constitutional framework provides the foundation for individual interaction. Those constitutional rules should be designed to create a framework that channels individual actions away from predatory zero-sum and negative-sum action toward action that is positive-sum and mutually advantageous. Brennan and Buchanan (1985, p. 5) reference Hobbes to say that we benefit from a set of rules that govern people's interactions with each other because " ... without them we would surely fight. We would fight because the object of desire for one individual would be claimed by another. Rules define the private spaces within which each of us can carry out our own activities".

What Brennan and Buchanan do not say is that when some people write and interpret the rules, one would expect them to write rules that favor themselves, and interpret any rules in ways that favor themselves. Buchanan and Congleton (1998) conclude that rules that are relatively permanent and that apply generally to everyone will receive widespread approval from the masses. What this line of reasoning does not take into account is that the elite write, interpret, and enforce the rules. Writing the rules is the first step in the process. Even in this first step, those who write the rules must be constrained to write them in a way that benefits everyone, not just the elite who write them. Then, the elite must be constrained to interpret the rules in an even-handed manner that does not favor themselves over the masses. And then, rules must not be selectively enforced so that enforcement favors those who have political power over those who do not. The analysis that follows takes the first

---

[3] This contrasts with the vision of democracy held by the American Founders, who designed a government with constitutionally limited enumerated powers, and designed constraints to try to prevent government from actions not specifically permitted by the Constitution. In this view, democracy is a method of selecting who exercises the power of government, but not a method for determining what those powers are. The more modern view, Holcombe (2002) explains, envisions democratic governments as furthering the public interest, where the public interest is revealed through a democratic political process.

step as given, and examines how rules can be interpreted and enforced in a way that does not favor the elites (who interpret and enforce the rules) over the masses.

One might ask whether this framework, which depicts the elite as controlling the political process for their benefit, overstates their influence over public policy. There is an extensive literature written by authors ranging from the political right to the political left who make just this observation. Nader (2014) argues that objections to the coalition of economic and political elites are so widely recognized from one end of the political spectrum to the other that they form an unstoppable coalition that will put an end to the cronyism and corporatism that everyone observes.[4] Stockman (2013, p. 52) says, "Trying to improve capitalism, modern economic policy has thus fatally overloaded the state with missions and mandates far beyond its capacity to fulfill. The result is crony capitalism—a freakish deformation that fatally corrupts free markets and democracy". Bartels (2008) refers to this situation as the new gilded age. Gilens (2012) cites growing inequality in political power that is creating an increasingly divided society.

The idea that the political process is run by the elite for their benefit is well-supported in the academic literature. Even if that literature overstates the power of the elite to benefit themselves at the expense of the masses, there is still good reason to design an institutional framework in which the ability of some to use it to benefit themselves at the expense of others is limited. How can constitutional constraints on government power be enforced, when those who enforce them have an incentive to use their enforcement powers to benefit themselves?

4. Democracy

One mechanism for enabling the 99 percent to exercise oversight over the 1 percent is democracy. Democratic elections allow citizens to select who exercises the power of government, and create a process whereby citizens can peacefully replace those with political power if they are unsatisfied with their performance. Downs (1957) develops a model in which competition for elected office results in the election of candidates who run on the platform most preferred by the median voter. Holcombe (1989) explains that this model has often been used to conclude that governments do what the median voter most prefers.

Beyond the median voter model, voting models in public choice generally conclude that the collective choice of a group is determined by aggregating the votes of the individuals in the group. The implication is that the policy outcomes implemented by government are those chosen by the voters. Even in models showing perverse outcomes, such as McKelvey's (1976) demonstration that that, in general, there is no stable equilibrium in majority rule voting, the conclusion, Riker (1980) explains, is that political processes are unstable. This potential instability has been widely recognized since the beginnings of the subdiscipline of public choice, and Arrow (1963) begins his well-known book with an example of a cyclical majority. Yet Tullock (1982) observes that political outcomes appear to be much more stable than economic outcomes, so if economists can argue that equilibrium models are descriptive of market outcomes, surely the concept of equilibrium outcomes applies more to government than to markets.

One explanation for the apparent stability of political outcomes, given in the previous section, is that voters do not choose those outcomes. Public policy is chosen by an elite few—the 1 percent—not the electorate. The elite are a small group who are able to bargain with each other to produce public policies that are most favorable to themselves because, following Coase (1960), transaction costs are low within that elite group. When transaction costs are low, political exchange produces a stable outcome for the same reason market exchange produces a stable outcome. Voters do not decide public policy outcomes. The elite negotiate among themselves to produce outcomes most valuable to them.

---

[4] Nader may be overly optimistic on the success of this coalition, because while there is widespread agreement that the elite control the political process, there is not agreement on the remedy. Those on the left tend to favor more government control, while those on the right see the problem as being caused by government and argue for less government interference in economic affairs.

Just as with externalities in markets, the masses are in a high transaction cost group and are unable to bargain to prevent costs from being imposed on them.

Public choice theory offers many reasons to question whether voters really do exercise any effective control over the politicians they elect. One reason, given by Downs himself, is that it would be so rare for any election outcome (except with a very small number of voters) to be determined by a single vote that individual voters have no incentive to become informed. They are rationally ignorant because they realize their one vote will have no effect. Uninformed voters are not in a position to exercise control over those who they elect. Elections have symbolic value to elected officials by making it appear that what they do has been chosen by the electorate, Edelman (1964) observes, but all this does is give those who hold political power even more discretion to act to further their own interests rather than in the interests of those who elected them. Elected officials can claim that they are carrying out the will of the people, as revealed through the democratic political process.

Even those who are very interested in following politics will be unable to effectively monitor those who they elect. For one thing, being a politician is a full-time job, so anyone really interested in monitoring elected representatives would have to devote full time to it. Because there are many elected representatives, there would not be enough time to monitor all of them. Furthermore, the people who participate in political decision-making specialize in it, and have an understanding beyond what outsiders could hope to achieve. Just as citizens would not expect to have as much medical knowledge as a doctor, or as much knowledge about the operation of an automobile as an auto mechanic, it is unrealistic to expect citizens to have sufficient knowledge to monitor those who specialize in politics.

While there is a market and individual choice for those who are looking for medical services or auto repair services, there is no similar market for politicians. Those who exercise political power claim a monopoly over it, and while they can be challenged in elections, challengers are only making claims about what they would do if elected, so their claims cannot be verified as with incumbents who are actually practicing politics. Voters cannot observe their actual performance until after they have been elected, and few people think that campaign promises are as credible as, for example, automobile advertisements. Voters do not have reliable information, and even when such information is available, they have an incentive to remain rationally ignorant.

Because the general public has little incentive to organize to further their political interests, Olson (1965) explains that concentrated interests are able to effectively organize to provide political benefits to themselves by imposing costs on the masses. Public policy tends to favor special interests—the 1 percent—rather than working in the interest of the general public—the 99 percent. A well-established body of public choice literature helps explain why democratic oversight is likely to be an ineffective mechanism for enforcing constitutional constraints on government actions.

Public choice voting models nearly always assume that voters vote instrumentally; that is, they vote as if their votes can affect an election's outcome. But Downs' (1957) rational ignorance hypothesis rests on the conclusion that voters know their individual votes will not affect an election outcome, so they have no incentive to become informed or to vote instrumentally. Citizens do vote in large numbers, and Brennan and Lomasky (1993) conclude that because they know their individual votes will not affect election outcomes, they tend to vote expressively rather than instrumentally. They vote for outcomes that make them feel good rather than those that actually are in their individual interests, which Tullock (1971) notes can result in outcomes antithetical to their interests. Caplan (2007) goes one step further to argue that voters cast votes that are rationally irrational. They have no incentive to rethink any irrational public policy beliefs they hold, because their individual opinions will have no effect on public policy.

Wittman (1989, 1995) challenges the assessment given above, arguing that there are many mechanisms that direct public policy to follow the preferences of the voters. Political advertising and party brand name identification help provide voters with information, and voters can join special interest groups like the National Education Association and the National Rifle Association to have their collective preferences represented. Wittman explicitly notes that there are counter-arguments to all his point. Indeed, he recognizes that he is presenting counter-arguments to generally-accepted models in public choice.

The point in mentioning Wittman's analysis is to note that while the arguments presented above about the influence of concentrated interests, rationally ignorant voters, and expressive voting are well-accepted in public choice, there are arguments going the other way. Despite any counter-arguments, the public choice literature provides many reasons for thinking that democratic oversight will not be an effective way to interpret and enforce constitutional rules. The essential point is that constitutional rules are designed, interpreted, and enforced by an elite few—the 1 percent—and the masses—the 99 percent—have essentially no say over them. One cannot expect the powerless 99 percent to police the activities of the elite. Public choice theory gives ample reasons why democratic oversight will be an ineffective constraint.

5. Checks and Balances

One of the celebrated innovations embodied in the Constitution of the United States was a set of checks and balances that enabled one branch of government to check and balance the power of the others. James Madison, in *Federalist No. 51* (1788), discusses the role of checks and balances, and explicitly recognizes that the reason they are required is to counter the potential for elite control of government to oppress the masses, saying "Ambition must be made to counter ambition ... It may be a reflection of human nature, that such devices should be necessary to control the abuses of government". Constitutional rules will not be constraining unless those who interpret and enforce them are also constrained, and if an elite few interpret and enforce the rules, any checks on the power of those elites must come from other elites. The masses do not have the power to constrain elites, either through democratic oversight or by other means.

Persson et al. (1997) note that a system of checks and balances requires a separation of powers within the structure of government. But separation of powers is not the same as checks and balances, and by itself can lead to outcomes worse for the masses. Brennan and Hamlin (1994) show that if powers are merely separated, that can give those with some powers the ability to act unilaterally to the detriment of all others. Separation of powers can create a common pool problem, where some can use their (separate) powers for their benefit, imposing costs on others—others in different branches of government, and others in the broader citizenry.

Checks and balances mean that along with a separation of powers, one branch of government cannot act unilaterally without the agreement of another. But even this is not sufficient. The different branches of government should be designed so that they have conflicting interests, but must reach an agreement to take collective action. If their interests are all the same, they will act together to accomplish their common ends rather than checking and balancing each other. With conflicting interests, the interests of one branch can then check the interests of another. Persson et al. (1997) provide an example of an executive branch that can propose a total budget and a legislative branch that determines the components of the budget. By constraining the total size of the budget, the executive branch can check the legislative branch's ability to enlarge its individual components, and by controlling its components, the legislative branch can check the executive branch's appetite for expenditures.

La Porta et al. (2004) note that an independent judiciary and constitutional review work as a judicial check on the abuse of power by other branches of government. Different elements of government can act as "veto players" who can prevent other elements from unilateral action. Keefer (2002) looks at the effects of veto players on the ability of a central bank to undertake independent monetary policy, and Beck et al. (2002) provide data on veto players in government. This literature on veto players points to a productive way to view checks and balances, but veto players are not necessarily the product of constitutional design.

For example, when a parliament contains members of many parties, a coalition of parties will be required to take action, making the coalition members veto players. But, if a single party gains a majority of seats, it eliminates other parties as veto players, even though the constitutional design remains unchanged. Ideally, a system of checks and balances will be built into the constitutional structure rather than be the result of political factionalization. Durable checks and balances are a part of the institutional structure within which government operates.

The system of checks and balances works on the principle that the individual branches of government guard their powers from being usurped by other branches. The key feature here is that some elites check and balance the power of others. If the masses have a minimal ability to check the power of government, the only way checks and balances can be effective is if institutions separate elites into groups with competing interests that have veto power over the actions of each other.

The United States Constitution embodies this idea by establishing executive, legislative, and judicial branches of government that can check and balance each other. As Madison said, ambition must be made to counter ambition. Actions taken by one branch require the cooperation of the others, and as originally conceived, the House of Representatives and Senate were designed as a part of this system. House members were elected by citizens and Senators were chosen by their state governments, with the idea that for legislation to pass, it had to be approved by the representatives of the people in the House and the representatives of the state governments in the Senate, as described by Zywicki (1997). This check was nullified in 1913 by the 17th Amendment to the Constitution, which required direct election of Senators. While Tarabar and Hall (2015) note that it appeared to have little immediate effect, the fact that its supporters pursued the difficult process of amending the Constitution indicates that they expected this weakening of checks and balances to make a difference. By eliminating this element of competing interests, the elite were able to remove one point of conflict that could act as a check on their abuse of power.

The US Constitution took some inspiration from British government, where the power of the crown was checked and balanced by the House of Lords and the House of Commons. Courts also had a place in checking the powers of the crown and Parliament. A comparison of British and American checks and balances shows that the functional division of power may play a minor role when compared to designing a system in which one group of elites has the ability to check and balance the power of others. Congleton (2012) describes the evolution of liberal political institutions in Europe over the last several hundred years, The key point is that over time institutions evolved to create political systems in which there was a division of power, and in which no branch of government could act independently without the cooperation of others.

With regard to contemporary American politics, Mann and Ornstein (2012) argue that constitutional checks and balances have eroded substantially since the nation's founding, and especially beginning in the twentieth century with increasing authority moving into the executive branch of government.[5] More generally, Acemoglu et al. (2013) argue that checks and balances have been eroded because the economic elite are better organized and are better able to influence politicians absent those checks and balances internal to the operation of government.

6. Other Checks and Balances

The checks and balances discussed above apply to a single government that is designed so that its various branches can check and balance each other. Madison, in *Federalist No. 51* (1788) says "In the compound republic of America, the power surrendered by the people is first divided between two distinct governments, and then the portion allotted to each subdivided among distinct and separate departments. Hence a double security arises to the rights of the people". An additional check is a federal system of government in which the state governments check the power of the federal government and the federal government checks the power of the states. This check was

---

[5] Mann and Ornstein (2012) attribute much of the breakdown of checks and balances to the increase in partisan extremism, especially with reference to the Republican party, but that is beside the point for present purposes.

clearly embodied in the original Constitution of the United States by specifying that Senators would be chosen by their state governments, so for any legislation to be approved by both Houses to become law, it would have to meet with the approval of the representatives of the state governments, as Ostrom (1971) explains. This check was eliminated by the passage of the 17th Amendment in 1913, which specified that Senators be elected by a direct vote of the citizens.[6]

Intergovernmental competition can also provide a check on the powers of competing governments, Tiebout (1956) explains, pushing governments to respond to the demands of their citizens, yielding another benefit of a federal system. Decentralized political systems allow more local control, another possible check on the power of government. Local elites still control local government, but there is less distance, socially as well as geographically, between local elites and the general public. Local control, intergovernmental competition, and the ability of one level of government to check another are mechanisms that a federal system provides to check and balance the power of the elites who hold political power.

A free press is another mechanism that checks the power of government, which was recognized by the American Founders and embodied in the First Amendment to the Constitution. Coyne and Leeson (2009) note the impact of a free press on institutions, both reinforcing institutions that provide general benefits and undermining institutions that allow elites to abuse their power. This is a check that rests outside of government, but that can be enabled or inhibited by government control of the media.

7. Conclusions

The important role constitutional constraints on government play in protecting the rights and well-being of citizens has been well-recognized for centuries. Hume [1777] (1987, Essay VI) says "Political writers have established it as a maxim, that, in contriving any system of government, and fixing the several checks and controuls of the constitution, every man ought to be supposed a knave, and to have no other end, in all his actions, than private interest ... Without this, they say, we shall in vain boast of the advantages of any constitution, and shall find, in the end, that we have no security for our liberties or possessions, except the good-will of our rulers; that is, we shall have no security at all". Constitutional political economy has focused heavily on designing rules that give those who hold political power the incentive to act in the public interest, but given those rules, they can only be effective if they are effectively enforced.

Checks and balances are a requirement for enforcement, because an elite few write, interpret, and enforce the rules. The 99 percent cannot regulate a process that is run by the 1 percent. The role of checks and balances is to have subsets of the 1 percent check and balance the power of others in that elite group.

The twenty-first century ideology of Progressive Democracy has weakened the constitutional constraints on government, because it justifies government policies that benefit some at the expense of others, and because it legitimizes the actions of a democratic government by depicting those actions as carrying out the will of the citizens, as revealed through a democratic political process. The ideology of twenty-first century Progressive Democracy encourages the 99 percent to demand the government take action to address a variety of issues, rarely recognizing that the 99 percent are transferring additional power to the 1 percent who write, interpret, and enforce the rules. Then, the 99 percent are surprised when the 1 percent uses their additional power for their own benefit, and in response the 99 percent again demand that the government should do something, which transfers even more power to the 1 percent.

---

[6]   The Articles of Confederation, the original US constitution, designed a government with only one legislative body whose members were chosen by the state governments, providing even more of a check on the power of the federal government.

Democracy is an ineffective constraint on abuse of government power, because it is based on the illusion that the 99 percent can exercise control over the 1 percent—the elite who actually design and enforce public policy. Public choice theory explains that the 99 percent are rationally ignorant (Downs 1957), that concentrated interests are able to use the political system for their benefit at the expense of the masses (Olson 1965), that government regulation works for the benefit of those who are regulated (Stigler 1971), and that the elite are able to design institutions to transfer power to themselves and away from the masses (Acemoglu and Robinson 2008). One cannot expect the powerless to control the powerful, even if the powerless well-outnumber the powerful.

The elite control government, so the most effective way to constrain government and enforce constitutional rules is to design institutions that give some elites the power to check the power of others. Checks and balances work to enforce constitutional rules through a separation of power, so that no single elite group can act without the cooperation of others. Separation of powers is not enough. Institutions must be designed so that elites have conflicting interests that give them the incentive to protect their own power by checking abuse of power by other elites. Institutions must be designed so that any abuse of power by one set of elites can be countered by the power of another set, and those different sets of elites must have the incentive to counter, to protect their own power.

The arguments presented here rest on a foundation that depicts government as ruled by an elite few, with the masses having essentially no power to design, interpret, and enforce the rules that constrain government. A more democratic vision of government depicts government as controlled through democratic processes that begin with elections in which the masses vote to elect the elite few who are able to exercise the power of government. Thus, in evaluating these arguments, one should consider which vision of government appears to be more descriptive of actual political institutions.

The constitutional political economy literature, tracing its origins back to Buchanan and Tullock (1962) and Buchanan (1975), depicts a set of constitutional constraints designed by a process that requires agreement among those who are subject to those constraints. Yeager (1985, 2001) argues that these models of hypothetical collective agreement to some set of rules have the pernicious effect of making government actions that are taken by an elite few and that are based on force appear as if they have been somehow agreed to by citizens. Recognizing that all government action is backed by the threat of force for noncompliance, and recognizing that an elite few are in a position where they can exercise government power, there is good reason for constitutional political economy, as a subdiscipline, to focus more attention on the types of institutions that can objectively interpret and enforce constitutional rules. It is not enough to have good rules if those rules are not objectively interpreted and enforced. If the elite really do control the state, there is good reason to think that democratic oversight will be ineffective and that checks and balances are necessary to constrain those who hold the power of government from abusing that power.

Funding: This research received no external funding.

Conflicts of Interest: The author declares no conflict of interest.

References

Acemoglu, Daron, and James A. Robinson. 2008. Persistence of Power, Elites, and Institutions. *American Economic Review* 98: 267–93. [CrossRef]

Acemoglu, Daron, James A. Robinson, and Ragnar Torvik. 2013. Why Do Voters Dismantle Checks and Balances? *Review of Economic Studies* 80: 845–75. [CrossRef]

Aidt, Toke S. 2016. Rent Seeking and the Economics of Corruption. *Constitutional Political Economy* 27: 142–57. [CrossRef]

Allison, John A. 2013. *The Financial Crisis and the Free Market Cure*. New York: McGraw Hill.

Arrow, Kenneth J. 1963. *Social Choice and Individual Values*, 2nd ed. New Haven: Yale University Press.

Bartels, Larry M. 2008. *Unequal Democracy: The Political Economy of the New Gilded Age*. Princeton: Princeton University Press.

Beck, Thorsten, George Clarke, Alberto Groff, Philip Keefer, and Patrick Walsh. 2002. *New Tools in Comparative Political Economy: The Database of Political Institutions*. Washington: World Bank.

Brennan, Geoffrey, and James M. Buchanan. 1985. *The Reason of Rules: Constitutional Political Economy.* Cambridge: Cambridge University Press.

Brennan, Geoffrey, and Alan Hamlin. 1994. A Revisionist View of the Separation of Powers. *Journal of Theoretical Politics* 6: 345–68. [CrossRef]

Brennan, Geoffrey, and Loran Lomasky. 1993. *Democracy & Decision: The Pure Theory of Electoral Preference.* Cambridge: Cambridge University Press.

Buchanan, James M. 1975. *The Limits of Liberty: Between Anarchy and Leviathan.* Chicago: University of Chicago Press.

Buchanan, James M., and Roger D. Congleton. 1998. *Politics by Principle, Not Interest: Toward Nondiscriminatory Democracy.* Cambridge: Cambridge University Press.

Buchanan, James M., and Gordon Tullock. 1962. *The Calculus of Consent: Logical Foundations of Constitutional Democracy.* Ann Arbor: University of Michigan Press.

Caplan, Bryan. 2007. *The Myth of the Rational Voter: Why Democracies Choose Bad Policies.* Princeton: Princeton University Press.

Coase, Ronald H. 1960. The Problem of Social Cost. *Journal of Law & Economics* 3: 1–44.

Congleton, Roger D. 2012. *Perfecting Parliament: Constitutional Reform, Liberalism, and the Rise of Western Democracy.* Cambridge: Cambridge University Press.

Coyne, Christopher J., and Peter T. Leeson. 2009. Media as a Mechanism of Institutional Change and Reinforcement. *Kyklos* 62: 1–14. [CrossRef]

Downs, Anthony. 1957. *An Economic Theory of Democracy.* New York: Harper & Row.

Edelman, Murray. 1964. *The Symbolic Uses of Politics.* Urbana: University of Illinois Press.

Gilens, Martin. 2012. *Affluence and Influence: Economic Inequality and Political Power in America.* Princeton: Princeton University Press.

Holcombe, Randall G. 1989. The Median Voter Model in Public Choice Theory. *Public Choice* 61: 115–25. [CrossRef]

Holcombe, Randall G. 2002. *From Liberty to Democracy: The Transformation of American Government.* Ann Arbor: University of Michigan Press.

Holcombe, Randall G. 2018. *Political Capitalism: How Economic and Political Power Is Made and Maintained.* Cambridge: Cambridge University Press.

Hume, David. 1987. *Essays Moral, Political, Literary.* Indianapolis: Liberty Fund. First published 1777.

Keefer, Philip. 2002. Politics and the Determinants of Banking Crises: The Effects of Political Checks and Balances. In *Banking, Financial Integration and International Crises.* Edited by Leonardo Hernandez and Klaus Schmidt-Hebel. Santiago: Central Bank of Chile, pp. 85–112.

Krueger, Anne O. 1974. The Political Economy of the Rent-Seeking Society. *American Economic Review* 64: 291–303.

La Porta, Rafael, Florincio Lopez-de-Silanes, Cristian Pop-Eleches, and Andrei Shleifer. 2004. Judicial Checks and Balances. *Journal of Political Economy* 112: 445–70. [CrossRef]

Mann, Thomas E., and Norman J. Ornstein. 2012. *It's Even Worse Than It Looks: How the American Constitutional System Collided with the New Politics of Extremism.* New York: Basic Books.

McKelvey, Richard D. 1976. Intransitivities in Multi Dimensional Voting Models and Some Implications for Agenda Control. *Journal of Economic Theory* 12: 472–82. [CrossRef]

Mills, C. Wright. 1956. *The Power Elite.* New York: Oxford University Press.

Nader, Ralph. 2014. *Unstoppable: The Emerging Left-Right Alliance to Dismantle the Corporate State.* New York: Nation Books.

North, Douglass C. 1991. Institutions. *Journal of Economic Perspectives* 5: 97–112. [CrossRef]

Olson, Mancur. 1965. *The Logic of Collective Action.* Cambridge: Harvard University Press.

Olson, Mancur. 1982. *The Rise and Decline of Nations: Economic Growth, Stagflation, and Social Rigidities.* New Haven: Yale University Press.

Ostrom, Vincent. 1971. *The Political Theory of a Compound Republic: A Reconstruction of the Logical Foundations of American Democracy as Presented in "The Federalist".* Blacksburg: Center for Study of Public Choice.

Persson, Torsten, Gerard Roland, and Guido Tabellini. 1997. Separation of Powers and Political Accountability. *Quarterly Journal of Economics* 112: 1163–202. [CrossRef]

Riker, William H. 1980. Implications from the Disequilibrium of Majority Rule of the Study of Institutions. *American Political Science Review* 74: 432–46. [CrossRef]

Schweizer, Peter. 2013. *Extortion: How Politicians Extract Your Money, Buy Votes, and Line Their Own Pockets.* New York: Houghton Mifflin.

Stigler, George J. 1971. The Theory of Economic Regulation. *Bell Journal of Economics and Management Science* 2: 3–21. [CrossRef]

Stiglitz, Joseph E. 2012. *The Price of Inequality: How Today's Divided Society Endangers the Future*. New York: W.W. Norton.

Stockman, David A. 2013. *The Great Deformation: The Corruption of Capitalism in America*. New York: Public Affairs Press.

Tarabar, Danko, and Joshua C. Hall. 2015. The Seventeenth Amendment, Senate Ideology and the Growth of Government. *Applied Economics Letters* 22: 637–40. [CrossRef]

Tiebout, Charles M. 1956. A Pure Theory of Local Expenditures. *Journal of Political Economy* 64: 416–24. [CrossRef]

Tullock, Gordon. 1967. The Welfare Costs of Tariffs, Monopolies, and Theft. *Western Economic Journal* 5: 224–32. [CrossRef]

Tullock, Gordon. 1971. The Charity of the Uncharitable. *Economic Inquiry* 9: 379–92. [CrossRef]

Tullock, Gordon. 1982. Why So Much Stability? *Public Choice* 37: 38–59. [CrossRef]

Wittman, Donald A. 1989. Why Democracies Produce Efficient Results. *Journal of Political Economy* 97: 1395–424. [CrossRef]

Wittman, Donald A. 1995. *The Myth of Democratic Failure*. Chicago: University of Chicago Press.

Yeager, Leland B. 1985. Rights, Contract, and Utility in Policy Espousal. *Cato Journal* 5: 259–94.

Yeager, Leland B. 2001. *Ethics as a Social Science*. Cheltenham: Edward Elgar.

Zywicki, Todd J. 1997. Beyond the Shell and Husk of History: The History of the Seventeenth Amendment and Its Implications for Current Reform Proposals. *Cleveland State Law Review* 45: 165–234.

economies

MDPI

Article

A New Quota Approach to Electoral Disproportionality

Miguel Martínez-Panero [1,*], Verónica Arredondo [2], Teresa Peña [1] and Victoriano Ramírez [3]

1   PRESAD Research Group, BORDA Research Unit, IMUVa, Departamento de Economía Aplicada, Universidad de Valladolid, 47011 Valladolid, Spain; maitepe@eco.uva.es
2   PRESAD Research Group, Unidad Académica de Matemáticas, Universidad Autónoma de Zacatecas, Zacatecas 98000, Mexico; veronica.arredondo@alumnos.uva.es
3   Departamento de Matemática Aplicada, Universidad de Granada, 18071 Granada, Spain; vramirez@ugr.es
*   Correspondence: panero@eco.uva.es; Tel.: +34-983-186591

Received: 10 January 2019; Accepted: 26 February 2019; Published: 5 March 2019

Abstract: In this paper electoral disproportionality is split into two types: (1) Forced or unavoidable, due to the very nature of the apportionment problem; and (2) non-forced. While disproportionality indexes proposed in the literature do not distinguish between such components, we design an index, called "quota index", just measuring avoidable disproportionality. Unlike the previous indexes, the new one can be zero in real situations. Furthermore, this index presents an interesting interpretation concerning transfers of seats. Properties of the quota index and relationships with some usual disproportionality indexes are analyzed. Finally, an empirical approach is undertaken for different countries and elections.

Keywords: electoral systems; proportionality; electoral quota; disproportionality indexes; measurement; Spain; Sweden; Germany

1. Introduction

Electoral systems are mechanisms by which votes become seats in a parliament. In order to reflect the overall distribution of voters' preferences, some of these systems advocate for proportional representation, so that political parties will receive percentages of seats corresponding to their respective percentages of votes. Since a seat cannot be divided, it is impossible to assign exactly the obtained vote shares in seat terms. This apportionment problem generates something known as electoral disproportionality. Consequently, some parties are overrepresented while others become underrepresented. Even more, disproportionality may increase, due to the existence of many districts and electoral thresholds.

There is not an agreement about an instrument to determine such distortions generated during the process of translating votes into seats and many efforts have been made to measure them. Disproportionality indexes are usually employed to this aim and there exists a wide literature on this approach.

A survey compilation of indexes resulting from the application of different techniques is presented by Taagepera and Grofman (2003) (see also Taagepera 2007; Karpov 2008; Chessa and Fragnelli 2012; Goldenberg and Fisher 2017). These authors also develop an interesting analysis of the properties that they fulfill. From a computational point of view, Ocaña and Oñate (2011) presents a software for calculating nine disproportionality indexes. On the other hand, Koppel and Diskin (2009) and Boyssou et al. (2016) propose axiomatizations for some indexes measuring disproportionality. Finally, relationships among some disproportionality indexes appear in Borisyuk et al. (2004) and Bolun (2012).

All the proposed indexes measure deviations (in some way) from exact proportionality, which is not affordable in practice. Balinski and Young (2001, pp. 79–83) deals with a more realistic requirement concerning the apportionment problem: No party's representation should deviate from its quota (number of seats that should be received by the parties in exact proportionality) by more than one unit. In other words, no party should get less than its quota rounded down, nor more than its quota rounded up. This property is called "staying within the quota" or "verification of the quota rule". Taking into account that usually the quota is not an integer number, votes-seats disproportionality could be non-forced (if the quota rule is not satisfied), or forced, otherwise.

This paper presents a new index that just measures non-forced disproportionality, avoiding that inherent to the fact that exact proportionality is unfeasible, as pointed out. Remarkably, this index is zero if and only if the quota condition is satisfied. Even more, from this index, it is possible to obtain the minimum number of seats that would be necessary to transfer from some parties to others, so that the distribution of parliament seats will satisfy the quota condition.

The paper has the following structure: Section 2 introduces the notation and basic concepts, paying particular attention to the quota. Section 3 presents some of the most used disproportionality indexes, namely: The maximum deviation, Loosemore-Hanby and Gallagher indexes. Section 4 introduces a new index, which will be called "quota index". Section 5 shows the properties that the last index verifies and some relationships with the previous disproportionality indexes. In Section 6 the aforementioned indexes are computed for different elections in Spain, Sweden and Germany, and comparisons among them are established. In Section 7, some conclusions are presented. Finally, technical proofs, electoral results and data resources are left in Appendices A–C, respectively.

2. Notation and Basic Concepts

Let V be the number of voters, n the number of parties and S the number of seats to be distributed; $(V_1, V_2, \ldots, V_n)$ is the vector whose components are the votes obtained by each party, so that $V = \sum_{i=1}^{n} V_i$; on the other hand, $(S_1, S_2, \ldots, S_n)$ is the vector whose components are the seats assigned to each party, where $S = \sum_{i=1}^{n} S_i$; finally, we denote by v_i and s_i the proportion of votes and seats that party i receives. Thus, $v_i = V_i/V$ and $s_i = S_i/S$ are the vote and seat shares, respectively, for each party i.

A party i is overrepresented when $s_i > v_i$, and underrepresented when $s_i < v_i$. Any of these inequalities represents a distortion with respect to the voters' real preferences.

The quota (or "fair share") is the number of seats that the party i should receive in exact proportionality after obtaining V_i votes. That is, the quota for party i results $q_i = \frac{V_i}{V}S$.

In terms of the quota, a party is underrepresented if $S_i < q_i$ and overrepresented if $S_i > q_i$. Since $\sum_{i=1}^{n} S_i = \sum_{i=1}^{n} q_i$, if a party is underrepresented, at least another one will be overrepresented.

The lower quota is the closest integer number that does not exceed q_i; it will be denoted by $\lfloor q_i \rfloor$. Likewise, the upper quota is the smallest integer number bigger than or equal to q_i; it will be denoted by $\lceil q_i \rceil$. In other terms, the lower quota is obtained by rounding down q_i, and the upper quota by rounding up q_i.

Usually, for each party, quotas are fractional numbers and hence $\lceil q_i \rceil = \lfloor q_i \rfloor + 1$. Otherwise, if q_i is an integer number, then $\lfloor q_i \rfloor = \lceil q_i \rceil$. The interval whose extremes are lower and upper quotas will be called quota interval.

An apportionment satisfies the quota rule if the number of seats S_i assigned to each party differs from its quota less than one, this is: $|q_i - S_i| < 1$, or equivalently, $\lfloor q_i \rfloor \leq S_i \leq \lceil q_i \rceil$ for each $i = 1, 2, \ldots, n$.

On the other hand we will say that a party is overrepresented with respect to the upper quota if $S_i > \lceil q_i \rceil$; and is underrepresented with respect to the lower quota if $S_i < \lfloor q_i \rfloor$. Obviously, these are more restrictive requirements for parties than being merely overrepresented or underrepresented.

3. Some Indexes of Electoral Disproportionality and Their Relationship

The literature on indexes is devoted to measuring the quality of an electoral system, in some way. One of the most important issues in this context is electoral disproportionality, which could be defined as the deviation level of vote and seat shares of the participating parties in an election.

In order to determine electoral disproportionality various indexes have been proposed. As aforementioned, compilations of these indexes have been made by different authors (Taagepera and Grofman 2003; Karpov 2008). Among them, the maximum deviation index, the Loosemore-Hanby index proposed by Loosemore and Hanby (1971) and the least squares index, presented by Gallagher (1991), are some of the most frequently used ones.

3.1. Maximum Deviation Index

This index measures the maximum difference between vote and seat shares in absolute terms. The mathematical expression for this index is:

$$I_{MD} = \max_{i=1,\dots,n} |s_i - v_i|.$$

As it can be observed, the maximum deviation index only provides information of one party that can be either the most underrepresented or overrepresented one, regardless of the deviation sizes of the other parties.

3.2. Loosemore-Hanby Index

This index adds all the deviations generated during the allocation, meaning the sum of absolute values of the differences between the vote and seat shares. Mathematically the index is defined as

$$I_{LH} = \frac{1}{2} \sum_{i=1}^{n} |s_i - v_i|.$$

The sum of absolute values of the differences between the vote and seat shares for overrepresented parties coincides with the same sum for underrepresented ones. Hence, the total sum appearing in I_{LH} is divided by two in order to obtain the seat share that has not been distributed in a completely proportional way.

3.3. Gallagher Index

The least squares index is also known as Gallagher index, and it is defined as the square root of the sum of the squared differences between vote and seat shares of every party divided by two. Formally:

$$I_G = \sqrt{\frac{1}{2} \sum_{i=1}^{n} (s_i - v_i)^2}.$$

This index takes into account both big and small deviations in the proportion of assigned seats and obtained votes. However, small differences have less influence than big differences. Consequently, this index is less sensitive than the previous one to the appearance of small parties.

3.4. Relationship among Disproportionality Indexes

Obviously, $I_{LH} = I_{MD} = I_G = 0$ if and only if there exists exact proportionality, i.e., the percentage of votes equals that of seats for each party. Some further relations among these indexes can be established. It is straightforward that $I_{LH} = I_{MD}$ if and only if there exists either just one overrepresented or just one underrepresented party. On the other hand, if there are at least two overrepresented parties jointly with another two underrepresented ones, it is straightforward that $I_{LH} > I_{MD}$.

On the other hand, Borisyuk et al. (2004) proved that $I_G \leq I_{LH}$. Besides, it is easy to check that $I_G = I_{LH}$ if and only if there is exactly one overrepresented party jointly with just one underrepresented party. In both cases, also I_{MD} reaches the same value.

Finally, taking into account the aforementioned relationships concerning the considered indexes we can assert that, if there are at least two overrepresented parties jointly with another two underrepresented ones, then $I_{LH} > \max\{I_{MD}, I_G\}$.

4. The Quota Index

All the aforementioned indexes measure deviations between vote and seat shares, and hence, in an implicit way, they take into account the quota as a point of reference. For example, the Loosemore-Hanby index can be expressed in quota terms as

$$I_{LH} = \frac{1}{2}\sum_{i=1}^{n}|s_i - v_i| = \frac{1}{2S}\sum_{i=1}^{n}\left|\frac{S_i}{S}S - \frac{V_i}{V}S\right| = \frac{1}{2S}\sum_{i=1}^{n}|S_i - q_i|.$$

Note that $I_{LH} = 0$ if and only if $S_i = q_i$ for all the parties (this is also true for the previously considered indexes). However, as the seats are indivisible, this situation requires all q_i to be integer numbers, and this is extremely unlikely. Therefore, exact proportionality becomes almost impossible in real elections.

On the other hand, in terms of seat transference I_{LH} can be understood as the proportion of seats that we need to transfer from overrepresented parties to underrepresented ones in order to achieve exact proportionality. However, this is merely a theoretical value because, again, such exact proportionality would require the seats to be divided.

This is the reason why we have focused our attention not in exact apportionments, but in those staying within the quota, which is a more plausible condition. These considerations do not mean that we advocate for apportionment methods verifying the quota rule, as the largest remainders (a.k.a. Hamilton) rule. That is, regardless of the used method, our aim is measuring *post hoc* deviations from the quota interval.

If the quota q_i is not an integer number for some party, depending on the value of S_i, two kinds of disproportionality can be considered. We will say that in an allocation of seats, there exists non-forced disproportionality if some party does not verify the quota condition (i.e., it is overrepresented with respect to the upper quota or underrepresented with respect to the lower quota). Otherwise, the quota rule is satisfied for all the parties and we will talk about forced disproportionality, unavoidable due to the nature of the apportionment problem. Such considerations are illustrated in Figure 1.

These ideas have been taken into account in our proposal, in which we only measure non-forced disproportionality (i.e., beyond de quota interval): That is, only distances of overrepresented parties from their upper quotas or underrepresented parties from their lower quotas are considered. In this way, we have defined an index, called quota index, as

$$I_q = \frac{1}{S}\max\left\{ \sum_{\substack{i=1 \\ S_i > q_i}}^{n}(S_i - \lceil q_i \rceil), \quad \sum_{\substack{i=1 \\ S_i < q_i}}^{n}(\lfloor q_i \rfloor - S_i) \right\}.$$

The value of I_q is between zero and one. The zero value corresponds to any distribution that verifies the quota rule, while the maximum disproportionality will be reached when all the seats are assigned to parties with no votes. It is worth noting that, while Loosemore-Hanby and the other aforementioned indexes are zero if and only if the apportionment is exact, I_q can be zero without this requirement. But, obviously, I_q is also zero if there exists exact proportionality.

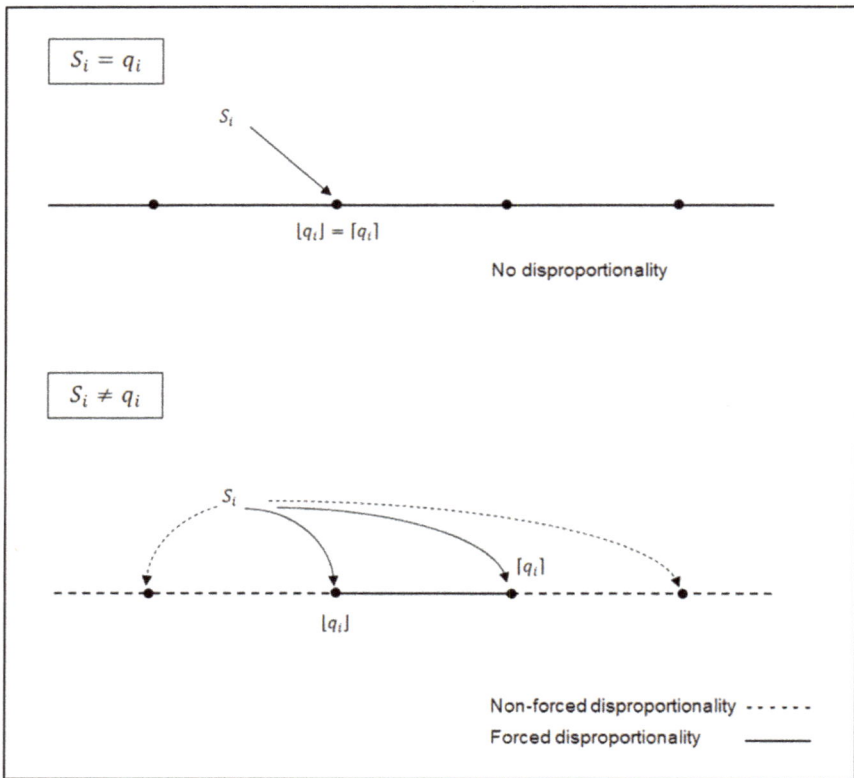

Figure 1. Types of disproportionality taking into account the quota rule.

Moreover, our index has an interesting interpretation in transference terms: The quota index I_q is the minimum proportion of seats in a parliament of S seats that we would need to transfer from overrepresented parties with respect to the upper quota to others underrepresented (or from overrepresented parties to others underrepresented with respect to the lower quota), for the quota rule to be verified. And $S \cdot I_q$ will be exactly the minimum number of seats that would have to be transferred from some parties to others for the distribution to verify the quota condition at a global level. This fact will be illustrated in Section 6 concerning 2016 Spanish elections.

5. Quota Index Analysis and Relationships with Other Indexes

Karpov (2008), Taagepera and Grofman (2003) and Taagepera (2007) propose some reasonable properties and analyze their fulfillment for several disproportionality indexes, the maximum deviation, the Loosemore-Hanby index and the Gallagher indexes among them. In this section, after showing the difference of perspectives between the above-mentioned indexes and the new one, we will test for I_q the most relevant properties appearing in the literature.

In what follows, we will formulate the above-mentioned disproportionality indexes in terms of the quota. In Section 4 we have shown that:

$$I_{LH} = \frac{1}{2S} \sum_{i=1}^{n} |S_i - q_i|.$$

In a similar way, it is easy to check that:

$$I_{MD} = \frac{1}{S} \max_{i=1,\dots,n} |S_i - q_i|,$$

and

$$I_G = \frac{1}{S} \sqrt{\frac{1}{2} \sum_{i=1}^{n} (S_i - q_i)^2}.$$

These expressions are intended to establish in an easy way their relationships with the quota index. It will be also used in further computations.

5.1. Quota Index and Disproportionality Indexes: Difference of Scopes

In Section 4, disproportionality has been split into two types. As shown in the previous expressions, traditional approaches to this issue measure the distances from quotas, and hence they take into account both forced and non-forced disproportionality. On the other hand, the quota index just measures distances to the quota interval, and therefore just consider non-forced disproportionality. In other words, usual disproportionality indexes contemplate underrepresented on overrepresented parties, while the quota index just considers those over the upper quota or below the lower quota.

The following example illustrates these aspects.

Example 1. *Consider parties A and B, and let the number of seats to allocate $S = 10$. Suppose that $S_A = 8$ and $q_A = 7.6$ are the number of seats and the respective quota of the party A. Also consider that $S_B = 2$ and $q_B = 2.4$ are the number of seats and the quota of the party B, respectively. Then, we obtain:*

$$I_{MD} = I_{LH} = I_G = 0.04.$$

However, as the quota rule is verified, $I_q = 0$. Notice that with these data all the appearing disproportionality is forced (unavoidable).

5.2. Disproportionality Indexes Properties and Quota Index

Following Karpov (2008), some compelling properties are taken into account:

1.   *Anonymity*: Any permutation of party labels does not change the value of the index.
2.   *Principle of transfers*: If we transfer a seat from an overrepresented party to an underrepresented one, then the value of the index should not increase.
3.   *Independence from split*: Suppose there are many parties with equal vote and seat shares, and these parties are grouped into one. Then, the value of the index calculated for all the parties in the group should be equal to the value of the index for the group considered as a whole.
4.   *Scale invariance (homogeneity)*: The index should not depend on any proportional change in the number of votes or seats
5.   *Zero normalization*: This property is satisfied if, when $v_i = s_i$ for all $i = 1, \dots, n$, then the value of the index is 0.

Next, we will check the fulfillment of the previous properties by I_q.

Proposition 1. *The index I_q satisfies anonymity, principle of transfers and zero normalization.*

(The proof can be found in Appendix A).
Now, Example 2 shows that I_q does not satisfy the property of independence from split.

Example 2. *Suppose nine parties whose quotas and assigned seats appear in Table 1, where $S = 6$.*

Table 1. Electoral data for testing independence from split (before grouping).

Results	Parties								
	A	**B**	**C**	**D**	**E**	**F**	**G**	**H**	**I**
q_i	1.4	1.4	0.4	0.4	0.4	0.5	0.5	0.5	0.5
S_i	3	3	0	0	0	0	0	0	0

Calculating separately I_q for all the appearing parties, we obtain:

$$I_q = max\left\{ \frac{3 - \lceil 1.4 \rceil + 3 - \lceil 1.4 \rceil}{6}, 0 \right\} = \frac{2}{6} = 0.33.$$

Now, in Table 2, I_q is calculated for parties with equal percentage of seats and quotas as unique coalitions:

Table 2. Electoral data for testing independence from split (after grouping).

Results	Parties Coalitions		
	A + B	**C + D + E**	**F + G + H + I**
q_i	2.8	1.2	2
S_i	6	0	0

And hence

$$I_q = max\left\{ \frac{6 - \lceil 2.8 \rceil}{6}, \frac{\lfloor 1.2 \rfloor - 0 + (2 - 0)}{6} \right\} = \frac{3}{6} = 0.5.$$

Table 3 shows the properties that I_{MD}, I_{LH}, I_G and I_q satisfy or do not (Karpov (2008) and Taagepera and Grofman (2003) for the three first indexes). A "+" sign means that the index satisfies the property and "−" means that it does not. Occasionally, these signs may appear enclosed into parentheses to point out that the corresponding property is or not satisfied under specific circumstances.

Table 3. Summary of indexes and properties.

Index	Anonymity	Transfer Principle	Independence from Split	Scale Invariance	Zero Normalizing
I_{MD}	+	(+)	−	+	+
I_{LH}	+	(+)	+	+	+
I_G	+	(+)	−	+	+
I_q	+	+	−	(−)	+

Parentheses appearing in the column relative to the Principle of Transfers in Table 3 mean that I_{MD}, I_{LH} and I_G may violate the principle of transfers in some situations, as shown in Example 3.

Example 3. *Consider parties A and B, and S = 10. Suppose that $q_A = 7.6$, $S_A = 8$, $q_B = 2.4$ and $S_B = 2$. That is, A is overrepresented and B is underrepresented. In this situation:*

$$I_{MD} = I_{LH} = I_G = 0.04.$$

Now, if we transfer a seat from A to B :

$$I_{MD} = I_{LH} = I_G = 0.06.$$

Note that, in this example, after the seat transference the overrepresented party becomes underrepresented, and vice versa.

However, it is easy to check that I_{MD}, I_{LH} and I_G satisfy a weaker Principle of Transfers establishing that, if a seat is transferred from an overrepresented party verifying $S_i - q_i > 0.5$ to an underrepresented one that satisfies $q_i - S_i > 0.5$, then the value of these indexes should not increase. In particular, this situation happens when a seat is transferred from an overrepresented party with respect to the upper quota to an underrepresented one with respect to the lower quota. Concerning different versions of the Principle of Transfers in electoral disproportionality and their connection with the original Dalton's Principle in more general inequality contexts, see Taagepera and Grofman (2003), Van Puyenbroeck (2008) and Goldenberg and Fisher (2017).

On the other hand, the parentheses appearing in the column relative to Scale Invariance in Table 3 means that I_q violates this property just with proportional changes in the number of seats, but not in the number of votes, as shown in Example 4.

Example 4. *Consider again parties A and B, and $S = 10$. Suppose that $q_A = 7.6$, $S_A = 8$, $q_B = 2.4$ and $S_B = 2$. Note that in this situation the quota rule is satisfied and hence $I_q = 0$. If we multiply by 10 the number of seats, that is, $S = 100$, we obtain $q_A = 76$, $S_A = 80$, $q_B = 24$ and $S_B = 20$. Now, the quota rule is not verified and $I_q = 0.04$.*

However, this fact should not be considered as a drawback of the index because the first situation cannot be improved by transferring seats in any way, while in the second situation if we transfer $S * I_q = 4$ seats from party A to B, the quota rule is verified. Even more, in this case the apportionment becomes exact.

Concerning this issue, Boyssou et al. (2016) assert that although the homogeneity with respect the number of seats "seems rather reasonable for large parliaments, a good disproportionality index should perhaps be sensitive to the size of the parliament, at least for small parliaments".

Obviously, proportional changes in the number of votes (maintaining the number of seats to allocate) do not affect the quota and consequently neither the value of I_q.

Some other properties can be considered for a disproportionality index (Taagepera and Grofman 2003; Taagepera 2007), among them:

- Informationally complete (makes use of all s_i and v_i)
- Uses data for all parties uniformly
- Does not depend on the number of parties
- Varies between 0 and 1 (or 100%)

As shown by the previous authors, these properties are satisfied by the disproportionality indexes considered along this paper, except the first one by I_{MD}. On the other hand, it is straightforward that I_q also verifies all of them.

5.3. Relationships among I_q and Disproportionality Indexes

The relationships existing among different disproportionality indexes have been shown in various ways (Borisyuk et al. 2004; Bolun 2012). In the present paper some relationships that the quota index has with the disproportionality indexes appearing above will be analyzed.

Proposition 2. *The value of the quota index is always minor than or equal to the Loosemore-Hanby index:*

$$I_q \leq I_{LH}.$$

(The proof can be found in Appendix A).

Proposition 3. *The values of the quota and the maximum deviation indexes verify the following inequality:*

$$I_q \geq I_{MD} - \frac{1}{S}.$$

(The proof can be found in Appendix A).

Obviously, $I_q = I_{LH} = I_{MD} = I_G = 0$ if there exists exact proportionality. If not, other relations can be established. It is obvious that $I_q = I_{LH}$ if and only if q_i are integer numbers for all the overrepresented parties and the maximum of the expression of I_q is reached for these ones, or q_i are integer numbers for all the underrepresented parties and the maximum is reached for them. As these situations are extremely unlikely, in general $I_q < I_{LH}$.

On the other hand, it is straightforward that $I_q = I_{MD}$ if and only if there exists either just one overrepresented party with respect to the upper quota and, in addition, its quota is an integer number or just one underrepresented party with respect to the lower quota and, in addition, its quota is an integer.

Finally, it is easy to check that $I_q = I_G$ if there is just one overrepresented party whose quota is an integer number and, in addition, there is exactly one underrepresented party. In both cases, also I_{MD} reaches the same value. Otherwise both inequalities might appear between I_q and I_G. For example, in any allocation verifying the quota with no exact proportionality, $I_q = 0 < I_G$. But if the quota condition is not satisfied, the inequality might be reversed and, in fact, $I_q < I_G$ is unlikely (see results in Section 6).

5.4. Discussion about Indexes

It can be observed that, as appearing in Table 3, none of the indexes considered along the paper is optimal. This situation is somehow analogous (in another context) to those in Social Choice theory, where is well known that there do not exist perfect voting systems nor apportionment methods, as proven by Arrow and Balinski-Young theorems, respectively.

In fact, it is possible to find examples where all the considered indexes present some weaknesses, as will be shown in what follows.

In an electoral situation where there exist non integer quotas (in fact, this is the most usual case), it is impossible to achieve exact proportionality, but it is always possible to find an apportionment verifying $I_q = 0$. It is a simple question of adjustment of each S_i in its quota interval, so that, at the end of the process $\sum_{i=1}^{n} S_i = S$. In such a situation, there are several possibilities of seat distribution staying within the quota, and this fact might be considered as a criticism, as shown in Example 5.

Example 5. *Consider parties A and B, and let the number of seats to allocate $S = 5$. Suppose that $q_A = 2.4$ and $q_B = 2.6$. In this situation there are two possibilities of seat distribution staying within the quota: $S_A = 2$, $S_B = 3$ and $S'_A = 3$, $S'_B = 2$. Hence, $I_q = I'_q = 0$.*

However, the second allocation is less compelling than the first one, because the most voted party obtains the least representation. In other terms, there exists a lack of vote/seat monotonicity in the last apportionment.

Now, notice that for the first allocation, we have $I_{MD} = I_{LH} = I_G = 0.08$, while for the second allocation, $I'_{MD} = I'_{LH} = I'_G = 0.12$. Consequently, these indexes point out the first allotment as better than the second one.

Nonetheless, Example 6 illustrates that the lack of monotonicity might not be captured (even more, it can be inversely reflected) when the usual disproportionality indexes are used.

Example 6. *Suppose eight parties whose quotas and assigned seats (in two different apportionments) appear in Table 4, where $S = 10$.*

The first seat distribution is intentionally arbitrary (in fact, it cannot be obtained by any divisor or quotient method). However, the second distribution is obtained by any divisor method in the parametric family (Balinski and Ramírez 1999) between Webster (Sainte-Laguë) and Jefferson (D'Hondt).

After some computations, the obtained values for quota and maximum deviation indexes in both allotments are $I_q = I'_q = 0$ and $I_{MD} = I'_{MD} = 0.09$. The first apportionment presents two pair of parties, (A, B) and (C, D), where, in each of them, the most voted is the least represented. However, in this example, unlike the *previous one, Loosemore-Hanby and Gallagher do no detect this lack of monotonicity. Even worse, they work in the opposite way to that expected:* $I_{LH} = 0.16$, $I'_{LH} = 0.17$ *and* $I_G = 0.094$, $I'_G = 0.099$.

Table 4. Electoral data for testing indexes suitability.

Results	A	B	C	D	E	F	G	H
q_i	4.2	4.1	0.4	0.3	0.3	0.3	0.2	0.2
S_i	4	5	0	1	0	0	0	0
S'_i	5	5	0	0	0	0	0	0

6. Implementation of the Quota Index in Some Countries and Elections

We first study in depth the case of Spain along the last 25 years, paying special attention to the transfer analysis in the 2016 elections, as well as to the overall correlation of the disproportionality indexes previously calculated.

Afterwards, we merely calculate the considered indexes for another two countries, Sweden and Germany, jointly with some comments on the results.

As a caveat, we note that slight (and hence negligible) differences might appear in the results, due to the treatment (grouped or not) of small parties without representation.

All electoral data resources appear in Appendix C.

6.1. Spain (1993–2016)

In Spain there exists a party list proportional representation system. The Spanish Chamber of Deputies has 350 members chosen in 52 districts. An exclusion threshold of 3% of the valid votes in each district is applied. All these elements have not been modified from 1977. Disproportionality partially occurs in Spain because population/representation shares are not balanced among districts. Furthermore, due to the small size of districts, some parties whose votes are scattered all over the country may obtain significantly fewer seats than other parties with a similar number of votes, if geographically concentrated. Other causes of disproportionality in Spain are the use of the D'Hondt rule, intended to favor larger parties.

Table 5 shows the values of maximum deviation, Loosemore-Hanby, Gallagher and the quota indexes for the eight most recent elections in Spain.

Table 5. Disproportionality indexes for recent Spanish elections (in percentage).

Index	1993	1996	2000	2004	2008	2011	2015	2016
I_{LH}	12.01	8.07	8.58	7.95	8.08	11.29	10.51	7.80
I_q	11.42	7.10	8.00	7.42	7.42	10.57	9.71	7.14
I_G	6.81	5.32	5.60	4.63	4.50	6.91	5.92	5.23
I_{MD}	6.33	5.39	7.04	3.97	3.92	7.89	6.21	5.86
				$S = 350$				

In all analyzed elections, I_{LH} is bigger than I_q (as theoretically proven), while I_G is the smallest (hence, in particular, $I_q > I_G$ in all the cases). Remarkably, the quota rule never is globally satisfied, given that always $I_q \neq 0$.

Focusing our attention in 2016, it can be observed that all the obtained values have decreased from those corresponding to the previous elections. An important fact that can partially explain this issue is that IU, a left-wing party, traditionally penalized by vote dispersion, formed a coalition with the emergent party Podemos.

Following with the last Spanish elections, it is worth noting that $I_{LH} = 7.8\%$ and $S \cdot I_{LH} = 27.3$. This value corresponds to the number of seats to be transferred from some parties to others in order to achieve exact proportionality. This is a theoretical value because seats cannot be divided. On the other hand, $I_q = 7.14\%$, and hence $S \cdot I_q = 25$, which means that this is the minimum number of seats to be transferred for the apportionment to verify the quota. This is a feasible goal. Concretely, in order to achieve this aim, 20 seats belonging to PP and 5 more seats from PSOE should be transferred to C's (14), PACMA (4) and Podemos-IU-EQUO (2). The remaining 5 seats should be moved, one by one, to any other unrepresented party (see Appendix B for details).

Despite the fact that I_q solely measures non-forced disproportionality and the remaining indexes are disproportionality ones, in what follows a correlation analysis among them is undertaken in order to explore their relationships. Table 6 shows the results coming from data appearing in Table 5.

Table 6. Correlation among indexes for elections in Spain.

Indexes	I_{LH}	I_q	I_G	I_{MD}
I_{LH}	1			
I_q	0.9990	1		
I_G	0.8991	0.9033	1	
I_{MD}	0.7051	0.7110	0.9311	1

The highest correlation value appears between I_{LH} and I_q. This fact relies on the formal expression of I_q which is somehow inspired by that of I_{LH}, although the first one only measures avoidable (beyond the quota interval) disproportionality. Hence, both indexes have different interpretations, as aforementioned. On the other hand, I_{MD} and I_{LH} have the smallest correlation.

6.2. Other Countries

As aforementioned, we next calculate the considered disproportionality indexes for another two countries, Sweden (proportional system) and Germany (mixed-member system).

6.2.1. Sweden (1998–2014)

Sweden is ranked in the third position worldwide according to the 2017 democratic index developed by *The Economist Intelligence Unit* (www.eiu.com). The Swedish Parliament (Riksdag) is composed of 349 seats elected under a proportional system. 310 of them belong to fixed constituency seats and the remaining 39 are adjustment seats. Any particular party must receive at least 4% of the national votes to be assigned a seat. Fixed seats are allocated among the parties using a method known as the adjusted odd numbers method (or modified Sainte-Laguë).

The purpose of the 39 adjustment seats is to make sure that the distribution of seats among the parties over the whole country should be as proportional in relation to the number of votes as possible. The whole country is viewed as it was a single constituency and is then compared with the distribution of votes in the 29 constituencies. The adjustment seats are allocated first according to party and then according to the constituency (see www.riksdagen.se for details).

Table 7 shows the values of the I_{LH}, I_q, I_G and I_{MD} indices in all the Swedish Riksdag elections held from 1998 to 2014.

Table 7. Disproportionality indexes for recent Swedish elections (in percentage).

Index	1998	2002	2006	2010	2014
I_{LH}	2.52	2.92	6.67	2.07	4.04
I_q	1.72	2.01	5.44	1.72	3.15
I_G	1.27	1.58	3.17	1.25	2.64
I_{MD}	1.12	1.44	2.67	1.42	3.13
			$S = 349$		

It can be observed, as in the previously studied case, that I_q is always between I_G and I_{LH}. Notice also that now the obtained results are lower than those for Spain. In fact, the Swedish electoral system produces a high proportionality unless one or several political parties have a percentage of votes just a little below the electoral threshold (4%). Concretely, this situation happened in 2006 and 2014 because the Sweden Democrats and the Feminist Initiative parties obtained 2.9% and 3.1% of the national votes, respectively.

6.2.2. Germany (1976–2017)

Germany's electoral system is a combination of "first-past-the-post" election of constituency candidates (first votes) and proportional representation on the basis of votes for the parties' States (Länder) lists (second votes). Hence, it is a mixed-member electoral system.

Concretely, half of the Members of the German Parliament (Bundestag) are elected directly from Germany's 299 constituencies, the other half via party lists in Germany's sixteen Länder. Accordingly, each voter casts two votes in the elections to the German Bundestag. The first vote, allowing voters to elect their local representatives to the Bundestag, decides which candidates are sent to Parliament from the constituencies. The second vote is cast for a party list. The 598 seats are distributed among the parties that have gained more than 5% of the second votes or at least three constituency seats. Each party receives the minimum between the number of seats obtained on the basis of the first votes and those corresponding to the second votes. The Sainte-Laguë/Schepers method is used to convert the votes into seats

In some circumstances, Parliament's size may increase during the process of allocating the seats, due to what are known as "overhang seats" and additional "balance seats" in order to maintain proportionality (see www.bundestag.de for further details).

Table 8 shows the values of the I_{LH}, I_q, I_G and I_{MD} indices in the German Bundestag elections held from 1976 to the most recent in 2017.

Table 8. Disproportionality indexes for recent German elections (in percentage).

Size	Index	1990	1994	1998	2002	2005	2009	2013	2017
	I_{LH}	8.05	3.61	4.72	8.45	4.33	6.01	15.69	5.00
	I_q	7.40	3.27	4.19	8.33	3.75	5.63	15.21	4.51
	I_G	4.62	2.22	2.75	6.15	2.28	3.14	7.33	1.95
	I_{MD}	3.85	2.15	3.11	7.98	2.05	3.92	6.29	1.45
S		662	672	669	672	614	622	631	709

Notice that, again, the values of I_q are always between those of I_G and I_{LH}. Paying attention to the historical sequence of data, the magnitude of the results obtained in 2013 is shocking. This high disproportionality arose because, in this year, parties that did not overcome the electoral threshold represented approximately 16% of the votes.

7. Conclusions

In this paper, the quota index (I_q) has been introduced and analyzed. It is worth mentioning that this index is zero if and only if the quota rule is satisfied by all the parties, i.e., when only forced (i.e., unavoidable) disproportionality arises.

Remarkably, in our approach, $I_q = 0$ can occur even if the apportionment is not exact (in fact, exact proportionality is almost impossible, due to the very nature of the apportionment problem). Moreover, I_q corresponds to the minimum percentage of seats that is necessary to transfer among parties for the quota rule to be verified. From this value it is possible to obtain the minimum number of seats (being an integer number) that it would be necessary to transfer from some parties to others, so that the seat distribution of the parliament will satisfy the quota condition.

After an electoral process, it is usual for the main party to be overrepresented. If the underrepresentation is distributed among all the other parties and none of them stays below its lower quota, then I_q will represent the surplus of the winning party calculated from its upper quota.

Notice also that, contrary to other well-known disproportionality indexes, the existence of many small parties with a quota less than the unit and without seat representation do not increase the value of I_q.

We have proven that the quota index verifies some compelling properties appearing in the literature. In particular, it is worth noting that I_q gain an advantage over some of the most relevant disproportionality indexes (maximum deviation, Loosemore-Hanby and Gallagher) when the principle of transfers is considered. On the other hand, we have checked that the quota index is not homogenous with respect to the number of seats, although it has been justified that this fact can make sense in our context.

Finally, quantitative relationships have been established among the quota and the aforementioned disproportionality indexes and all of them have been calculated for several elections in Spain, Sweden and Germany. The obtained results show that there exists a high correlation among the Loosemore-Hanby and quota indexes, but a major argument to use the last one is its interpretability in terms of seat transfer.

Author Contributions: All the authors have equally participated in the research aspects of the work reported.

Funding: We are grateful for the financial support of the Spanish Ministerio de Economía y Competitividad (project ECO2016-77900-P).

Acknowledgments: The authors acknowledge and appreciate the comments of two anonymous referees.

Conflicts of Interest: The authors declare no conflict of interest.

Appendix A. Proofs of the Propositions

Proposition 1. *The index I_q satisfies anonymity, principle of transfers and zero normalization.*

Proof:

- *Anonymity*

  Given that the value of I_q is the maximum of two arguments:

$$\sum_{\substack{i=1 \\ S_i > q_i}}^{n} (S_i - \lceil q_i \rceil) \text{ and } \sum_{\substack{i=1 \\ S_i < q_i}}^{n} (\lfloor q_i \rfloor - S_i),$$

this property is immediate since it relies on commutative property for real numbers.

- *Principle of transfers*

  Consider S_h and q_h, number of seats assigned and quota for an overrepresented party h, respectively. Let S_j and q_j be the number of seats assigned and the quota for an underrepresented party j, respectively. When a seat is transferred from h to j, the following cases can happen:

(1) If party h continues being overrepresented, then

$$S_h - \lceil q_h \rceil > (S_h - 1) - \lceil q_h \rceil \geq 0.$$

(2) If party h becomes underrepresented, then

$$\lfloor q_h \rfloor - (S_h - 1) = 0.$$

In such scenarios we can find any of these situations:

(a) If party j continues being underrepresented, then

$$\lfloor q_j \rfloor - S_j > \lfloor q_j \rfloor - (S_j + 1) \geq 0.$$

(b) If party j becomes overrepresented, then

$$(S_j + 1) - \lceil q_j \rceil = 0.$$

Taking this into account, if a seat is transferred from an overrepresented party to an underrepresented one I_q does not increase its value in any of the arguments of the maximum appearing in its expression.

- *Zero normalization*

If $v_i = s_i$ for all $i = 1, \ldots, n$, then $\frac{V_i}{V} = \frac{S_i}{S}$ and $\frac{V_i}{V}S = S_i$. Furthermore, we know that $q_i = \frac{V_i}{V}S$, because $q_i = S_i$. Given that the number of assigned seats S_i is an integer number and $\sigma_i = S_i$, q_i is also an integer number, and then $\lceil q_j \rceil = \lfloor q_i \rfloor = q_i$. Therefore:

$$
I_q = \tfrac{1}{S}\max \left\{ \sum_{\substack{i=1 \\ S_i > q_i}}^{n} (S_i - \lceil q_i \rceil), \ \sum_{\substack{i=1 \\ S_i < q_i}}^{n} (\lfloor q_i \rfloor - S_i) \right\} =
$$

$$
= \tfrac{1}{S}\max \left\{ \sum_{\substack{i=1 \\ S_i > q_i}}^{n} (S_i - S_i), \ \sum_{\substack{i=1 \\ S_i < q_i}}^{n} (S_i - S_i) \right\} = 0. \quad \square
$$

Proposition 2. *The value of the quota index is always minor than or equal to the Loosemore-Hanby index:*

$$I_q \leq I_{LH}.$$

Proof: As aforementioned in Section 4, the Loosemore-Hanby index can be expressed in terms of the quota as

$$I_{LH} = \frac{1}{2S} \sum_{i=1}^{n} |S_i - q_i|.$$

On one hand, given that the sum of the terms corresponding to overrepresented parties is equal to that corresponding to underrepresented ones, we obtain

$$I_{LH} = \frac{1}{S} \sum_{\substack{i=1 \\ S_i > q_i}}^{n} (S_i - q_i) = \frac{1}{S} \sum_{\substack{i=1 \\ S_i < q_i}}^{n} (q_i - S_i).$$

On the other hand,

$$\sum_{\substack{i=1 \\ S_i > q_i}}^{n} (S_i - q_i) \geq \sum_{\substack{i=1 \\ S_i > q_i}}^{n} (S_i - \lceil q_i \rceil), \quad \sum_{\substack{i=1 \\ S_i < q_i}}^{n} (q_i - S_i) \geq \sum_{\substack{i=1 \\ S_i < q_i}}^{n} (\lfloor q_i \rfloor - S_i).$$

Thus, the maximum of the two terms appearing in the definition of I_q is less than or equal to I_{LH}.

$\square$

Proposition 3. *The value of the quota indexes and the maximum deviation verify the following inequality:*

$$I_q \geq I_{MD} - \frac{1}{S}.$$

Proof: Taking into account that

$$I_{MD} = \frac{1}{S} \max_{i=1,\dots, n} |S_i - q_i|,$$

we consider two cases:

(a) If $\max\limits_{i=1,\dots, n} |S_i - q_i|$ is reached for underrepresented party u, then $\max\limits_{i=1,\dots,n} |S_i - q_i| = (q_u - S_u)$.
Therefore:

$$\sum_{\substack{i=1 \\ S_i < q_i}}^{n} (\lfloor q_i \rfloor - S_i) \geq \lfloor q_u \rfloor - S_u \geq (q_u - S_u) - 1,$$

where the last inequality takes into account that $\lfloor q_u \rfloor \geq q_u - 1$. Dividing both extreme members by S, we have

$$\frac{1}{S} \sum_{\substack{i=1 \\ S_i < q_i}}^{n} (\lfloor q_i \rfloor - S_i) \geq \frac{(q_u - S_u)}{S} - \frac{1}{S} = \frac{\max\limits_{i=1,\dots,n} |S_i - q_i|}{S} - \frac{1}{S}, I_q \geq I_{MD} - \frac{1}{S}$$

(b) If $\max\limits_{i=1,\dots,n} |S_i - q_i|$, is reached for a party o that is overrepresented, then $\max\limits_{i=1,\dots,n} |S_i - q_i| = (S_o - q_o)$.
Therefore:

$$\sum_{\substack{i=1 \\ S_i > q_i}}^{n} (S_i - \lceil q_i \rceil) \geq S_o - \lceil q_o \rceil \geq (S_o - q_o) - 1,$$

where the last inequality takes into account that $q_o + 1 \geq \lceil q_o \rceil$. Dividing both extreme members by S, we have

$$\frac{1}{S} \sum_{\substack{i=1 \\ S_i > q_i}}^{n} (S_i - \lceil q_i \rceil) \geq \frac{(q_o - S_o)}{S} - \frac{1}{S} = \frac{\max\limits_{i=1,\dots,n} |S_i - q_i|}{S} - \frac{1}{S}.$$

In consequence, $I_q \geq I_{MD} - \frac{1}{5}$. $\square$

Appendix B.

Table A1. Spanish Electoral Results (2016).

Parties	Votes	Quotas	Seats
PP	7906.185	116.48	137
PSOE	5424.709	79.92	85
PODEMOS-IU-EQUO	3201.170	47.16	45
C's	3123.769	46.02	32
ECP	848.526	12.50	12
PODEMOS-COMPROMÍS-EUPV	655.895	9.66	9
ERC-CATSÍ	629.294	9.27	9
CDC	481.839	7.10	8
PODEMOS-EN MAREA-ANOVA-EU	344.143	5.07	5
EAJ-PNV	286.215	4.22	5
EH Bildu	184.092	2.71	2
CCa-PNC	78.080	1.15	1
PACMA	284.848	4.20	
RECORTES CERO-GRUPO VERDE	51.742	0.76	
UPyD	50.282	0.74	
VOX	46.781	0.69	
BNG-NÓS	44.902	0.66	
PCPE	26.553	0.39	
GBAI	14.289	0.21	
EB	12.024	0.18	
FE de las JONS	9.862	0.15	
SI	7.413	0.11	
SOMVAL	6.612	0.10	
CCD	6.264	0.09	
PH	3.288	0.05	
SAIn	3.221	0.05	
P-LIB	3.103	0.05	
CENTRO MODERADO	2.986	0.04	
CCD-CI	2.668	0.04	
UPL	2.307	0.03	
PCOE	1.812	0.03	
AND	1.695	0.02	
JXC	1.184	0.02	
IZAR	854	0.01	
CILUS	847	0.01	
PFyV	838	0.01	
PxC	722	0.01	
MAS	718	0.01	
UNIDAD DEL PUEBLO	684	0.01	
PREPAL	640	0.01	
Ln	617	0.01	
REPO	569	0.01	
INDEPENDIENTES-FIA	556	0.01	
IMC	351	0.01	
FME	338	0.00	
PUEDE	330	0.00	
ENTABAN	257	0.00	
FE	254	0.00	
ALCD	210	0.00	
HRTS-Ln	82	0.00	
UDT	54	0.00	
Total	23,756.674	350	350

Source: Ministry of Interior (Spain).

Appendix C. Electoral Data Resources

Spain: www.infoelectoral.mir.es/infoelectoral/min/.
Sweden: www.electionresources.org/se/.
Germany: www.bundeswahlleiter.de/bundestagswahlen/2017/publikationen.html.

References

Balinski, Michael, and Victoriano Ramírez. 1999. Parametric methods of apportionment, rounding and production. *Mathematical Social Sciences* 37: 107–22. [CrossRef]

Balinski, Michael, and H. Peyton Young. 2001. *Fair Representation: Meeting the Ideal of One Man, One Vote.* Washington, DC: Brookings Institution Press.

Bolun, Ion. 2012. Comparison of indices of disproportionality in PR systems. *Computer Science Journal of Moldova* 20: 246–71.

Borisyuk, Galina, Colin Rallings, and Michael Thrasher. 2004. Selecting indexes of electoral proportionality: General properties and relationships. *Quality and Quantity* 38: 51–74. [CrossRef]

Boyssou, Denis, Marchant Thierry, and Marc Pirlot. 2016. Axiomatic Characterization of Some Disproportionality and Malapportionment Indices. Available online: https://editorialexpress.com/cgi-bin/conference/download.cgi?db_name=SCW2016&paper_id=287 (accessed on 7 January 2019).

Chessa, Michela, and Vito Fragnelli. 2012. A note on Measurement of disproportionality in proportional representations systems. *Mathematical and Computer Modelling* 55: 1655–60. [CrossRef]

Gallagher, Michael. 1991. Proportionality, disproportionality and electoral systems. *Electoral Studies* 10: 33–51. [CrossRef]

Goldenberg, Josh, and Stephen D. Fisher. 2017. The Sainte-Laguë index of disproportionality and Dalton's principle of transfers. *Party Politics.* [CrossRef]

Karpov, Alexander. 2008. Measurement of Disproportionality in Proportional Representations Systems. *Mathematical and Computer Modelling* 48: 1421–38. [CrossRef]

Koppel, Moshe, and Abraham Diskin. 2009. Measuring disproportionality, volatility and malapportionment: Axiomatization and solutions. *Social Choice and Welfare* 33: 281–86. [CrossRef]

Loosemore, John, and Victor J. Hanby. 1971. The theoretical limits of maximum distortion: Some analytic expressions of electoral systems. *British Journal of Political Science* 1: 467–77. [CrossRef]

Ocaña, Francisco A., and Pablo Oñate. 2011. IndElec: A software for analyzing party systems and electoral systems. *Journal of Statistical Software* 42: 1–28. [CrossRef]

Taagepera, Rein. 2007. *Predicting Party Sizes. The Logic of Simple Electoral Systems.* Oxford: Oxford University Press.

Taagepera, Rein, and Bernard Grofman. 2003. Mapping the indices of seats-votes disproportionality and inter-election volatility. *Party Politics* 9: 659–77. [CrossRef]

Van Puyenbroeck, Tom. 2008. Proportional Representation, Gini Coefficients, and the Principle of Transfers. *Journal of Theoretical Politics* 20: 498–526. [CrossRef]

economies

MDPI

Article

On the Samaritan's Dilemma, Foreign Aid, and Freedom

Joao Ricardo Faria [1,*] **and Daniel Arce** [2]

[1] Department of Economics, Florida Atlantic University, Boca Raton, FL 33431, USA
[2] School of Economics, Political and Policy Sciences, University of Texas at Dallas, Richardson, TX 75080, USA; darce@utdallas.edu
[*] Correspondence: jfaria@fau.edu; Tel.: +1-561-297-2397

Received: 28 August 2018; Accepted: 21 September 2018; Published: 8 October 2018

Abstract: This paper presents an extension of the two-period Samaritan's Dilemma in order to analyze the potential for foreign aid to promote freedom. An example is the United States' recent opening towards Cuba. It is shown that a donor nation's dual concern for economic reforms and greater freedoms can exacerbate the Samaritan's Dilemma, even when economic aid is coupled with targets for freedom. By contrast, a policy that is focused on freedom alone can potentially resolve the Samaritan's Dilemma. Such a policy requires the donor to temper the degree of altruism that motivates its provision of economic aid to the recipient nation.

Keywords: Altruism; Leading by example; Policy formulation; Hierarchical games

JEL Classification: D78; F35; F59; C73

1. Introduction

Donor nations may seek to attain multiple goals when providing foreign aid to a recipient nation. For example, if the recipient nation is a dictatorship, then the donor may be interested in fostering both economic growth and political freedoms. By contrast, the recipient dictatorship might not be interested in achieving both goals, particularly if political freedoms would lead to a reduction in power. In such a situation, what is a donor nation to do?

Cuba is a motivating example of this phenomenon. In the first 30 years of communist rule it was a USSR satellite in that Cuba's economy critically depended on Soviet aid (Morris 2007). Given the effects of the United States (U.S.) embargo that resulted from Cuba's nationalization of U.S. oil refineries, it was impossible for Cuba to sustain its economy without receiving external support (Pérez 2002). With the demise of the Soviet Union, Cuba's primary source of aid dried up and it looked for new partners to economically and financially support the communist regime. Subsequently, Hugo Chavez's Venezuela became the main provider of aid to Cuba (Amegashie et al. 2013). Yet, under the combination of falling oil prices and the death of Chavez, Venezuela could no longer afford to support Cuba (Piccone and Trinkunas 2014). Brazil, under the Lula and Rousseff administrations, then became Cuba's new life-line.[1] Over time, the Brazilian government was plagued by corruption and also committed itself to vast expenditures associated with its hosting of The World Cup and Rio Olympics. Finally, during Rousseff's presidency, the Brazilian economy entered into the nadir of a recession (Economist 2016), at which point it could no longer maintain its support of Cuba.

This history of aid to Cuba characterizes the regime as *parasitic* in the sense of Buchanan's (Buchanan 1975) Samaritan's Dilemma. That is, sponsors directed international aid to Cuba primarily

---

[1] For the Brazilian foreign policies see Dauvergne and Farias (2012).

for the purpose of maintaining Cuba's communist regime, and, knowing this, Cuba has had no incentive to conduct meaningful economic reform. Cuba's leaders were well-aware that aid would not be withdrawn in the absence of reform because the maintenance of Cuba's communist system was of first-order importance to its donors. This is consistent with Gibson et al.'s (2005) characterization of the Samaritan's Dilemma as being a motivational problem, rather one than stemming from the asymmetry or absence of information. Moreover, Gibson et al. (2005) recognize that the dynamics of the Samaritan's Dilemma are such that not only is meaningful reform unlikely, but also aid recipients may actually lose skills and motivation over time (p. 39).

Such behavior is not limited to Cuba. For example, North Korea and other dictatorial clientele states do the same; they have an incentive to avoid reforming their own economies in order to extract rents from the rest of the world in the form of foreign aid. Although not framed within the context of the Samaritan's Dilemma, Bapat (2011) notes that donors of anti-terrorism aid face a similar situation. Specifically, it is the existence of terrorism in the recipient nation that prompts the need for aid. This then begs the question as to the incentive for true counterterror efforts within the recipient nation if counterterror success leads to less aid.

What happens if, in addition to economic performance, the donor is also interested in promoting freedom? For example, as outlined above, without the help of the Soviet Union, Venezuela, or Brazil the Cuban regime had no obvious source of aid. Within this vacuum, the Obama administration saw a clear opportunity to engage Cuba and reestablish diplomatic and commercial relations with it. For the Obama administration, opening its relationship with Cuba was seen as an opportunity to renew its leadership in the Americas "and promote more effective change that supports the Cuban people and our national security interests" [https://www.whitehouse.gov/issues/foreign-policy/cuba]. In particular,

> "A critical focus of these actions will include continued strong support for improved human rights conditions and democratic reforms in Cuba. The promotion of democracy supports universal human rights by empowering civil society and a person's right to speak freely, peacefully assemble, and associate, and by supporting the ability of people to freely determine their future. The U.S. efforts are aimed at *promoting the independence of the Cuban people so they do not need to rely on the Cuban state*".

> [https://www.whitehouse.gov/issues/foreign-policy/cuba, emphasis added]

In sum, the aim of the Obama administration's policy was to improve Cuba's economic performance, and, at the same time, increase the freedom of its people so that they do not have to rely on the Cuban state.[2] Indeed, promoting freedom is often used as a justifying rationale for foreign aid. For freedom promotion to work, it would appear that, at a minimum, the donor must resolve the Samaritan's Dilemma. Moreover, we show how changes to this policy under the Trump administration will have the effect of testing the administration's resolve.

The issues here are quite general and extend beyond U.S.-Cuba relations. Consequently, this paper introduces an explicitly dynamic model as a context for analyzing the possible outcomes of a change in donor-recipient relations that emphasizes both increased economic performance and freedoms. In particular, we ask whether a focus on resolving the Samaritan's Dilemma with respect to the aid-income relationship is enough to successfully increase freedoms as well. That is, is a focus on the Samaritan's Dilemma an example of Kerr's (Kerr 1975) classic trap of rewarding A while hoping for B? Here, 'A' is rewarding recipient economic reform with increased aid, consistent with resolving the Samaritan's Dilemma. The 'B' is the donor's objective of increased freedoms for the recipient population.

---

[2] The evolution of this policy under the Trump administration is addressed below.

Within this context, we consider three different types of policies and two policymaking environments. The policies are (i) an aid policy that is targeted on recipient economic performance; (ii) a policy that couples aid with freedom and (iii) a freedom target that affects the recipient's economic performance indirectly via entrepreneurial reforms. The two policy environments are Stackelberg (leader-follower) and Nash. The Stackelberg environment with the recipient treated as the leader is most closely associated with the Samaritan's Dilemma within two-period models (Pedersen 2001; Dijkstra 2007); hence, it serves as a benchmark. Within this environment, we show that a policy that is designed to avoid Kerr's (1975) trap by coupling aid with freedom neither resolves the Samaritan's Dilemma nor does it foster freedom. This leads us to consider Nash interaction between donor and recipient because Nash behavior involves sufficient donor commitment to resolve the two-period Samaritan's Dilemma (Gintis 2009). However, this turns out to be a classic case of rewarding A while hoping for B. Specifically, in a Nash environment, the policy of coupling aid with freedom resolves the Samaritan's Dilemma, but it does not commensurately increase freedoms within the recipient nation. Our final consideration, Nash play (representing donor commitment) and an explicitly freedom-based policy, succeeds at resolving both the Samaritan's Dilemma and increasing freedoms. To be successful; however, such a policy requires the donor to temper its altruistic motivation for supporting the recipient. This is especially true if the recipient is willing to test the donor's resolve.

The paper is organized as follows. The next section presents a literature review. Section 3 introduces a baseline dynamic version of a Samaritan's Dilemma between a donor and recipient. Section 4 considers several policies designed to resolve the Samaritan's Dilemma, and shows that in all cases, the recipient is able to accept donor aid and maintain its restrictions on freedoms. In Section 5 we analyze the effect of the donor pre-committing to a freedom-based target, and show how this causes meaningful reform within the recipient. Concluding remarks appear in Section 6.

2. Literature Review

Many countries engage in foreign aid and yet the literature on the efficacy of aid is equivocal. For example, Easterly (2003) disputes that aid promotes growth. By contrast, Dalgaard et al. (2004) show that aid increases long-run productivity. Boone (1996) finds that foreign aid has little impact reducing poverty, or increasing investment; its main effect is to increase the size of government. Tavares (2003) shows that foreign aid reduces corruption. Goldsmith (2001) finds a small, positive relationship between foreign aid and democracy or freedom in Africa. Conversely, Knack (2004) does not find any empirical evidence that aid promotes democracy for a sample of recipient nations over 1975–2000. Power and Ryan (2006) analyze recipient nations over a 30-year time span (1970–2000) and find no significant effect of foreign aid on economic freedom. Regarding the equivocal relationship between aid and freedom, it is our contention that such observations can be partially explained by mixed results on the part of donors to resolve the Samaritan's Dilemma.

Indeed, *The Elusive Quest for Growth* (Easterly 2002) raised awareness of the importance of accounting for economic and political incentives when it comes to development aid. Much earlier, Buchanan (1975) similarly observed that suitable incentives and institutions for both donors and recipients are necessary in order to be able to successfully institute aid-based reforms. Buchanan called such a situation the *Samaritan's Dilemma*, where a donor that is motivated by altruism (the proverbial Samaritan) might have to restrict the extent of their altruism in order to provide the necessary incentives for a recipient nation to conduct reform. For example, suppose that, as an altruist, a donor's aid to a recipient nation is negatively related to the recipient's GDP. Then, if the recipient nation's economy fares poorly—owing to the absence of economic reforms—the recipient nation may receive more aid than it would have under reforms that produced better economic outcomes. Buchanan (1975) calls such recipient behavior *parasitic*. Moreover, Buchanan (1975) sees the issue in terms of being as much of a problem of the donor's behavior as that of the recipient.

In particular, when a donor is altruistic, the donor's utility places positive weight on the recipient's utility. Aid has a direct cost in that it subtracts from the donor's income but it also constitutes an altruistic benefit for the donor because it increases the recipient's utility. Hence, if the recipient underachieves economically an altruistic donor finds it in its interest to augment the recipient's income via aid. In addition, in Buchanan's (1975) *active* Samaritan's Dilemma, the donor's utility is not only a function of the amount of aid given to the recipient but it is also a function of the recipient's actions. Typically, this means that the donor prefers that the recipient conduct economic reforms rather than exhibit parasitic behavior. In this paper, we put a twist on the donor's preferences over the recipient's actions. Specifically, donor aid policy is motivated by both a concern for recipient economic performance and also as a means for promoting freedom. Consequently, an altruistic donor prefers that aid results in actions by the recipient that ultimately lead to increased freedoms.

In order to avoid the counterproductive incentive structure between the lack of reform and the provision of aid, the donor nation may have to tie its hands and act against its altruistic interests. Whether or not the donor should abandon its altruistic tendencies, thereby temporarily penalizing both itself and the recipient, is the Samaritan's Dilemma. In making such a commitment, the donor must weigh the utility of the recipient in both the short and long run. Yet, the dynamic asymmetries present between donor and recipient are absent from Buchanan's (1975) model because it is a static game in strategic form. Consequently, a literature has emerged that examines the dynamic means for tying the hands of altruistic donors and aligning the incentives for the recipient with those of the donor.

Within a dynamic context the Samaritan's Dilemma typically arises when the recipient acts as a Stackelberg leader, thereby capitalizing on the donor's altruism to its full extent (Bruce and Waldman 1990). The Stackelberg relation applies because recipients know that the greater the need that an altruistic donor observes, the more aid the donor will give. To summarize Pedersen (2001, p. 698): upon observing a low level of recipient income, it is in the donor's interest to increase aid, which is exactly what the recipient anticipated the donor to do. This is because if the donor does not give extra aid it will lower the recipient's utility, and, by the donor's altruism, the utility of the donor itself. The recipient's understanding of this incentive structure allows for it to behave like a Stackelberg leader in that it anticipates the donor's likely response.

The solution therefore requires the donor to commit to not giving extra aid if the recipient underperforms economically. Gintis (2009) demonstrates that if the donor is able to commit to Nash play with the recipient, then the Samaritan's Dilemma may be resolved. It is also well-established that the two-period passive version of Buchanan's Samaritan's Dilemma can be resolved if the donor acts as a leader in the Stackelberg sense (e.g., Dijkstra 2007).[3] Another resolution is provided by Lagerlöf (2004), where the donor has incomplete information regarding the recipient's preferences over the aid-augmented term in the recipient's utility. As is often the case, the introduction of incomplete information increases the set of equilibria. In particular, equilibrium exists where the recipient truthfully signals its need for aid. In an alternative environment, where the donor has asymmetric information regarding the recipient's degree of reform, Svensson (2000) shows that a second-best solution can be achieved when the donor delegates its aid decision to an agent that is less altruistic than the donor. This is consistent with Buchanan's (1975) intuition that resolving the Samaritan's Dilemma requires the donor to tie its hands against its altruistic interests.

In terms of the literature reviewed above, there are two defining aspects of our analysis. First, the recipient is engaged in an active Samaritan's Dilemma with the donor, owing to the donor's concerns for freedoms that extend beyond its altruistic motivation for providing aid. That is, the donor is concerned with both the recipient's welfare and actions. Second, it is a complete information analysis. This is in keeping with donor's understanding of the recipient as a dictatorship with well-defined preferences for remaining in power. In addition, it is consistent with the treatment of the Samaritan's

---

[3] In the passive Samaritan's Dilemma the donor's payoffs are only dependent on the amount of aid the donor gives and are not dependent on the recipient's actions. Recall that we are instead examining the active version of the Samaritan's Dilemma, in which the recipient's actions also matter to the donor. In particular, the expansion of freedoms to augment recipient nation income matters to the donor nation.

Dilemma in the foreign aid literature as being a motivational problem for donor and recipient alike, rather than stemming from asymmetric information (Gibson et al. 2005). The corresponding model is presented in the following section.

3. The Model

Our framework is based on an explicitly dynamic version of the Samaritan's Dilemma. This two-period baseline model allows for us to begin by formally addressing Buchanan's (1975) assertion that the resolution of the Samaritan's Dilemma may require a commitment that is costly to an altruistic aid donor in order to convince the aid recipient that it is in the recipient's best interest to undertake reform. Moreover, the two-period horizon captures the inability of elected governments to commit to longer-term criteria for aid.

In expressing the model, the upper-case symbols U and V are used to denote the donor and recipient's two-period utility functions, respectively. The first-period components of the donor's and recipient's utilities are denoted as u and v, respectively, with the second-period component of the recipient's utility being denoted as $\hat{v}$. We do not specify a second-period component of the donor's utility because, by the definition of altruism, the donor's second-period utility will be a function of the recipient's utility, V.

The two-period utility function of the recipient's leadership, V, is defined to be consistent with that of a dictatorship.[4] In the first period, prior to receiving donor aid, the recipient's welfare depends positively on the state of its economy, as measured by its GDP, y, and negatively on the freedom, F, of its people. The greater the freedom, the lower the dictator's utility. These considerations are captured by the following partial derivatives of the first-period utility function, $v(y, F)$:

$$v_y > 0, v_{yy} < 0, v_F < 0, v_{FF} < 0, v_{yF} > 0. \tag{1}$$

For example, the cross-partial derivative $v_{yF} > 0$ reflects the following phenomena. Aid is a second-period decision for the donor Hence, one way that the recipient can augment its first period income in the absence of aid is by increasing freedoms that lead to increased entrepreneurship. In the Cuban example, when the Soviet Union fell, its aid and trade subsidization policies with Cuba ended as well. In order to make up the output gap, Cuba responded by legalizing microenterprises in various sectors during 1993–1995 (Ritter 1998). The tradeoff that is involved for a dictatorship considering such freedoms in the first period is captured by $v_F < 0, v_{FF} < 0$, implying that the dictatorship dislikes freedom; and, $v_{yF} > 0$, implying that entrepreneurial freedom is good for growth. The short-term use of entrepreneurial freedoms to augment growth is a hallmark of dictatorships.[5]

In the second period, aid from the donor is now possible. Aid/help from the donor is denoted by H, which adds to the recipient's second-period income; i.e., $y + H$. The recipient's second-period utility, $\hat{v}(y + H, F)$, is characterized by the following set of partial derivatives:

$$\hat{v}_1 > 0, \hat{v}_{11} < 0, \hat{v}_F < 0, \hat{v}_{FF} < 0, \hat{v}_{1F} = 0, \tag{2}$$

where $\hat{v}_1$ denotes the partial derivative of the recipient's second-period utility function, $\hat{v}$, with respect to its first argument, $y + H$. The possibility of aid in the second period means that freedom loses its income-augmenting appeal in the recipient's second-period utility function; which is captured by

---

4   In the case of a totalitarian dictatorship, such as the Castros', ideas, interests and institutions are molded by the state and influence society. The opposite is true of a liberal state (Moravcsik 1997).

5   The best historical example of this type of behavior, typical of communist dictatorships, is Russia's NEF [New Economic Policy—1921–1928], created by Lenin, which allowed for some market freedom during the 1920's, permitting the recuperation of the Soviet economy after the failed policies of war communism 1918–1921 (Radzinsky 1996). Then, by the end of the decade, in spite or because of its success, NEP was reversed in its tracks in favor of the collectivization of agriculture and the big push of state-led industrialization (Conquest 1991; Medvedev 1972).

$\hat{v}_{1F} = 0$. That is, in the second period the recipient behaves strategically by substituting aid for reform, as is the case in the Samaritan's Dilemma. The inconsistent way that the recipient views freedom when aid is not present (in the first period) versus how it views freedom when aid is a possibility (in the second period) is a characteristic of dictatorial behavior [see footnote 5].

The recipient's utility function for both periods is

$$V(y, F, H) = v(y, F) + \delta \hat{v}(y + H, F),\tag{3}$$

where $\delta > 0$ is the recipient's discount factor. Being a dictatorship, the recipient's control variable is its income, y. To wit, in choosing y the recipient is effectively determining its degree of economic reform. Moreover, given the relationship between entrepreneurial freedom and y, in selecting y the recipient imputes a corresponding level of F. Measures that have been used to monitor F are discussed below.

The donor acts as an altruistic agent, in that it wants to improve the well-being of the recipient's people via income-augmenting aid to the recipient at a material cost to itself. Specifically, aid/help (H) comes out of the donor's GDP, Y. The donor's two-period utility function is

$$U(Y, H, y, F) = u(Y - H) + \alpha V(y, F, H),\tag{4}$$

where $\alpha > 0$ is the donor's degree of altruism. The presence of altruism in this form is a defining characteristic of the Samaritan's Dilemma. The donor's first-period utility function is increasing and concave in its own net income, $Y-H$. That is, $u' > 0$ and $u'' < 0$. As an altruist, the donor's second-period utility is the α-weighted utility of the recipient. In particular, given that $\alpha \hat{v}_1 > 0$, if y is low, then an altruistic donor sees it as in its interest to augment the low y with aid, H. Hence, the potential for the Samaritan's Dilemma is present.

Given these utility functions, the interaction between the recipient and donor hinges upon two relationships. The first is dH/dy; i.e., the effect that the recipient's economic performance has on donor aid. A parasitic relationship exists when $dH/dy < 0$. Lower recipient economic performance leads to a lower value of y, which in turn induces the donor to give greater aid. This in keeping with the Samaritan's Dilemma approach to foreign aid. As an extension to this approach, note that one determinant of y is F. When freedoms increase this facilitates entrepreneurial behavior that spurs growth. Such freedoms reduce dictatorial power, however. It follows that if the dictatorship infringes on F this limits y. The dictator's cost of reducing economic-enhancing freedom is offset when $dH/dy < 0$ because aid can potentially make up the difference. This exacerbates the Samaritan's Dilemma. Moreover, this characterization of strategic interaction between recipient and donor captures the observed equivocal relationship between aid and freedom. Indeed, in resolving the Samaritan's Dilemma by creating an aid policy that leads to $dH/dy > 0$, the question remains as to how this will ultimately affect freedom. Kerr's (1975) trap is a potentiality. Only when the interaction between the donor and the recipient results in $dH/dF > 0$ is the donor aid policy in alignment with its desire to promote freedom for the recipient's people. We now turn to three aid policies that address this issue.

4. Aid without Commitment

In the Samaritan's Dilemma, if the donor is unable to commit to a policy of no aid when the recipient does not undertake economic reform, then the donor's altruism causes the donor to react optimally to the economic situation that is produced by the recipient's reforms or lack thereof. In terms of the model, this means that, if the donor cannot commit to an aid level that is independent of the recipient's economic situation, then altruism leads the donor to make its aid policy contingent on the recipient's economic situation. Expressed in terms of the choice variables, this means that the donor observes the recipient's choice of y and then the donor sets its choice of H. That is, the donor's policy is its best reply function. The donor's inability to commit is therefore indicative of a leader-follower relationship where the recipient is the leader and the donor is the follower. In this section we consider two cases that can arise in the absence of donor commitment. The difference between the two cases is whether the donor selects aid, H, in reaction to the recipient's choice of y (Case A); or, if the donor instead couples aid, H, with freedom, F. Case A is the classic Samaritan's Dilemma and Case B is a new wrinkle that recognizes the donor's ultimate rationale for engaging the recipient: increasing freedoms.

Case A: No Donor Link between Aid and Reform

The donor's choice variable is aid, H (help). In Case A, the donor selects aid in reaction to the current economic situation in the recipient nation, y. Solving the model backwards, for a given y the donor maximizes (4) with respect to H. The donor's first order condition is

$$-u'(Y - H) + \alpha \delta \hat{v}_1(y + H, F) = 0 \Rightarrow H = H(\alpha, y, Y), \tag{5}$$

which characterizes the donor's best reply function.

The result is a parasitic relationship, as the impact of y on H is negative [all comparative static calculations are derived in Appendix A]:

$$H_y = \frac{dH}{dy} = \frac{-\alpha \delta \hat{v}_{11}}{u'' + \alpha \delta \hat{v}_{11}} < 0. \tag{6}$$

Equation (6) describes a counterproductive incentive at play. When the recipient underperforms economically, this induces the donor to give more aid. This is a classic parasitic relationship in the sense of Buchanan (1975) Samaritan's Dilemma. A failing recipient economy leads to increased aid. Hence, this is our starting point for donor-recipient relations.

Given donor aid policy (the donor's best reply function), $H(\alpha, Y, y)$, the recipient maximizes (3) with respect to y, yielding

$$v_y(y, F) + \delta \hat{v}_1(y + H, F)(1 + H_y) = 0 \Rightarrow y_A^* = y(\alpha, F, H). \tag{7}$$

Equation (7) determines the optimal value of the recipient's income for Case A: y_A^*. Note that the impact of freedom on the optimal y_A^* is positive:

$$\frac{dy_A^*}{dF} = \frac{-v_{yF}}{v_{yy} + \delta(1 + H_y)^2 \hat{v}_{11}} > 0. \tag{8}$$

By Equation (8), a dictatorship's restrictions on freedom allows a parasite to underperform with respect to income, thereby further facilitating the parasitic relationship. This exacerbates the Samaritan's Dilemma.

Inserting y_A^* into Equation (5) yields the donor's optimal aid for Case A, H_A^* :

$$H_A^* = H(\alpha, y_A^*, Y) = H(\alpha, y_A^*(\alpha, F, Y), Y). \tag{9}$$

Now, one can assess the impact of donor aid on the freedom on the recipient's people [taking into account Equations (6) and (8)]:

$$\frac{dH_A^*}{dF} = \frac{dH}{dy_A^*} \frac{dy_A^*}{dF} < 0. \tag{10}$$

That is, although freedom has a positive impact on income, $dy_A^*/dF > 0$, this is offset by the parasitic donor-recipient relationship, $dH_A^*/dy_A^* < 0$. Increased freedoms that might be necessary for augmenting a regime's income are instead neglected, because the resulting decrease in income causes the altruistic donor to be more generous. Consequently, the recipient does not reform either economically or in the dimension of freedom for its people. As expected, this case is consistent with the Samaritan's Dilemma.

Figure 1 illustrates the inner workings of Case A. First, the top left graph depicts Equation (6): the negative relation between donor aid, H, and the recipient's income, y. If the recipient's income falls from y_0 to y_1, donor aid is increased from H_0 to H_1. This is the Samaritan's Dilemma: the recipient finds it in its interest to underperform economically in order to extract more aid. Second, the bottom left graph uses a 45° line in (y, y) space to transform the measurement of y, which is on the horizontal axis of the top left graph, to the measurement of y on the vertical axis of (F, y) space in the bottom right graph of Figure 1. Third, the bottom right graph depicts the relationship given in Equation (8): the positive relationship between freedom and the recipient's income. When the recipient makes its choice of income y_1 instead of y_0 it does not need the entrepreneurial freedoms, F_0, associated with y_0. Instead, it imputes that the freedoms necessary for y_1 are those that are given by F_1. Fourth, the top right graph depicts Equation (10): the impact of donor aid on the freedom of the recipient's people. It captures the tradeoff between these two variables, in which a decrease in freedoms from F_0 to F_1 leads to an increase in donor aid from H_0 to H_1. Figure 1 presents the two main tradeoffs identified within this paper: the Samaritan's Dilemma, which captures the tradeoff between income and aid; and, the resulting tradeoff between freedom and aid, which, to the best of our knowledge, has gone unidentified until now.

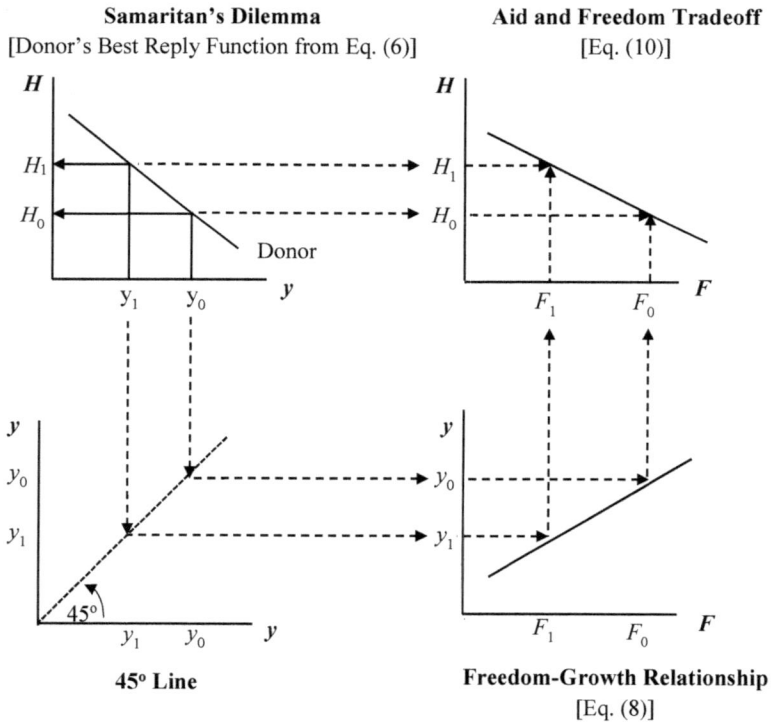

Figure 1. Case A: No Donor Link between Aid and Reform.

Case B: The Donor Couples Aid to Reform

Of course, both outcomes of Case A: (i) the recipient's parasitic ability to receive aid when it engages in less reform; and, (ii) the negative relationship between freedom and aid; run against the donor's goodwill and intentions. As an alternative, the donor can use aid to augment the recipient's income, but do so in a way that couples aid to freedom.

A coupled donor aid policy is expressed as the product FH, where H is again the donor's choice variable. This implies that rather than aid augmenting the recipient's income through the term $y +$

H, it does so through the term $y + FH$. From an operational perspective, the term FH can be directly estimated if F is a freedom index that lies along the $[0, 1]$ interval, where 0 represents no freedom and 1 the freedom level the donor is targeting. Such freedom scores allow for the monitoring of changes in freedom in the recipient nations, and have been used in empirical work on the composition and efficacy of aid (Amegashie et al. 2013; Power and Ryan 2006; Medvedev 1972). Therefore, the recipient's and donor's utility functions are, respectively,

$$V(y, F, H) = v(y, F) + \delta \hat{v}(y + FH); \tag{11}$$

$$U(Y, H, y, F) = u(Y - FH) + \alpha V(y, F, H). \tag{12}$$

Throughout this section, we retain the leader-follower structure consistent with an altruistic donor that makes its aid policy contingent upon the recipient's income. Consequently, the donor takes y as given and maximizes (12) with respect to aid, H, yielding the following best reply function:

$$-u'(Y - FH)F + \alpha \delta \hat{v}_1 (y + FH)F = 0 \Rightarrow H = H(\alpha, y, Y, F). \tag{13}$$

From (13), one can see that in this context the aid-income relationship remains parasitic:

$$H_y = \frac{dH}{dy} = \frac{-\alpha \delta \hat{v}_{11}}{[u'' + \alpha \delta \hat{v}_{11}]F} < 0. \tag{14}$$

Once again, it is in the recipient's interest to underperform economically, thereby receiving more aid.

Moreover, in contrast to Case A, from (13) F now has a direct impact on H:

$$\frac{dH}{dF} = \frac{-H}{F} < 0, \tag{15}$$

which can be best understood in terms of the elasticity of donor aid, H, with respect to freedom in the recipient, F:

$$\varepsilon_{HF} = \frac{dH}{dF} \frac{F}{H} = -1 \tag{13'}$$

As the absolute value of ε_{HF} is equal to one, $|\varepsilon_{HF}| = 1$, the donor's best reply function is of unit elasticity, i.e., the marginal impact of freedom on aid is equal to the average impact.

The recipient takes the donor's best reply in (13) into account and selects a level of reform that determines y. Effectively, the recipient maximizes (11) with respect to y given (13), yielding

$$v_y(y, F) + \delta \hat{v}_1 [y + FH(\alpha, y, Y, F)](1 + FH_y) = 0 \Rightarrow y_B^* = y(\alpha, Y, F). \tag{16}$$

Equation (16) determines the optimal recipient income in Case B: y_B^*. The impact of freedom on y_B^* is given by

$$\frac{dy}{dF} = \frac{-v_{yF} - \delta \hat{v}_{11}(FH_F + H)(1 + FH_y) - \delta \hat{v}_1 H_y}{[v_{yy} + \delta \hat{v}_{11}(1 + FH_y)^2]} \tag{17}$$

Substituting (16) into (13) yields the optimal donor aid for Case B: $H_B^* = H(\alpha, y_E^*, Y, F)$, which allows for an assessment of the impact of donor aid on the freedom when aid is coupled with freedom. Note that now there exists both a direct and an indirect impact of F on H_B^*. Policy FH results in the direct channel between F and H_B^*. The indirect channel between F and H_B^* occurs by combining of the effect of F on y with the effect of y on H via the chain rule:

$$\frac{dH_B^*}{dF} = \frac{dH}{dF} + \frac{dH}{dy_B^*}\frac{dy_B^*}{dF} = \frac{-H}{F} + \frac{(-\alpha \delta \hat{v}_{11})}{[u'' + \alpha \delta \hat{v}_{11}]F} \left[\frac{-v_{yF} - \delta \hat{v}_{11}(FH_F + H)(1 + FH_y) - \delta \hat{v}_1 H_y}{[v_{yy} + \delta \hat{v}_{11}(1 + FH_y)^2]} \right] \tag{18}$$

Given a positive effect of entrepreneurial freedom on growth, $\partial y / \partial F > 0$, by Equations (14) and (15), one must conclude that $\partial H_B^* / \partial F < 0$.

In both cases addressed in this section, a parasitic relationship exists between donor aid and recipient economic reform. Moreover, aid is a negative function of freedom in that the dictatorship uses restrictions on freedoms to inhibit growth, thereby exacerbating the Samaritan's Dilemma. Notably, this occurs even when the donor follows a policy that couples aid and freedom. The desired result is not obtained, and this is due to the structure of the game in which the donor does not commit to an aid level, but instead follows a policy in which aid is a best reply to the recipient's income level.

5. The Donor Pre-Commits Its Aid to the Recipient

In this section, we allow for the donor to commit to a particular aid strategy, rather than reacting to the prevailing economic situation in the recipient. Instead of a leader-follower relationship, in which the recipient takes the donor's best reply function as given, the two countries engage in Nash behavior, implying that in equilibrium the donor's aid policy is a best reply to the recipient's economic policy and vice-versa. In other words, each country creates the conditions under which the other sets its policy. We therefore analyze two aid strategies for the donor. In the first (Case C), the donor follows the aid-freedom coupling policy *FH*. In the second (Case D), the donor specifies aid as an increasing function of freedom in the recipient nation.

Case C: The Freedom-Aid Coupling Policy

Here, the donor again couples its aid to freedom; i.e., policy *FH*, but aid no longer moves in tandem with the recipient's income, *y*. The two are instead co-determined as part of a Nash equilibrium. Given policy *FH*, the donor's utility is as expressed in Equation (12) and the recipient's is as expressed in Equation (11). The first order conditions for the donor (with respect to *H*) and the recipient (with respect to *y*) are

$$-u'(Y - FH)F + \alpha\delta\hat{v}_1(y + FH)F = 0; \tag{19}$$

$$v_y(y, F) + \delta\hat{v}_1[y + FH] = 0. \tag{20}$$

When *y* and *H* are determined simultaneously, as is the case in Equations (19) and (20), by definition, there is no longer a parasitic relationship between the recipient and donor. Changing the game from a Stackelberg game in which the recipient is the leader, to a Nash game in which recipient income and donor aid are co-determined, eliminates the recipient's parasitism, thereby resolving the Samaritan's dilemma.

The impact of freedom on aid is given by (proof in Appendix A):

$$\frac{dH_C^*}{dF} = \frac{\alpha\delta\hat{v}_{11}v_{yF} - (Hu''[v_{yy} + \delta\hat{v}_{11}] + \alpha\delta H\hat{v}_{11}v_{yy})}{\Delta} < 0. \tag{21}$$

where $\Delta = [u''F + \alpha\delta F\hat{v}_{11}][v_{yy} + \delta\hat{v}_{11}] - \alpha\delta^2 F(\hat{v}_{11})^2 = [v_{yy} + \delta\hat{v}_{11}]u''F + \alpha\delta F\hat{v}_{11}v_{yy} > 0$.

Unfortunately, the tradeoff between freedom and aid persists, as $\partial H_C^* / \partial F < 0$. In Case C, the donor has fallen into Kerr's (1975) trap in that it has committed to a policy that couples aid with freedom, thereby resolving the Samaritan's Dilemma, but the ultimate goal of establishing a positive relationship between freedom and aid is not achieved. Per Equation (21), there is a tradeoff between freedom and aid. Therefore, the ability to pre-commit eliminates the recipient's parasitism, thereby resolving the Samaritan's Dilemma. At the same time, pre-commitment to aid coupled with freedom does not remove the tradeoff between freedom and aid.

Figure 2 illustrates Case C. The donor's best reply function is given by Equation (19), denoted as *D*. The recipient's best reply function is given by Equation (20), denoted as *R*. Strategies *H* and *y* are strategic substitutes for both the donor and recipient, as depicted by their downward-sloping best reply functions in (*y*, *H*) space. Indeed, the fact that aid and income are strategic substitutes lies at the heart of the Samaritan's Dilemma, because when the recipient can act as a Stackelberg leader, the recipient maximizes its utility function along the donor's negatively-sloped best reply function, implying that the recipient can substitute aid for income, as occurs in Cases A and B. In a Nash environment, the equilibrium instead takes place at the intersection of the best reply functions.

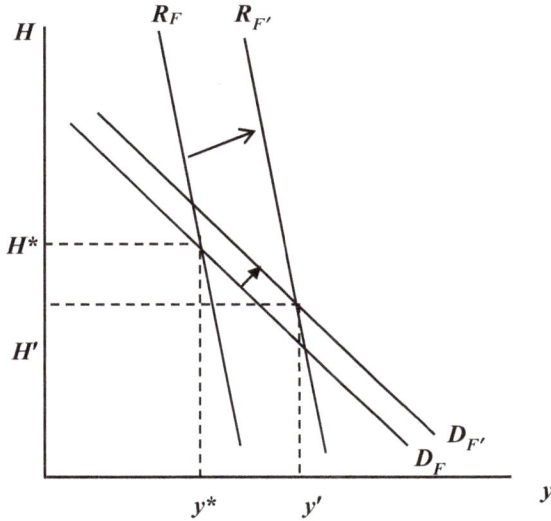

$$D = \text{Donor's Best Reply Function}$$
$$R = \text{Recipient's Best Reply Function}$$

Figure 2. Case C. The impact of freedom.

An increase in recipient freedom from F to F' shifts both best reply functions outward from the origin and the equilibrium changes from the original point (y^*, H^*) to (y', H'). Consequently, there is a tradeoff between F and H; i.e., optimal donor aid falls when the recipient's freedom increases.

Case D: The Donor Explicitly Targets Freedom

In this case the donor's aid is based on the following policy:

$$H = H(F) = hF, \ h > 0. \tag{22}$$

Under this policy, the donor aims at directly influencing freedom in the recipient, treating F as its strategy. Aid is no longer a policy itself but is instead the result of the policy that makes the donor's aid an increasing function of freedom in the recipient nation. Differently from the other cases, where the donor attempts to influence freedom indirectly through aid, in Case D, aid is explicitly tied to freedom. In other words, the donor recognizes the potential for Kerr's (1975) trap if it rewards economic reform with aid and hopes that freedom will be bolstered as well. Instead, the donor targets freedom directly. The utility functions of the recipient and donor are, respectively:

$$V(y, F, H) = v(y, F) + \delta\hat{v}(y + hF); \tag{23}$$

$$U(Y, H, y, F) = u(Y - hF) + \alpha V(y, F, H). \tag{24}$$

The first order conditions for a Nash equilibrium are

$$v_y(y, F) + \delta \hat{v}_1(y + hF) = 0; \tag{25}$$

$$-hu'(Y - hF) + \alpha \delta h \hat{v}_1(y + hF) = 0, \tag{26}$$

where in (25) the recipient maximizes its payoff with respect to its income, y, and in (26) the donor maximizes its payoff with respect to freedom, F.

For Case D, Equations (25) and (26) jointly determine the optimal levels of freedom, F_D^*, and income, y_D^*. With F_D^* one can calculate optimal aid, through Equation (22), to obtain H_D^*. In this case, the donor designs and enforces an aid policy which increases aid to the recipient only when freedom in the recipient increases. By definition, then, aid is an increasing function of freedom. It is clear that committing to the hF policy obtains the ultimate goal of the donor's aid policy. By targeting F instead of H the donor reduces the recipient's incentive to underperform economically via restrictions on freedom.

Interestingly, this creates a potential dilemma for a recipient dictatorship. As a dictatorship, the recipient may likely reject the freedom targets set by the donor. Absent any viable alternative donor, a rejecting recipient faces two alternatives. First, it could allow for growth-enhancing freedoms in order to reform itself out of the parasitic/clientele existence it has been sustaining via the Samaritan's Dilemma. But, this is tantamount to acquiescing to what the donor wanted in the first place. Second, the recipient could test the donor's resolve. For example, citing a need for U.S.-Cuban relations to be more closely tied with economic freedoms for the Cuban people, the Trump administration decided to rescind several Obama administration foreign-aid initiatives. Consequently, Cuba's government "has stopped allowing self-employed entrepreneurs to form company-like cooperatives" (Economist 2017). Again, like freedom scores, it is possible for donors to observe the evolution of such policies.

Recipient efforts at testing a freedom-targeting donor's resolve are captured by our model. Specifically, in the previous cases, altruism, α, is positively correlated with aid, H, and freedom, F (not shown). By contrast, under the hF policy this need not be the case:

$$\frac{dF_D^*}{d\alpha} = \frac{h\delta \hat{v}_{11}[v_{yy} + \delta \hat{v}_{11}]}{\Delta} < 0 \Leftrightarrow \Delta < 0 \Leftrightarrow \alpha \delta \hat{v}_{11} v_{yF} < h\{[u'' + \alpha \delta \hat{v}_{11}]v_{yy} + u''\delta\} \tag{27}$$

$$\frac{dH_D^*}{d\alpha} = \frac{h^2 \delta \hat{v}_{11}[v_{yy} + \delta \hat{v}_{11}]}{\Delta} < 0 \Leftrightarrow \Delta < 0 \tag{28}$$

One of Buchanan's (1975) primary points about the relationship between incentives and aid is that a donor may have to restrict the extent of their altruism to temper a recipient's incentive to underperform in order to receive more aid. This is captured by the two equations above. If the donor can reduce the way in which altruism enters into the aid decision, thereby lowering α, then *both* aid and freedom increase and the Kerr's (1975) trap is averted. Hence, the donor must be prepared to demonstrate resolve.

An even more convincing example of the need to reduce altruism in the aid decision is given by a fully cooperative model in which both donor and recipient are coordinated by an agreement in which they aim at maximizing the sum of their payoffs:

$$\underset{y,F}{Max} V(y, F, H) + U(Y, H, y, F) = u(Y - hF) + (1 + \alpha)V(y, F, H); \text{ i.e.}$$

$$\underset{y,F}{Max} u(Y - hF) + (1 + \alpha)[v(y, F) + \delta \hat{v}(y + hF)] \tag{29}$$

The impact of altruism in this fully cooperative case is negative for reasonable conditions [less restrictive than the one underlying (27) and (28)] (see calculations in the Appendix A):

$$\frac{dF_{coop}}{d\alpha} = \Delta^{-1}\{v_{yy}(v_F + h\delta\hat{v}_1) - v_y(v_{Fy} + h\delta\hat{v}_{11})\}(1+\alpha)^{-1} < 0$$
$$\Leftrightarrow \Delta > 0 \text{ and } v_{yy}(v_F + h\delta\hat{v}_1) < v_y(v_{Fy} + h\delta\hat{v}_{11})$$

(30)

In Equation (30), note that, in contrast with (27) and (28), the denominator Δ, must be positive, $\Delta > 0$, because it corresponds to the optimal second order condition of the maximization in Equation (29). According to (30), the marginal impact of altruism is negative on the optimal choice of freedom of the cooperative solution. This is because, in the cooperative solution, the joint externality between donor and recipient is internalized; namely, the penchant for the recipient to reduce income owing to the presence of the Samaritan's Dilemma. The effects of this externality are further decreased via a reduction in the donor's altruism.

Surprisingly, neither the cooperative solution, nor its comparative statics relative to the donor's level of altruism, have been characterized in prior treatments of the Samaritan's Dilemma. By doing so, we verify Buchanan's (1975) intuition that the donor needs to temper its altruism if it is to fully resolve the Samaritan's Dilemma.

6. Concluding Remarks

This paper presents a two-period game based on the Samaritan's dilemma to analyze the relationship between a foreign aid donor nation and a dictatorial recipient. Our model extends past analyses in that the donor nation is interested in fostering both economic growth and freedom within the recipient nation. This is consistent with many nations' underlying objectives for foreign aid. It is also consistent with the existing empirical literature, in which the observed relationship between aid and freedom is equivocal. This indeterminacy is often attributed to the existence of a Samaritan's Dilemma between donor and recipient. We show that it is further exacerbated by the donor's concern for freedom. Specifically, resolving the Samaritan's Dilemma can come at the cost of economic freedoms in the recipient nation.

In particular, prescriptions for resolving the Samaritan's Dilemma typically involve donor commitment to aid policies that force the recipient into a relationship where aid and economic performance are co-determined (in the Nash sense). Yet, we show that a focus on resolving the Samaritan's Dilemma represents a potential trap for the donor in that it need not ultimately foster recipient nation freedoms. An example of such a trap is an aid-freedom coupling policy. Within a Nash framework, the coupling policy resolves the Samaritan's Dilemma but recipient freedoms do not commensurately increase.

Finally, we examine an alternative policy that avoids this trap because the donor provides aid in direct proportion to increases in freedom. Given that the donor pre-commits, the Samaritan's Dilemma does not arise, and because aid increases with freedom, the donor achieves its dual goals of increasing economic performance and freedom in the recipient nation. Yet, the policy is not as simple as it may seem because the optimal commitment requires the donor to reduce its altruistic motivations for helping the recipient and replace them with a commitment to freedom targets. This may be difficult for altruistic policymakers, especially if the recipient is willing to test the donor's resolve. In the absence of such a policy, what this paper has identified is a fundamental tradeoff for a donor nation in terms of resolving the Samaritan's Dilemma versus promoting freedom. As such, this tradeoff should be recognized and accounted for in empirical analyses of the performance of foreign aid.

Author Contributions: J.R.F., model and research question; D.A., model and literature review.

Funding: This research received no external funding.

Conflicts of Interest: Authors declare no conflicts of interest.

Appendix A. Derivations

Case A:

Total differentiation of Equation (5) yields

$$- u''(dY - dH) + d\alpha \delta \hat{v}_1(y + H, F) + \alpha \delta \hat{v}_{11}(dy + dH) = 0. \tag{A1}$$

Therefore we obtain an expression for dH:

$$dH = \frac{u'' dY - \delta \hat{v}_1 d\alpha - \alpha \delta \hat{v}_{11} dy}{u'' + \alpha \delta \hat{v}_{11}}, \tag{A2}$$

from which Equation (6) is derived.

Total differentiation of Equation (7) yields $\left[\text{recall that } \hat{v}_{yF} = 0\right]$:

$$v_{yy} dy + v_{yF} dF + \delta \hat{v}_{11}(dy + dH)(1 + H_y) + \delta \hat{v}_1 H_{y\alpha} d\alpha = 0. \tag{A3}$$

Substituting (A2) into (A3):

$$v_{yy} dy + v_{yF} dF + \delta(1 + H_y)\hat{v}_{11}\left(dy + \frac{u'' dY - \delta \hat{v}_1 d\alpha - \alpha \delta \hat{v}_{11} dy}{u'' + \alpha \delta \hat{v}_{11}}\right) + \delta \hat{v}_1 H_{y\alpha} d\alpha = 0. \tag{A4}$$

From (A4) we obtain an expression for dy:

$$dy = \frac{-v_{yF} dF - \delta(1 + H_y)v_{11}\left(\frac{u'' dY - \delta \hat{v}_1 d\alpha}{u'' + \alpha \delta \hat{v}_{11}}\right) - \delta \hat{v}_1 H_{y\alpha} d\alpha}{u_{v_{yy}} + \delta(1 + H_y)\hat{v}_{11} - \frac{\alpha(1 + H_y)(\delta \hat{v}_{11})^2}{u'' + \alpha \delta \hat{v}_{11}}} \tag{A5}$$

Note that the definition of H_y in Equation (6) implies that the denominator of (A5) reduces to $v_{yy} + \delta(1 + H_y)^2 \hat{v}_{11} < 0$. From (A5) we derive Equation (8).

Case B:

Total differentiation of Equation (13) yields

$$- u''(dY - HdF - FdH) + \alpha \delta \hat{v}_{11}(dy + HdF + FdH) + \delta \hat{v}_1 d\alpha = 0. \tag{A6}$$

From (A6) we obtain the following expression for dH:

$$dH = \frac{u'' dY - (u'' + \alpha \delta \hat{v}_{11})HdF - \alpha \delta \hat{v}_{11} dy - \delta \hat{v}_1 d\alpha}{[u'' + \alpha \delta \hat{v}_{11}]F}. \tag{A7}$$

From (A7) we derive Equations (14) and (15).

Total differentiation of (16) yields

$$v_{yy} dy + v_{yF} dF + \delta \hat{v}_{11}[dy + F(H_\alpha d\alpha + H_y dy + H_Y dY + H_F dF) + HdF](1 + FH_y) + \delta \hat{v}_1(H_y dF + FdH_y) = 0. \tag{A8}$$

$$dy = \frac{[-v_{yF} dF - \delta \hat{v}_{11}[F(H_\alpha d\alpha + H_Y dY + H_F dF) + HdF](1 + FH_y) - \delta \hat{v}_1(H_y dF + FdH_y)]}{[v_{yy} + \delta \hat{v}_{11}(1 + FH_y)^2]} \tag{A9}$$

From (A9) and (15) we derive Equation (17).

Case C:

Total differentiation of Equations (19) and (20):

$$- u'' (dY - HdF - FdH) + \alpha \delta \hat{v}_{11}(dy + HdF + FdH) + \delta \hat{v}_1 d\alpha = 0; \tag{A10}$$

$$v_{yy}dy + v_{yF}dF + \delta \hat{v}_{11}[dy + FdH + HdF] = 0. \tag{A11}$$

Rearranging (A10) and (A11) in matrix form:

$$\begin{bmatrix} u'' F + \alpha \delta F \hat{v}_{11} & \alpha \delta \hat{v}_{11} \\ \delta F \hat{v}_{11} & v_{yy} + \delta \hat{v}_{11} \end{bmatrix} \begin{bmatrix} dH \\ dy \end{bmatrix} = \begin{bmatrix} u'' dY - (Hu'' + \alpha \delta H \hat{v}_{11})dF - \delta \hat{v}_1 d\alpha \\ -[v_{yF} + \delta H \hat{v}_{11}]dF \end{bmatrix} \tag{A12}$$

$$\Delta = [u'' F + \alpha \delta F \hat{v}_{11}][v_{yy} + \delta \hat{v}_{11}] - \alpha \delta^2 F(\hat{v}_{11})^2 = [v_{yy} + \delta \hat{v}_{11}]u'' F + \alpha \delta F \hat{v}_{11}v_{yy} > 0 \tag{A13}$$

$$\frac{dH}{dF} = \frac{\alpha \delta \hat{v}_{11}[v_{yF} + \delta H \hat{v}_{11}] - (Hu'' + \alpha \delta H \hat{v}_{11})[v_{yy} + \delta \hat{v}_{11}]}{\Delta} = \frac{\alpha \delta \hat{v}_{11} v_{yF} - (Hu''[v_{yy} + \delta \hat{v}_{11}] + \alpha \delta H \hat{v}_{11}v_{yy})}{\Delta} < 0 \tag{A14}$$

$$\frac{dy}{dF} = \frac{-[v_{yF} + \delta H \hat{v}_{11}][u'' F + \alpha \delta F \hat{v}_{11}] + \delta F \hat{v}_{11}(Hu'' + \alpha \delta H \hat{v}_{11})}{\Delta} = \frac{-v_{yF}[u'' F + \alpha \delta F \hat{v}_{11}]}{\Delta} > 0 \tag{A15}$$

Equation (A14) is Equation (21) in the text.

Case D:

Total differentiation of Equations (25) and (26):

$$v_{yy}dy + v_{yF}dF + \delta \hat{v}_{11}(dy + hdF) = 0; \tag{A16}$$

$$- hu'' (dY - hdF) + \alpha \delta h \hat{v}_{11}(dy + hdF) + \delta h \hat{v}_{11}d\alpha = 0. \tag{A17}$$

Rearranging (A16) and (A17) in matrix form:

$$\begin{bmatrix} v_{yF} + h\delta \hat{v}_{11} & v_{yy} + \delta \hat{v}_{11} \\ h^2[u'' + \alpha \delta \hat{v}_{11}] & \alpha \delta h \hat{v}_{11} \end{bmatrix} \begin{bmatrix} dF \\ dy \end{bmatrix} = \begin{bmatrix} 0 \\ hu'' dY - \delta h \hat{v}_{11}d\alpha \end{bmatrix} \tag{A18}$$

$$\Delta = \alpha \delta h \hat{v}_{11}[v_{yF} + h\delta \hat{v}_{11}] - h^2[u'' + \alpha \delta \hat{v}_{11}][v_{yy} + \delta \hat{v}_{11}] = \alpha \delta h \hat{v}_{11}v_{yF} - h^2[u'' + \alpha \delta \hat{v}_{11}]v_{yy} - h^2 u'' \delta \hat{v}_{11} \tag{A19}$$

$$\frac{dF}{d\alpha} = \frac{h\delta \hat{v}_{11}[v_{yy} + \delta \hat{v}_{11}]}{\Delta} > 0 \Leftrightarrow \Delta > 0 \Leftrightarrow \alpha \delta \hat{v}_{11}v_{yF} > h\{[u'' + \alpha \delta \hat{v}_{11}]v_{yy} + u'' \hat{\varepsilon}\} \tag{A20}$$

$$\frac{dF}{dY} = \frac{-hu''[v_{yy} + \delta \hat{v}_{11}]}{\Delta} < 0 \Leftrightarrow \Delta > 0 \tag{A21}$$

$$\frac{dy}{d\alpha} = \frac{-h\delta \hat{v}_{11}[v_{yF} + h\delta \hat{v}_{11}]}{\Delta} \gtrless 0 \tag{A22}$$

$$\frac{dy}{dY} = \frac{hu''[v_{yF} + h\delta \hat{v}_{11}]}{\Delta} \gtrless 0 \tag{A23}$$

Cooperative Case:

$$\underset{y,F}{Max} u(Y - hF) + (1 + \alpha)[v(y, F) + \delta \hat{v}(y + hF)] \tag{A24}$$

The first order conditions for a maximum are:

$$- hu'(Y - hF) + (1 + \alpha)[v_F(y, F) + h\delta \hat{v}_1(y + hF) = 0 \tag{A25}$$

$$(1 + \alpha)[v_y(y, F) + \delta \hat{v}_1(y + hF) = 0 \tag{A26}$$

Economies **2018**, *6*, 53

Total differentiation yields:

$$
\begin{bmatrix}
v_{yF} + h\delta\hat{v}_{11} & v_{yy} + \delta\hat{v}_{11} \\
v_{FF} + h^2(\delta\hat{v}_{11} + u'') & v_{yF} + h\delta\hat{v}_{11}
\end{bmatrix}
\begin{bmatrix}
dF_{coop} \\
dy_{coop}
\end{bmatrix}
=
\begin{bmatrix}
-\frac{(v_y + \delta\hat{v}_1)}{(1+\alpha)} d\alpha \\
-\frac{(v_F + h\delta\hat{v}_1)}{(1+\alpha)} d\alpha + \frac{hu'' \, dY}{(1+\alpha)}
\end{bmatrix}
\tag{A27}
$$

References

Amegashie, J.A., Ouattara Bazoumana, and Eric Strobl. 2013. Moral Hazard and the Composition of Transfers: Theory and Evidence from Cross-Border Transfers. *Economics of Governance* 14: 279–301. [CrossRef]

Bapat, Navin A. 2011. Transnational Terrorism, U.S. Military Aid, and the Incentive to Misrepresent. *Journal of Peace Research* 48: 303–18. [CrossRef]

Boone, Peter. 1996. Policies and the Effectiveness of Foreign Aid. *European Economic Review* 40: 289–329. [CrossRef]

Bruce, Neil, and Michael Waldman. 1990. Rotten-Kid Theorem Meets the Samaritan's Dilemma. *The Quarterly Journal of Economics* 105: 155–65. [CrossRef]

Buchanan, James M. 1975. The Samaritan's Dilemma. In *Altruism, Morality and Economic Theory*. Edited by Edmund S. Phelps. New York: Russell Sage, pp. 71–85.

Conquest, Robert. 1991. *Stalin, Breaker of Nations*. New York: Penguin Books.

Dalgaard, Carl-Johan, Henrik Hansen, and Finn Tarp. 2004. On the Empirics of Foreign Aid and Growth. *The Economic Journal* 114: F191–F216. [CrossRef]

Dauvergne, Peter, and Déborah BL Farias. 2012. The Rise of Brazil as a Global Development Power. *Third World Quarterly* 33: 903–17. [CrossRef]

Dijkstra, Bouwe R. 2007. Samaritan versus Rotten Kid: Another Look. *Journal of Economic Behavior and Organization* 64: 91–110. [CrossRef]

Easterly, William R. 2002. *The Elusive Quest for Growth*. Cambridge: MIT Press.

Easterly, William R. 2003. Can Foreign Aid Buy Growth? *Journal of Economic Perspectives* 17: 23–48. [CrossRef]

Economist. 2016. Brazil's Fall. Available online: http://www.economist.com/news/leaders/21684779-disaster-looms-latin-americas-biggest-economy-brazils-fall (accessed on 2 January 2016).

Economist. 2017. Donald Trump Closes the Door to Cuba—A Bet. Available online: https://www.economist.com/the-americas/2017/06/22/donald-trump-closes-the-door-to-cuba-a-bit (accessed on 22 June 2017).

Gibson, Clark C., Krister Andersson, Elinor Ostrom, and Sujai Shivakumar. 2005. *The Samaritan's Dilemma: The Political Economy of Development Aid*. Oxford: Oxford University Press.

Gintis, Herbert. 2009. *Game Theory Evolving*. Princeton: Princeton University Press.

Goldsmith, Arthur A. 2001. Foreign Aid and Statehood in Africa. *International Organization* 55: 123–48. [CrossRef]

Kerr, Steven. 1975. On the Folly of Rewarding A, While Hoping for B. *Academy of Management Journal* 18: 769–83. [PubMed]

Knack, Stephen. 2004. Does Foreign Aid Promote Democracy? *International Studies Quarterly* 48: 251–66. [CrossRef]

Lagerlöf, Johan N.M. 2004. Efficiency-Enhancing Signaling in the Samaritan's Dilemma. *The Economic Journal* 144: 55–68. [CrossRef]

Medvedev, Roy. 1972. *Let History Judge*. New York: Alfred A. Knopf.

Moravcsik, Andrew. 1997. Taking Preferences Seriously: A Liberal Theory of International Politics. *International Organization* 51: 513–53. [CrossRef]

Morris, Emily. 2007. How Exceptional is the Cuban Economy? In *Debating Cuban Exceptionalism*. Edited by Bert Hoffmann and Laurence Whitehead. New York: Palgrave, pp. 37–59.

Pedersen, Karl Rolf. 2001. The Samaritan's Dilemma and the Effectiveness of Development Aid. *International Tax and Public Finance* 8: 693–703. [CrossRef]

Pérez, Louis A. 2002. Fear and Loathing of Fidel Castro: Sources of U.S. Policy toward Cuba. *Journal of Latin American Studies* 34: 227–54.

Piccone, Ted, and Harold Trinkunas. 2014. The Cuba-Venezuela Alliance: The Beginning of the End? Latin America Initiative Foreign Policy at Brookings, Policy Brief. June. Available online: https://www.brookings.edu/wp-content/uploads/2016/06/CubaVenezuela-Alliance-Piccone-Trinkunas.pdf (accessed on 16 June 2014).

Power, Benjamin, and Matt E. Ryan. 2006. Does Development Aid Lead to Economic Freedom? *The Association of Private Enterprise Education* 22: 1–21.

Radzinsky, Edvard. 1996. *Stalin*. New York: Doubleday.

Ritter, Archibald R.M. 1998. Entrepreneurship, Microenterprise and Public Policy in Cuba: Promotion, Containment or Asphyxiation? *Journal of Interamerican Studies and World Affairs* 40: 63–94. [CrossRef]

Svensson, Jakob. 2000. When is Foreign Aid Policy Credible? Aid Dependence and Conditionality. *Journal of Development Economics* 61: 61–84. [CrossRef]

Tavares, Jose. 2003. Does Foreign Aid Corrupt? *Economics Letters* 79: 99–106. [CrossRef]

economies

MDPI

Article

Chronicle of a Failure Foretold: 2017 Rector Election at Ghent University

Raúl Pérez-Fernández [1,*], José Luis García-Lapresta [2] and Bernard De Baets [1]

[1] KERMIT, Department of Data Analysis and Mathematical Modelling, Ghent University, 9000 Ghent, Belgium; bernard.debaets@ugent.be

[2] PRESAD Research Group, BORDA Research Unit, IMUVA, Departamento de Economía Aplicada, Universidad de Valladolid, 47011 Valladolid, Spain; lapresta@eco.uva.es

* Correspondence: raul.perezfernandez@ugent.be

Received: 17 September 2018; Accepted: 30 November 2018; Published: 8 January 2019

Abstract: After more than half a year of elections (yielding three voting stages and nine voting rounds), the 2017 Rector election at Ghent University (Belgium) resulted in a victory for the duo leading all nine voting rounds, and in a resounding defeat for the electoral system. Significant regulation changes were needed in order to break the institutional deadlock in which Ghent University found itself. In this paper, we follow the timeline of the election and dissect what went wrong in the election planning.

Keywords: election; rector; Ghent University; majority decision; majority judgment

---

1. Some Preliminary Notions on Majority Decisions

Since Rousseau published his acclaimed book 'Du Contrat Social' (Rousseau 1762), countless discussions on the (non)existence of the 'general will' built up the field of social choice, whose main goal is to identify what is best for this general will. Associated with the search for what is best, a collective will often find itself with the need of reaching a collective decision by calling an election. Although very early election systems can be traced back to Ancient Greece (and even to some small bands of primitive hunter-gatherers), it is considered that the fundaments for election systems were established after the stimulating discussion between Borda (1781) and Condorcet (1785) about the appropriate election system for new members of the French Academy of Sciences. It is a couple of centuries later that Arrow points out his despairing impossibility theorem Arrow (1963): in case there are more than three candidates, there is no election system that satisfies some basic and deeply-expected properties. Fortunately, things become easier when selecting among only two candidates.

Simple majority decision is one of the most widespread and studied methods for selecting among two candidates (Fishburn 1970; Inada 1969; May 1952; Sen 1966). A candidate is said to defeat another candidate by simple majority if the number of voters who prefer the former candidate to the latter one is greater than the number of voters who prefer the latter candidate to the former one. In the two-candidate setting, it assures that a winner will be proclaimed letting aside the scenario of a tie (which is impossible when the number of voters is odd and unlikely when the number of voters is large). In case more than two candidates are considered, the method of simple majority might result in the famous voting paradox in which a majority cycle could arise (Condorcet 1785).

A closely related concept is that of absolute majority (Fishburn 1973), where a candidate is said to defeat another candidate by absolute majority if the number of voters who prefer the former candidate to the latter one is greater than half of the number of voters. Note that, in case no abstention is allowed, both simple majority and absolute majority coincide. However, when voters are allowed to abstain from voting, the proclamation of a winner by absolute majority is no longer assured even in a two-candidate election.

Although simple and absolute majority probably are the most common examples of majority decisions, other types of majorities have also called the attention of social choice theorists. The strongest type of majority is that of unanimous majority (Fishburn 1973). A candidate is said to defeat another candidate by unanimous majority if every voter prefers the former candidate to the latter one. Note that the proclamation of a winner is rarely assured under the unanimous majority decision. In between the notions of absolute majority and unanimous majority lie the so-called qualified majorities (Ferejohn and Grether 1974). Qualified majorities require the proportion of voters who prefer the former candidate to the latter one to be greater than or equal to a certain quota α (where $\alpha \in \,]0.5, 1]$), fixed before the election. Note that any $\alpha < \frac{r+1}{2r}$ (where r is the number of voters) corresponds to absolute majority and $\alpha = 1$ corresponds to unanimous majority. Finally, the last type of majorities discussed here is that of majorities based on difference of votes (García-Lapresta and Llamazares 2001; Llamazares 2006). This type of majorities lies in between the notions of simple majority and unanimous majority, and requires the difference between the number of voters who prefer the former candidate to the latter one and the number of voters who prefer the latter candidate to the former one to be greater than or equal to a fixed threshold $t \in \{1, \ldots, r\}$. Note that $t = 1$ corresponds to simple majority and $t = r$ corresponds to unanimous majority.

2. The Context of the 2017 Rector Election at Ghent University

Ghent University was founded on 9 October 1817, physician Jean-Charles Van Rotterdam being the first Rector of the institution. In the year of its 200-year anniversary, a new Rector election took place. The election was ruled by the regulations issued by the Board of Governors on 10 February 2017 (as an amend of the special decree dated 26 June 1991 relating to Ghent University and the University Centre of Antwerp). In the following, we summarize the most important aspects of the considered regulations (originally written in Dutch).

As stated in Articles 7 and 8 of stated regulations, the candidatures had to be listed as a duo, i.e., one candidate for the position of Rector and one candidate for the position of Vice-Rector. It was a requirement for the duo to be a gender-balanced pair of full professors at Ghent University that could not reach the age of 66 years during the course of their (potential) four-year mandate.

The electoral college consisted of four groups of voters (Article 4): professional staff (ZAP), assistant academic staff (AAP), administrative and technical staff (ATP) and students (STU). All members of the electoral college had to be invited to vote via a link to the election application on the intranet sent to their personal Ghent University e-mail address. The personal link mentioned could only be accessed during the election period. A voter could decide whether to vote for one of the duos or to vote 'blanco'. It comes without saying that all votes were strictly confidential.

The percentage of votes for each of the duos had to be computed in each category of the electoral college. Then, the percentages of votes had to be aggregated by applying the following weights for the different categories (Article 12): 0.67 for ZAP, 0.085 for AAP, 0.085 for ATP and 0.16 for STU. After computing the aggregated percentage for each duo, the duo reaching a (weighted) two-thirds majority of the votes had to be proclaimed the winner (Article 13). Note that a two-thirds weighted majority was a requirement regardless of how many duos presented their candidature. If no duo reached the required two-thirds weighted majority, then a second voting round had to be organised. The regulations clearly stated that up to five voting rounds had to be conducted until a duo reached a two-thirds weighted majority. In case the fifth round concluded without a winning duo, Article 16 stated that the voting rounds were terminated, and that the election procedure had to be restarted.

Talking in terms of majority decisions, we can see that the considered method requiring a two-thirds (weighted) majority is a weighted version of what some call supermajority, i.e., a qualified majority with $\alpha = \frac{2}{3}$. Note that a problem the chosen election system needs to face is the increasing difficulty of reaching the chosen quota $\alpha = \frac{2}{3}$ as the number of candidates increases. Fortunately, as will be discussed later, the number of candidatures turned out to be only two in each of the voting rounds. Nevertheless, as we will also discuss later, the changes in the regulations solved this potential problem by considering the common plurality with runoff in which the two candidates with the most votes are compared by simple majority in a second voting round (Richelson 1980).

3. A Failure Foretold

3.1. First Voting Stage

On 17 March, the candidatures for the 2017 Rector election were officially announced. The announced duos were Rik Van de Walle and Mieke Van Herreweghe (**RM**) and Guido Van Huylenbroeck and Sarah De Saeger (**GS**).

The planned schedule for the first voting stage was the following:

(i)   First voting round: From Wednesday 19 April (9:00 a.m.) to Friday 21 April (12:00 p.m.).
(ii)   Second voting round (if necessary): From Wednesday 26 April (9:00 a.m.) to Friday 28 April (12:00 p.m.).
(iii)   Third voting round (if necessary): From Wednesday 3 May (9:00 a.m.) to Friday 5 May (12:00 p.m.).
(iv)   Fourth voting round (if necessary): From Monday 8 May (9:00 a.m.) to Tuesday 9 May (12:00 p.m.).
(v)   Fifth voting round (if necessary): From Thursday 11 May (9:00 a.m.) to Friday 12 May (12:00·p.m.).

After the first-voting-round counting on Friday 21 April, no duo reached the fixed two-thirds weighted majority. Although there was a significant difference in support between both duos (57.76% of the votes for **RM** opposed to 36.20% of the votes for **GS**), the leading duo actually was considerably far from the fixed quota.

The second voting round surely was meant to be a critical moment in the first voting stage. The difference in support between both duos in the first voting round hinted that **GS** would probably be unable to reach a two-thirds weighted majority. It was unsure whether sufficient voters would switch their votes deciding to support the leading duo in order to avoid an election deadlock. The results of the second voting round were not promising. The percentage of abstentions decreased (from 6.05% to 4.44%) and the turnout significantly increased (from 11,084 to 13,922), but the support for **RM** only increased up to 59.62%. After the second round, three more voting rounds were conducted (all first-cycle voting results are provided in Table 1[1]) but the support for **RM** no longer increased beyond that of the second voting round while the abstentions kept increasing round after round.

Table 1. Results of the first voting stage.

Round	Turnout	RM	GS	Blanco
First	11,084	57.76%	36.20%	6.05%
Second	13,922	59.62%	35.94%	4.44%
Third	14,445	58.18%	35.95%	5.86%
Fourth	12,021	58.69%	34.11%	7.19%
Fifth	14,544	58.10%	32.57%	9.32%

Although foreseen after the results of the third voting round and the questionable choice of voting system, the first voting stage ended with the fifth voting round not yielding a duo carrying the required support. Together with the results of the first voting stage, a brief statement appeared on the election website: "New candidates can present themselves from Monday 29 May (9:00 a.m.) until

---

[1]   For more details, we refer to the News Bulletin of Ghent University (2017), 21 April 2017, 28 April 2017, 5 May 2017, 9 May 2017 and 12 May 2017.

Wednesday 31 May (12:00 p.m.)" (News Bulletin of Ghent University 2017, 12 May 2017). Despite **RM** clearly being ahead their adversary, no duo could be proclaimed Rector and Vice-Rector with the then-current regulations.

3.2. Second Voting Stage

It was not until 31 May that the duos for the second voting stage were officially announced. Leading duo **RM** appeared as the only candidate. At the same time, some controversial modifications in the Rectoral team structure were announced:

"After lengthy deliberations and starting from reciprocal trust that has been built up step by step, we have arrived at a common programme that contains the most important elements of our original programmes and that we can all fully embrace. We are convinced that the implementation of this programme would be very beneficial to our university and to the UGhentians" (News Bulletin of Ghent University 2017, 31 May 2017).

"The explicit desire—expressed by us and by many other people—to bring visions together, to let us all come together and to realise an ambitious project has led to the question of expanding the rectoral team. We make a plea for the possibility to appoint extra vice-rectors at our university (which by the way has long been possible at other Flemish universities), who would become full members of the rectoral team, together with the elected rector and vice-rector" (News Bulletin of Ghent University 2017, 31 May 2017).

In particular, the proposal was to appoint five Vice-Rectors instead of one[2], former Rector/Vice-Rector candidates Guido Van Huylenbroeck and Sarah De Saeger being two of the proposed Vice-Rectors. Quoting a message by **GS** privately sent to the corporate e-mail address of the electorate, "A request to the board of governors and the parlement has been formulated to create the possibility (also in a decree) to appoint extra vice-rectors. If, against all expectations, this proves to be impossible, Rik and Mieke have engaged themselves to take us on board of their rectoral team be it with other titles."

The planned schedule for the second voting stage was the following:

(i)   First voting round: From Monday 19 June (8:00 a.m.) to Tuesday 20 June (8:00 a.m.).
(ii)   Second voting round (if necessary): From Wednesday 21 June (8:00 a.m.) to Thursday 22 June (8:00 a.m.).
(iii) Third voting round (if necessary): From Friday 23 June (8:00 a.m.) to Saturday 24 June (8:00 a.m.).
(iv)   Fourth voting round (if necessary): From Monday 26 June (8:00 a.m.) to Tuesday 27 June (8:00 a.m.).
(v)   Fifth voting round (if necessary): From Wednesday 28 June (8:00 a.m.) to Thursday 29 June (8:00 a.m.).

The result of the first-voting-round counting on Tuesday 20 June was indeed surprising: **RM** remained at 58.62% of the votes, 41.38% of the votes being abstentions. Not even an increasing turnout (from 8560 to 10,391) and support (from 58.62% to 60.34%) in the second voting round prevented **RM** to announce their withdrawal before the start of the third voting round (all second-cycle voting results are provided in Table 2[3]). The same day of the withdrawal announcement, an official announcement appeared on the election website: "The Board of Governors of Ghent University will now establish the further course of the elections" (News Bulletin of Ghent University 2017, 22 June 2017).

---

2   Ultimately, the proposal of appointing five Vice-Rectors was not presented to the Board of Governors of Ghent University.
3   For more details, we refer to the News Bulletin of Ghent University (2017), 20 June 2017 and 22 June 2017.

Table 2. Results of the second voting stage.

Round	Turnout	RM	Blanco
First	8560	58.62%	41.38%
Second	10,391	60.34%	39.66%

One could conjecture that the problem in this voting stage was not the election system itself; instead, the popular exasperation towards the new proposal of Rectoral team was to be blamed. Anyway, the 2017 Rector election at Ghent University reached a deadlock starting 22 June.

3.3. Third Voting Stage

On 16 August, it was announced that "new elections for a rector and vice-rector will be held in September. The Board of Governors has adapted the election regulations" (News Bulletin of Ghent University 2017, 16 August 2017). Mainly, the new regulations stopped counting abstentions towards the majority decision, reduced the number of voting rounds in the voting stage, and reduced the required quota to a (strict)[4] one-half weighted majority in the last voting round of the voting stage. More precisely, the new regulations distinguish three cases: (a) there were more than two duos as candidates; (b) there were two duos as candidates; (c) there was only one duo as a candidate. In the first case, the first voting round would be conducted as in the previous voting stages; in a potential second round, only the two most voted duos would be compared and required to have a two-thirds weighted majority (without counting abstentions); and, in a potential third round, the quota would be reduced to a one-half weighted majority (without counting abstentions). In the second case, the first voting round would be conducted as in the previous voting stages; and, in a potential second round, the quota would be reduced to a one-half weighted majority (without counting abstentions). In the third case, the votes would be either yes, no, or abstention, and it would be required to reach a two-thirds weighted majority in the first round and a one-half weighted majority in the potential second round (without counting abstentions).

The planned schedule for the third voting stage was the following:

(i)   First voting round: From Monday 18 September (8:00 a.m.) to Tuesday 19 September (8:00 a.m.).
(ii)   Second voting round (if necessary): From Thursday 21 September (8:00 a.m.) to Friday 22 September (8:00 a.m.).
(iii)   Third voting round (if necessary): From Monday 25 September (8:00 a.m.) to Tuesday 26 September (8:00 a.m.).

On 25 August, the candidatures for the last voting stage were announced. The announced duos were the already-acquainted **RM** and the new duo Karin Raeymaeckers and Patrick De Baets (**KP**).

Adding a little bit more of drama to the elections, the day of the counting of the first voting round, Sas van Rouveroij—chairman of the election commission—announced the cancellation of the voting round: "Today, the proverbial Murphy's law has hit. [...] A technical failure has caused the election email of Karin and Patrick not to be sent to all intended recipients. The principle of equality is particularly important in this—all students and staff are entitled to the same communication—hence this unanimous decision of the electoral commission, in which all ranks are represented" (News Bulletin of Ghent University 2017, 19 September 2017). Apparently, due to a technical defect, the campaign message of **RM** reached 61,187 voters while the campaign message of **KP** reached only 13,507 voters. A new schedule was announced:

---

[4]   Note that two candidates can potentially tie if the requirement is to reach a one-half weighted majority, so the requirement is to reach a strict one-half weighted majority, i.e., an α-weighted majority with $\alpha > 0.5$ (and not $\alpha \geq 0.5$). Interestingly, in the election regulations, the technically-incorrect term "majority of half the votes plus one" is used: for an odd number of votes, say $2n + 1$ with n being a natural number, a strict one-half majority means more than $n + 1$ votes, while half of the votes plus one means more than $\frac{2n+1}{2} + 1$ votes (or, equivalently, more than $n + 2$ votes).

(i) First voting round: From Thursday 21 September (8:00 a.m.) to Friday 22 September (8:00 a.m.).
(ii) Second voting round (if necessary): From Monday 25 September (8:00 a.m.) to Tuesday 26 September (8:00 a.m.).

The first recount yielded no duo carrying a two-thirds weighted majority, but **RM** presented a comfortable lead (60.25% against 39.75%). Interestingly, it was the first time in the whole election that **RM** did not win in all the categories of the electoral college: **KP** carried 51.58% of the student vote in opposition to the 48.42% carried by **RM**.

This same day at 3:00 p.m. it was announced that **KP** had decided to withdraw their candidature, and that there would be only one candidate in the second voting round. It was also reminded that "Votes cast for the one team that is left shall be either yes, no or abstention". Finally, on Tuesday 26 September, **RM** obtained the required one-half weighted majority in the last round of the voting stage, thus being elected as the new Rector and Vice-Rector. All third-cycle voting results are provided in Tables 3 and 4[5].

Table 3. Results of the third voting stage (with abstentions).

Round	Turnout	RM	KP	No	Blanco
First	8171	57.40%	37.81%	-	4.79%
Second	7945	67.95%	-	26.75%	5.30%

Table 4. Results of the third voting stage (without abstentions).

Round	Turnout	RM	KP	No
First	7710	60.25%	39.75%	-
Second	7515	71.74%	-	28.26%

4. A Further Analysis of the Voting System

In the eighteenth century, Rousseau (1762) already encouraged the use of qualified majorities or majorities based on difference of votes for important decisions: "The more the deliberations are important and serious, the more the opinion that carries should approach unanimity." Mostly, these deliberations are linked to a unipolar decision, i.e., one votes for or against a unique given option. For instance, 'do you agree with duo x being appointed as Rector and Vice-Rector?'. In these cases, the fact that the candidate's proclamation is not supported by the chosen majority decision is understood as a defeat of the candidate.

In case there are two candidates, the deliberations are linked to a bipolar decision, i.e., one votes for either one or another option among two given ones. For instance, 'do you prefer duo x or duo y being appointed as Rector and Vice-Rector?'. These differences between the semantics of a unipolar decision and a bipolar decision are illustrated in Figure 1. In a bipolar decision, the proclamation of a winner may turn cumbersome if one requires a (moderately) large quota/threshold. Naturally, it holds that the larger the quota/threshold, the higher the chance of the election procedure reaching a deadlock. Furthermore, one could note that the fact that a certain duo reaches a large quota/threshold does not mean that the duo is seen by the electorate as a good option for the Rectorship— neither does it mean that the other duo is not. Only relative information on how both candidates are positioned w.r.t. each other is available. Of course, the use of a moderately-large quota/threshold might be justified in order to add some stability that may prevent the outcome to be susceptible to small changes in the votes (for instance, the result of a simple majority decision could ultimately depend on just one undecided voter). Unfortunately, the use of a large quota/threshold inevitably leads to a reduced decisive spectrum

---

[5] For more details, we refer to the News Bulletin of Ghent University (2017), 22 September 2017 and 26 September 2017.

of election results. In national elections, this problem is normally avoided by allowing for coalitions between parties, but, obviously, this solution is simply not possible in a Rector election.

A potential solution for avoiding an electoral deadlock could be to fix a small (but non-negligible) quota/threshold. This will result in a 'guarantee' of a winner being selected after some voting rounds, while not electing a candidate that has just one more vote than its adversary. Subsequently, the proclamation (or not) of this winner could confront a (for instance) two-thirds majority voting procedure since it is now indeed a unipolar decision. In Figure 2, we illustrate an example of this two-stage procedure in which a 52%-majority (without counting abstentions) is required at the first stage and the winning candidate is then confronted to a two-thirds majority voting at the second stage. In the general setting in which there are more than two candidates, only the first stage is to be adapted by considering a ranking rule for elections with more than two candidates, e.g., the plurality rule (a small threshold could also be fixed).

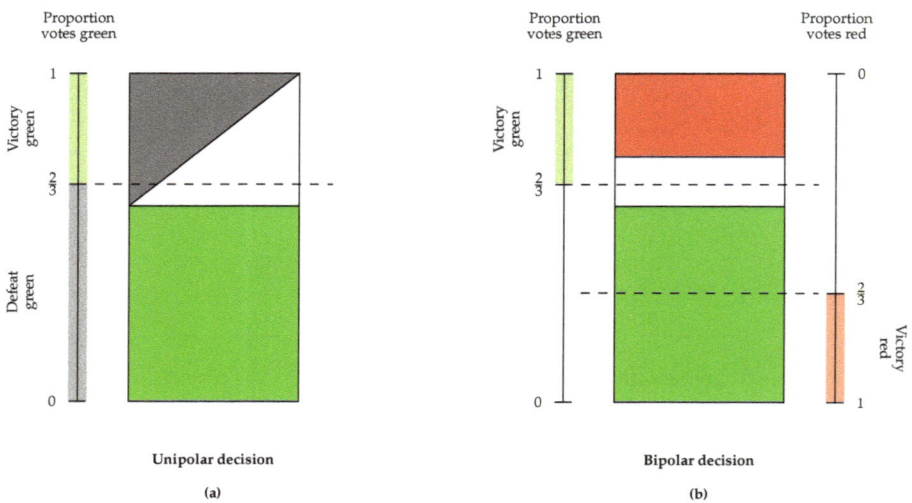

Figure 1. (a) representation of a two-thirds majority requirement for a unipolar decision concerning one candidate in which the proportion of votes for the unique candidate is coloured in green and the proportion of votes against the candidate and abstentions is coloured in white and grey, respectively; (b) representation of a two-thirds majority requirement for a bipolar decision concerning two candidates in which the proportion of votes for one candidate is coloured in red, the proportion of votes for the other candidate is coloured in green and the proportion of abstentions is coloured in white (right).

A more elegant solution would require to totally reformulate the semantics of the election in an approval-voting fashion (Brams and Fishburn 1983). Instead of 'which candidate do you prefer?', the question to be asked would now be 'which candidates do you approve?'. The bipolar question would then turn into two (or more, depending on the number of candidates) unipolar questions. However, quoting Balinski and Laraki (2014) on approval voting, "why limit the judgment to accept/not accept or pass/fail?" In the following section, we propose a potential procedure for the next Rector elections: Balinski and Laraki's Majority Judgment (Balinski and Laraki 2007, 2010).

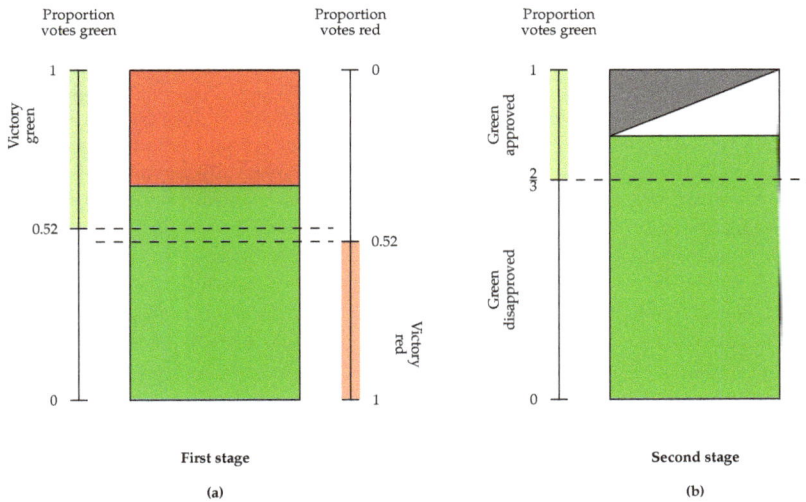

Figure 2. Two-stage procedure in which (a) a 52%-majority is required (no abstentions considered) at the first stage and, subsequently, (b) the winning candidate confronts a two-thirds majority voting procedure at the second stage.

5. A Proposal for Upcoming Elections

Social choice theory is a field full of paradoxes (Nurmi 1999), probably Arrow's and Condorcet's paradoxes being the two most famous ones. On the one hand, Arrow's paradox states that, in an election with at least three candidates, it is possible for a candidate to win, yet with the same set of rank-order preferences a second candidate wins when a third candidate withdraws. A famous interpretation of this paradox is often attributed to philosopher Sidney Morgenbesser (Hausman 2011): "After finishing dinner, Sidney Morgenbesser decides to order dessert. The waitress tells him he has two choices: apple pie and blueberry pie. Sidney orders the apple pie. After a few minutes the waitress returns and says that they also have cherry pie at which point Morgenbesser says: In that case I'll have the blueberry pie". Although this anecdote technically concerns individual decisions rather than collective decisions, we could illustrate the point in a similar manner by considering three friends that are offered apple pie and blueberry pie, initially vote and decide to order the apple pie and, after being offered the cherry pie, decide to order the blueberry pie instead. As silly as this sounds, Arrow's impossibility theorem (Arrow 1963) proves that there is no natural method[6] that avoids this paradox[7], leaving aside dictatorships.

On the other hand, Condorcet's paradox states that, in an election with at least three candidates, the transitivity of the voters' preferences does not imply the transitivity of the majority rule. Coming back to the example of the pies, one could understand this paradox with the following example. Alice's favourite pie is apple pie, but she sure does prefer blueberry pie to cherry pie. Bob has always liked berries, thus, he would rather eat a blueberry pie, or, in case this is not possible, a cherry pie. A third diner, Carol, has expressed her desire of enjoying a cherry pie, but she would actually be fine with the house-special apple pie. Inconveniently, when choosing which desert to share, they realize that

---

[6] Understanding 'natural' as a method satisfying Pareto Efficiency (also referred to as unanimity), i.e., if every voter prefers a candidate to another candidate, then this also holds for the collective preference.

[7] A method that avoids Arrow's paradox for any set of rank-order preferences is said to satisfy Independence of Irrelevant Alternatives.

they collectively prefer the apple pie to the blueberry pie, the blueberry pie to the cherry pie, and the cherry pie to the apple pie. Thus, they forget about sharing, and just proceed to order one piece of each. We conclude that, although each voter expresses transitive preferences, cycles might (and often do!) appear in the collective preference.

Balinski and Laraki (2007) recently advocated for totally restructuring the form in which we understand and perform voting systems: "[...] if Arrow's and Condorcet's paradoxes are to be avoided, then the traditional model and paradigm must be abandoned. [...] Not only do rank-order inputs not permit voters to express themselves as they wish, but they are the culprits that lead to all of the impossibilities and incompatibilities" (Balinski and Laraki 2014). They proposed a method called *Majority Judgment* Balinski and Laraki (2010) that proceeds as follows. First, a common language of grades (labels in a linearly ordered scale) needs to be agreed upon. Afterwards, each of the voters is required to evaluate each of the candidates independently according to this common language of grades. Then, for each candidate x, the grades are ordered in an increasing manner. We denote by s_i^x the i-th greatest grade assigned to candidate x. Subsequently, the majority value is computed for each candidate x, i.e., the sequence

$$m^x = (s_t^x, s_{t+1}^x, s_{t-1}^x, s_{t+2}^x, s_{t-2}^x, \ldots, s_{2t-1}^x, s_1^x),$$

if there is an odd number of voters $r = 2t - 1$, or

$$m^x = (s_t^x, s_{t-1}^x, s_{t+1}^x, s_{t-2}^x, s_{t+2}^x, \ldots, s_{2t-2}^x, s_1^x),$$

if there is an even number of voters $r = 2t - 2$. Finally, candidates are lexicographically ordered[8] according to their majority values by ranking a candidate x ahead of a candidate y if the value at the first position at which m^x and m^y differ is greater in m^x than in m^y. Note that two candidates can only be tied if they have the same grades.

Example 1. *Consider the list of grades used by OpinionWell poll during the French 2012 presidential election (Balinski and Laraki 2014):*

Outstanding $\succ$ Excellent $\succ$ Very Good $\succ$ Good $\succ$ Acceptable $\succ$ Poor $\succ$ To reject .

Consider that there are five voters and three candidates x, y and z. Candidate x received two times the grade Outstanding and three times the grade Excellent; candidate y received one time the grade Outstanding, three times the grade Excellent and one time the grade Very good; candidate z received two times the grade Very Good and three times the grade Good.

The ordered grades assigned to each candidate are thus the following ones:

$$s^x = (Outstanding, Outstanding, Excellent, Excellent, Excellent) ,$$
$$s^y = (Outstanding, Excellent, Excellent, Excellent, Very good) ,$$
$$s^z = (Very good, Very good, Good, Good, Good) .$$

---

8   Balinski and Laraki have proposed different tie-breaking methods in case two candidates x and y have the same $s_i^x = s_i^y$ (this value being referred to as the lower middlemost). The one considered here is the one proposed in Balinski and Laraki (2014) that amounts to successively removing the lower middlemost in both sets of grades until one candidate has a strictly greater lower middlemost than the other.

Thus, the majority values for each candidate are the following ones:

$$m^x = (Excellent, Excellent, Outstanding, Excellent, Outstanding),$$
$$m^y = (Excellent, Excellent, Excellent, Very\ good, Outstanding),$$
$$m^z = (Good, Good, Very\ good, Good, Very\ good).$$

Since x has a greater grade than y at the third position (first position at which m^x and m^y differ) and a greater grade than z at the first position (first position at which m^x and m^z differ), we conclude that candidate x should be proclaimed the winner according to the method of Majority Judgment.

The number of advantages of this method over classical ones based on ranking is substantial. From a practical point of view, the method of Majority Judgment is easy to understand for the voters and, unlike many classical methods based on ranking, its implementation is computationally friendly even for a large electorate. From a theoretical point of view, both Arrow's and Condorcet's paradoxes are assured to be avoided, and among other properties, it is proved to be fairly resistant to manipulation. Moreover, in case of elections with only two candidates, which was the actual case of the Rector elections at Ghent University, provides a(n arguably) more natural outcome than the simple majority rule since "the method of majority decision takes no account of intensities of preference, and it is certainly arguable that what matters is not merely the number who prefer x to y and the number who prefer y to x, but also by how much each prefers one alternative to the other" (Sen 1970). Indeed, as suggested by Balinski and Laraki, in the next Rector elections at Ghent University, we might need to judge, rather than vote.

6. Conclusions

One hundred and fifty-nine days passed from the first voting round of the Rector elections at Ghent University to the last one, and we wonder whether this time lapse could have been greatly reduced just by considering a more suitable electoral system. The requirement of the two-thirds weighted majority proved to be too strong, while the ultimate restriction to a one-half weighted majority seems to be an 'ad hoc' solution just trying to assure the end of the electoral deadlock. We conjecture that the use of a two-stage voting procedure in which a candidate is selected in a first voting stage subsequently being confronted to a two-thirds (weighted) majority voting in a second voting stage probably would have reduced the election time lapse considerably (and would have reduced voters' fatigue towards the election). In addition, the use of Majority Judgment in future elections is strongly encouraged by the authors.

Author Contributions: R.P.-F. gathered the data; R.P.-F., J.L.G.-L. and B.D.B. wrote the paper.

Funding: Raúl Pérez-Fernández acknowledges the support of the Research Foundation of Flanders (FWO17/PDO/160). The Spanish *Ministerio de Economía y Competitividad* (project ECO2016-77900-P) and ERDF are acknowledged.

Conflicts of Interest: The authors declare no conflict of interest.

References

Arrow, Kenneth J. 1963. *Social Choice and Individual Values*, 2nd ed. New Haven: Yale University Press.
Balinski, Michel, and Rida Laraki. 2007. A theory of measuring, electing and ranking. *Proceedings of the National Academy of Sciences USA* 104: 8720–25. [CrossRef] [PubMed]
Balinski, Michel, and Rida Laraki. 2010. *Majority Judgment: Measuring, Ranking, and Electing*. Cambridge: MIT Press.
Balinski, Michel, and Rida Laraki. 2014. Judge: Don't vote! *Operations Research* 62: 483–511. [CrossRef]
Borda, Jean Charles. 1781. *Mémoire sur les Élections au Scrutin*. Paris: Histoire de l'Académie Royale des Sciences.

Brams, Steven, and Peter C. Fishburn. 1983. *Approval Voting*. Boston: Birkhauser.

Condorcet, Marquis. 1785. *Essai sur l'Application de l'Analyse à la Probabilité des Décisions Rendues à la Pluralité des Voix*. Paris: De l'Imprimerie Royale.

Ferejohn, John A., and David M. Grether. 1974. On a class of rational social decision procedures. *Journal of Economic Theory* 8: 471–82. [CrossRef]

Fishburn, Peter C. 1970. Conditions for simple majority decision functions with intransitive individual indifference. *Journal of Economic Theory* 2: 354–67. [CrossRef]

Fishburn, Peter C. 1973. *The Theory of Social Choice*. Princeton: Princeton University Press.

García-Lapresta, José Luis, and Bonifacio Llamazares. 2001. Majority decisions based on difference of votes. *Journal of Mathematical Economics* 35: 463–81. [CrossRef]

Hausman, Daniel M. 2011. *Preference, Value, Choice, and Welfare*. Cambridge: Cambridge University Press.

Inada, Ken-ichi. 1969. The simple majority decision rule. *Econometrica* 37: 490–506. [CrossRef]

Llamazares, Bonifacio. 2006. The forgotten decision rules: Majority rules based on difference of votes. *Mathematical Social Sciences* 51: 311–26. [CrossRef]

May, Kenneth O. 1952. A set of independent necessary and sufficient conditions for simple majority decision. *Econometrica* 20: 680–84. [CrossRef]

News Bulletin of Ghent University. 2017. Available online: https://www.ugent.be/en/ (accessed on 15 February 2018).

Nurmi, Hannu. 1999. *Voting Paradoxes and How to Deal with Them*. Heidelberg/Berlin: Springer.

Richelson, Jeffrey T. 1980. Running off empty: Run-off point systems. *Public Choice* 35: 457–68. [CrossRef]

Rousseau, Jean Jacques. 1762. *Du Contrat Social*. Amsterdam: Marc Michel Rey.

Sen, Amartya K. 1966. A possibility theorem on majority decisions. *Econometrica* 34: 491–99. [CrossRef]

Sen, Amartya K. 1970. *Collective Choice and Social Welfare*. San Francisco: Holden–Day.

Article

Is Political Ideology Stable? Evidence from Long-Serving Members of the United States Congress

Franklin G. Mixon Jr. [1,*], Chandini Sankaran [2] and Kamal P. Upadhyaya [3]

[1]   Center for Economic Education, Columbus State University, Columbus, GA 31907, USA
[2]   Department of Economics, Boston College, Chestnut Hill, MA 02467, USA; sankarac@bc.edu
[3]   Department of Economics, University of New Haven, West Haven, CT 06516, USA;
      Kupadhyaya@newhaven.edu
*   Correspondence: mixon_franklin@columbusstate.edu; Tel.: +1706-507-8052

Received: 18 March 2019; Accepted: 30 April 2019; Published: 6 May 2019

Abstract: This study extends the political science and political psychology literature on the political ideology of lawmakers by addressing the following question: How stable is a legislator's political ideology over time? In doing so, we employ Nokken–Poole scores of legislators' political ideology for members of the United States (U.S.) House of Representatives and the U.S. Senate who were elected prior to the 103rd Congress that began in early 1991 and who served consecutively through the 115th Congress, which ended in early 2019. Results from individual time-series estimations suggest that political ideology is unstable over time for a sizable portion of the members of both major political parties who serve in the U.S. Congress, while analysis of the pooled data suggests that, after accounting for inertia in political ideology and individual legislator effects, Republican legislators become more conservative over time. These results run somewhat counter to the finding in prior studies that the political ideologies of lawmakers and other political elites are stable over time.

Keywords: political ideology; roll-call voting; public choice; public policy; United States Congress

JEL Classification: D70; D72

---

1. Introduction

The voting behavior of the electorate and the actions of elected officials are largely shaped by core political values and political party affiliations. In the United States (U.S.), the Republican Party is, as indicated in seminal studies by Carmines and Stanley (1990, 1992); Levine et al. (1997); Abramowitz and Saunders (1998), generally associated with conservative political ideology, while the Democratic Party tends to be associated with liberal political ideology. As Layman and Carsey (2000) point out, the studies listed above demonstrate that, as an element of political partisanship, political ideology has risen in importance relative to social structure and performance. Other studies in political science have shown that voters associate specific issue ownership to political parties (Seeberg 2017), that voters tend to vote for candidates from parties aligned with their own political ideologies (Wright et al. 1985; Goren 2005), and that shifting political ideologies explains party-switching decisions by incumbent lawmakers (Nokken and Poole 2004).

The psychology literature also addresses the political psychology of ideology formation. For example, Jost et al. (2009) discuss the number and types of dimensions individuals employ in formulating their political opinions. More specifically, these authors delve into what they refer to as "elective affinities" between the situational and dispositional needs of individuals in terms of political ideology, as well as the consequences of political ideology vis-à-vis voter attitudes and judgments (Jost et al. 2009). Next, a more recent study by Ksiazkiewicz et al. (2016) explores the genetics of political ideology, and finds that measures of cognitive style (i.e., the need for cognition, the need for cognitive closure) account for distinct genetic variance in political ideology. Lastly, a new study by Naumann et al. (2017) examines data from a sample of U.S.-born Mexican Americans and finds that strength of Mexican identity, stronger integration acculturation attitudes, weaker assimilation attitudes, and lower socioeconomic status are associated with exhibiting a more liberal political ideology.[1]

The current study extends the political science and political psychology literature on the political ideology of lawmakers, particularly the studies by Nokken and Poole (2004) and Jost et al. (2009), respectively, by addressing the following question: How stable is a legislator's political ideology over time? In doing so, we employ Nokken–Poole scores (Nokken and Poole 2004) of legislators' political ideology for members of the U.S. House of Representatives and the U.S. Senate who were elected prior to the 103rd Congress that began in early 1991 and who served consecutively through the 115th Congress, which ended in early 2019. Results from individual time-series estimations suggest that political ideology is unstable over time for a sizable portion of the members of both major political parties serving in the U.S. Congress. Additionally, analysis of the pooled data suggests that, after accounting for inertia in political ideology and individual legislator effects, Republican legislators become more conservative over time. These results, which run somewhat counter to the finding in prior studies of stability in the political ideologies of lawmakers and other political elites by Jennings (1992) and Jewitt and Goren (2016), not only have implications for how well legislators represent the interests of their constituents in representative democracy, they also provide a rationale for new avenues of empirical investigation in the public choice literature.

2. Prior Literature: A Brief Review

There is a body of emerging research that concerns "issue ownership" by local and national political parties. Issue ownership is defined in these studies as a "reputation for policy and program interest, produced by a history of attention, initiative and innovation towards problems which leads voters to believe that one of the parties is more sincere and committed to do something (Petrocik 1996, p. 826)." Overall, issue ownership is a key source of information used by voters in evaluating political parties and the legislative behavior of elected officials. Recent research on issue ownership has explored the concept of stability with regard to how voters attach issues to specific political parties over time. For example, Seeberg (2017) analyzes voter perceptions of political parties located at both ends of the ideology continuum (i.e., the liberal-conservative spectrum) for 17 countries across three decades and concludes that issue ownership is not only stable (and similar) over time and across countries, but it is also a "critical constant" in voting and party behavior. Other studies using large surveys to track the partisan attitudes of respondents in the United States over time have also found stability in the core political predispositions and partisan identities of the electorate (Sears and Funk 1999; and Goren 2005).

In addition to research on issue ownership, prior academic research has also found significant interstate variation in electorate political ideology. A seminal study by Wright et al. (1985) analyzes 76,000 responses to 51 separate CBS News and *New York Times* polls from 1974 through 1982 and finds that "both partisan and ideological differences matter in the behavior of state electorates, and that they are differentially important depending upon the nature of the choices offered to the voters (Wright et al. 1985, p. 488)." Moreover, while significant interstate variations continue to exist, the majority of more recent studies that explore the stability of state-level political ideology also show intra-state variability over time (e.g., see Berry et al. 1998, 2007).[2]

---

[1]   Naumann et al. (2017) conclude that political campaigns should pay attention to differences in cultural identifications and acculturation attitudes when targeting Latino constituents.

[2]   A study by Brace et al. (2004) finds that state political ideology does not change over time. However, Berry et al. (2007) dismiss the findings of this study as being logically and methodologically flawed.

As in the case of research on constituent ideology, there is large body of work, showing mixed results, on the stability of the political ideology of elected officials.[3] An important study by Jennings (1992) employing survey data finds that political party elites exhibit significantly more stable political preferences in terms of the traditional liberal-conservative dimension than do ordinary citizens, including those among the most politically active among the electorate.[4] An analysis of 16 million individual roll call votes over two centuries in seminal research by Poole and Rosenthal (1997) shows that over 80 percent of a legislator's voting decisions can be attributed to a consistent ideological position. On the other hand, Nokken and Poole (2004), using data on political party and roll call voting behavior between 1795 and 1995, find significant shifts in party-switching roll-call voting behavior during periods of high ideological polarization. More recent work by Lupton et al. (2015) contends that the political ideologies of political leaders fit the traditional unidimensional framework, while those of the general electorate are multidimensional.[5] Results from survey data similar to those used by Jennings (1992) comparing structural political ideologies of political leaders and those of the mass public from 1980 to 2004 support their contention. Relatedly, Jewitt and Goren (2016) also use these survey data to examine whether the political ideologies of more engaged members of the electorate, whom they count as holding strong ideological identities, who are politically informed, and who participate actively in public affairs, are similar in terms of structure and stability to those of political elites. In doing so they conclude that, in 1980, ideologically engaged citizens exhibited more stable political ideologies than their less engaged counterparts, but less stable political ideologies than those of political leaders. However, by 1992, stability in the political ideologies of engaged citizens reached parity with that of political elites (Jewitt and Goren 2016).[6]

Our study extends this body of research by investigating stability of political ideology through the voting behavior of long-serving members of the U.S. Congress. In doing so, we first present our conceptual approach to voting behavior using the unidimensional policy space described in the public choice literature (e.g., see Krehbiel 1998). After a discussion of our conceptual approach, we discuss the data and statistical analyses that are the main focus of this study.

3. Political Ideology in the U.S. Congress: A Conceptual Approach

As a foundation of our empirical exploration into the stability of the political ideology of long-serving federal legislators in the U.S., we assert that collective choice occurs through voting on proposals that can be arranged along a unidimensional policy space. Following Krehbiel (1998, p. 21), it "is convenient and intuitive to think of the policy space as a continuum on which liberal policies are located on the left, moderate policies are located in the center, and conservative policies are located on the right. Because the policy space is continuous, it is possible to consider policies at any point between liberal and conservative extremes." The policy space referred to above consists of the lawmakers' ideal points, where a given lawmaker's ideal point represents that policy that provides the lawmaker with greater benefits than all other policies (Krehbiel 1998, p. 22).[7]

---

[3] Although the current study focuses on stability of political ideology in the U.S., recent research focusing on other countries also abounds (e.g., Lee 2013; Leach 2015; Peña 2016; Harring and Sohlberg 2017; Melville 2018).

[4] Bartle (2000) finds that the political ideologies of more aware voters are more stable over time than those of less aware voters.

[5] Lupton et al. (2015) argue that political sophistication constrains the ideologies of political leaders to a single ideological dimension.

[6] This result runs counter to that in the earlier study by Jennings (1992).

[7] This conceptualization of the political ideology of political actors is not without its critics. Seminal work by Converse (1964), which indicates that only 2.5 percent of Americans qualify as political ideologues, argues for an absence of political ideology across the American political landscape. On the other end of the spectrum lies an alternative stream of research (e.g., Knoke 1979; Carmines and Stimson 1989; Abramowitz 1994; Carmines and Layman 1997) that considers political ideology to be multidimensional, consisting of distinct attitudes toward social welfare, racial, and cultural issues (see Layman and Carsey 2000). Despite these critiques, Jost et al. (2009) indicate that many of life's domains are explained along the type of left-right policy space described here, such as implicit and explicit preferences for tradition, conformity, order, stability, traditional values, and hierarchy (versus those for progress, rebelliousness, chaos, flexibility, feminism, and equality, respectively).

Figure 1 presents a spatial model of policy preferences in the U.S. Senate, where each point on the liberal-conservative continuum represents an ideal point for one of the 100 lawmakers in the U.S. Senate.[8] Here, the vertical line (see Figure 1) separates the most liberal lawmakers from the most conservative lawmakers. Lastly, in order to provide additional exposition, two individual lawmakers, m_1 and m_2, are highlighted in Figure 1. These two unnamed lawmakers represent pivotal lawmakers in the sense that they represent the potential majority vote on any bill under consideration by the U.S. Senate (Krehbiel 1998, p. 24).[9] For example, when Republicans hold a majority in the U.S., as they do in 2019, m_1, represents the majority pivot in the sense that any bill emanating from the Republican majority would have to win the favor of m_1, and all the lawmakers to his or right on the policy space, in order to win a majority of votes in that body (i.e., 51 votes).[10] Similarly, in a U.S. Senate administered by a Democratic majority, m_2 represents the majority pivot along the policy space.[11]

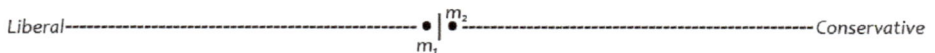

Liberal---• | m_2 •---Conservative
m_1

Figure 1. Spatial model of policy preferences.

The unidimensional (i.e., liberal-conservative) political ideology scores maintained by Boche et al. (2018) and Lewis et al. (2018) include the traditional NOMINATE measures developed in Poole and Rosenthal (1997, 2000) that have been employed extensively in the political science and public choice economics literature to construct the type of policy space presented in Figure 1. However, these estimates assume that a legislator's political ideology is static over the duration of his or her legislative career (Boche et al. 2018). The Nokken–Poole estimates, on the other hand, assume that each Congress is entirely separate in terms of a legislator's political ideology. To compute these scores, Nokken and Poole (2004) allow for movement of legislators along the unidimensional policy space from Congress to Congress.[12] As with the NOMINATE scores, the Nokken–Poole scores range from −1 to +1, with Democrats generally falling along the 0 to −1 policy space (i.e., the left half of the policy space in Figure 1), while Republicans typically occupy the 0 to +1 portion of the policy space (i.e., the right half of the policy space in Figure 1).

If converted into percentages, the Nokken–Poole scores discussed above range from −100% to +100%. Therefore, to facilitate efficient discussion of the Nokken–Poole scores, we follow the convention in finance of quoting interest rates using the permyriad concept of a basis point, which is equal to one-hundredth of one percent. Using this convention, the policy space in Figure 1 encompasses, using Nokken–Poole scores, 20,000 basis points, with half of this total constituting each half of the policy space. Thus, the maximum variation in political ideology for either Democrats or Republicans is expected to be (about) 10,000 basis points. In this case, an increase in one's Nokken–Poole score from 0.345 to 0.435, or 0.090, represents a movement of 900 basis points along the policy space. This would represent a relatively conservative member of the legislative body becoming more conservative in the absolute sense, and, if he or she moves to the right of another member of the legislative body, also more conservative in the relative sense.

4. Political Ideology in the U.S. Congress: Data and Methodology

In order to gather enough information on the stability of the political ideology of federal legislators, Nokken–Poole scores for members of the 115th U.S. Congress (i.e., 2017–2019) who were elected prior

---

8 Spatial models like that in Figure 1 follow that developed by Downs (1957), which is based on the work of Hotelling (1929).
9 This representation assumes that there are 50 Senators on each side of the vertical line in Figure 1.
10 Put differently, lawmaker m_1 occupies the fifty-first point from the right end of the policy space in Figure 1.
11 In other words, lawmaker m_2 occupies the fifty-first point from the left end of the policy space in Figure 1.
12 Nokken and Poole (2004) apply these scores in a comparison of legislators who switched political parties during their careers to those who maintained political party membership.

to 1991, and who held congressional seats without interruption over this period, are collected by the authors. We divided the sample into several subsamples. The *Early Cohorts* subsample include members of the U.S. Congress who were elected before 1976. Those elected from 1976 through 1980 are placed in the *Late 1970s Cohort*, while those elected from 1981 through 1985 are included in the *Early 1980s Cohort*. Lastly, those members of the U.S. Congress who were elected from 1986 through 1989 are placed in the *Late 1980s Cohort*. In all cases, members of party leadership are omitted from the subsamples.

Table 1 presents the demographic data for members of the U.S. Congress who are included in these subsamples. In each case, the member's name, political party, home state, Congressional Chamber and year elected are provided. As indicated near the top of Table 1, the *Early Cohorts* subsample includes three legislators, two Democrats and one Republican. Only two legislators, both Republicans, are included in the *Late 1970s Cohort*, while seven legislators are listed in the *Early 1980s Cohort*. Among these, three are Democrats and four are Republicans. Lastly, the *Late 1980s Cohort* is the largest of the four cohorts, with 14 members. Eight of these are Democrats, and six are Republicans.

Table 1. Demographics of congressional subsamples.

Name	Political Party-State	Congressional Chamber	Year Elected
Early Cohorts			
Conyers, John	D-MI	House	1965
Leahy, Patrick	D-VT	Senate	1975
Young, Donald	R-AK	House	1973
Late 1970s Cohort			
Cochran, Thad	R-MS	Senate	1979
Hatch, Orrin	R-UT	Senate	1977
Early 1980s Cohort			
Barton, Joe	R-TX	House	1985
Grassley, Charles	R-IA	Senate	1981
Kaptur, Marcy	D-OH	House	1983
Levin, Sander	D-MI	House	1983
Rogers, Hal	R-KY	House	1981
Smith, Christopher	R-NJ	House	1981
Visclosky, Peter	D-IN	House	1985
Late 1980s Cohort			
DeFazio, Peter	D-OR	House	1987
Duncan, John Jr.	R-TN	House	1989
Engel, Eliot	D-NY	House	1989
Lewis, John	D-GA	House	1987
Lowey, Nita	D-NY	House	1989
McCain, John	R-AZ	Senate	1987
Neal, Richard	D-MA	House	1989
Pallone, Frank Jr.	D-NJ	House	1989
Rohrabacher, Dana	R-CA	House	1989
Ros-Lehtinen, Ileana	R-FL	House	1989
Serrano, José	D-NY	House	1989
Slaughter, Louise	D-NY	House	1987
Upton, Frederick	R-MI	House	1987
Smith, Lamar	R-TX	House	1987

Given the relatively small size of the U.S. Senate, the number of long-serving legislators in the U.S. Senate is, as expected, smaller than that for the U.S. House of Representatives. In terms of the information contained in Table 1, only five of the 26 legislators across the four cohorts are members of the U.S. Senate. The remaining 21 legislators are members of the U.S. House of Representatives. As such, our empirical approach, which is explained below, provides a clearer picture of the stability of political ideology in this latter-mentioned branch of the U.S. Congress.

Our empirical investigation of stability of political ideology of lawmakers is two-pronged. First, we investigate political instability at the individual level by collecting both the largest and smallest Nokken–Poole scores over each U.S. Representative's legislative career, referred to here as NP_L and NP_S, respectively, and compute,

$$|NP_L - NP_S|, \tag{1}$$

for each Representative. Here, (1) captures the absolute deviation in political ideology (over time) for each lawmaker, where smaller (larger) values represent greater stability (instability) of political ideology.

An alternative approach to investigating stability of political ideology of lawmakers relies on regression analysis employing a legislator's Nokken–Poole scores. This entails estimation by Ordinary Least Squares (OLS) of the specification below,

$$IDEOL_t = a_0 + b_1 TREND_t + b_2 IDEOL_{t-2} + e_t, \tag{2}$$

where the dependent variable, $IDEOL_t$, is a given legislator's Nokken–Poole score in year t. This variable is explained by $TREND_t$, which is an indicator of the number of Congressional sessions served by a given legislator by year t, and $IDEOL_{t-2}$, which is the lagged value (by one Congressional session, or two years) of $IDEOL_t$.[13] The number of observations, n, in each case is determined by the length of each U.S. Representative's legislative career, which is measured in Congressional sessions.

One expects that a legislator's political ideology during a given Congressional session will exhibit a positive relationship to his or her political ideology during the previous Congressional session. If so, the coefficient estimate attached to $IDEOL_{t-2}$ will be positively-signed and statistically significant. Next, and more importantly, failure to reject the null hypothesis that b_1, the coefficient estimate attached to $TREND_t$, is equal to 0 would, in this case, support a finding of stability in one's political ideology from Congressional session to Congressional session. Of course, rejection of this null hypothesis would support a finding of instability in political ideology, with the sign of the estimate attached to b_1 indicating whether the member of Congress is becoming more liberal or more conservative from one Congressional session to the next. Here, a positively-signed coefficient estimate describes a trend toward greater conservatism, while a negatively-signed coefficient estimate describes a trend toward greater liberalism.

5. Political Ideology in the U.S. Congress: Empirical Results and Discussion

This section of the study presents the results of our empirical analyses of the Nokken–Poole data on legislator ideology in the U.S. Congress. Following this presentation, we (1) highlight the importance to economists and political scientists of our findings regarding the stability of ideology, and (2) discuss some of the limitations relating to the data employed on political ideology in our study.

5.1. Empirical Results

Our empirical analysis of the stability of political ideology of lawmakers begins with the four cohorts from the U.S. House of Representatives sample. As indicated near the top of Table 2, the *Early Cohorts* subsample includes two legislators, one Democrat and one Republican. In both

---

[13] For example, if t is equal to 1995, and the legislator under consideration is Frank Pallone (see Table 1), then $IDEOL_t$ is equal to −0.246, which represents Pallone's Nokken–Poole score for the Congressional session ending in 1995. This particular Congressional session was also Pallone's third session as a member of the U.S. House of Representatives. As such, $TREND_t$ is equal to 3 in this case. The second regressor, $IDEOL_{t-2}$, is in this case equal to −0.149, which is Pallone's Nokken–Poole political ideology score from the previous Congressional session, which ended in 1993. It is worth noting here that Pallone was more liberal in his voting patterns during the Congressional session ending in 1995 than he was during the preceding Congressional session. More specifically, his Nokken–Poole score fell by 970 basis points from one session to the next in this case.

cases, a noteworthy degree of instability of political ideology, as measured by (1) above, is exhibited. For example, the value of (1) for John Conyers, a Democrat from Michigan, is 0.423, meaning that variation in his political ideology over the course of his legislative career spans 4230 basis points. In the case of Donald Young, a Republican from Alaska, variation in exhibited political ideology spans 2470 basis points (from low to high) along the policy space. A graphical representation of the instability in political ideology in each of these two cases is presented in Figure 2. There, and throughout this study, the Republican's time series is depicted in red, while the time series representing his or her Democratic counterpart is depicted in blue.

Table 2. Political ideology in the U.S. House of Representatives.

Name	$|NP_L-NP_S|$	$TREND_t$	*p*-Value	*n*	AC
Early Cohorts					
Conyers, John	0.423	0.008*	0.004	26	no
Young, Donald	0.247	0.003	0.101	22	no
Late 1970s Cohort					
Early 1980s Cohort					
Barton, Joe	0.107	−0.003 †	0.052	16	no
Kaptur, Marcy	0.188	−0.004 †	0.090	17	no
Levin, Sander	0.099	−0.002 †	0.073	17	no
Rogers, Hal	0.173	0.3×10^{-3}	0.426	18	no
Smith, Christopher	0.249	0.008 ‡	0.027	18	no
Visclosky, Peter	0.199	−0.003	0.148	16	no
Late 1980s Cohort					
DeFazio, Peter	0.355	0.005	0.201	15	no
Duncan, John Jr.	0.776	0.032 ‡	0.013	14	no
Engel, Eliot	0.185	0.002	0.300	14	no
Lewis, John	0.144	-0.3×10^{-3}	0.458	15	yes
Lowey, Nita	0.084	−0.001	0.235	14	no
Neal, Richard	0.125	−0.003 †	0.075	14	yes
Pallone, Frank Jr.	0.484	−0.013 †	0.066	14	no
Rohrabacher, Dana	0.229	−0.005 *	0.008	14	no
Ros-Lehtinen, Ileana	0.129	−0.005	0.349	14	no
Serrano, José	0.141	−0.005	0.225	14	no
Slaughter, Louise	0.319	−0.001	0.395	15	no
Upton, Frederick	0.202	0.002	0.280	15	no
Smith, Lamar	0.231	0.006†	0.052	15	no

Notes: One-tailed *p*-values reported above. *(‡)[†] denote the 0.01(0.05)[0.10] level of significance. AC = autocorrelation. The null hypothesis of "no autocorrelation" is tested using the Durbin *t* test statistic.

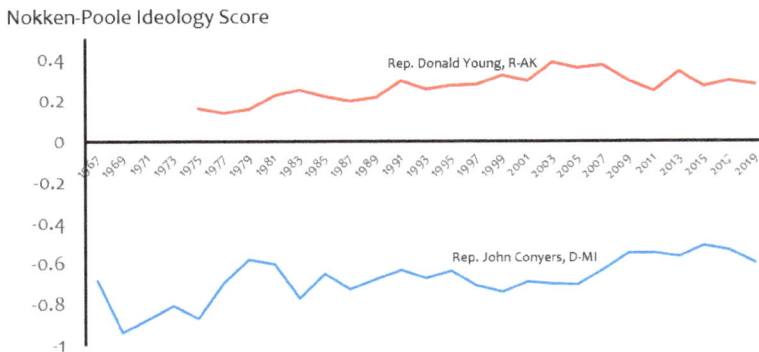

Figure 2. Early Cohorts, U.S. House of Representatives.

Next, the remaining portions of Table 2 present data on political ideology from the other, larger cohorts in the U.S. House of Representatives. In terms of the widest ranges, Christopher Smith, a Republican from New Jersey is first among the *Early 1980s Cohort*, with an ideology range of 2490 basis points, while Sander Levin, a Democrat from Michigan, exhibits the narrowest, although nontrivial (at 990 basis points), range along the policy space. Again, the size of each of the ideology ranges in this cohort points toward instability in political ideology. Figure 3 presents the Nokken–Poole time series for Smith and Peter Visclosky, a Democrat from Indiana, who exhibits the widest Nokken–Poole range among those Democrats in the *Early-1980s Cohort* of the U.S. House of Representatives. Visclosky's political ideology exhibits a range of 1990 basis points along the policy space.

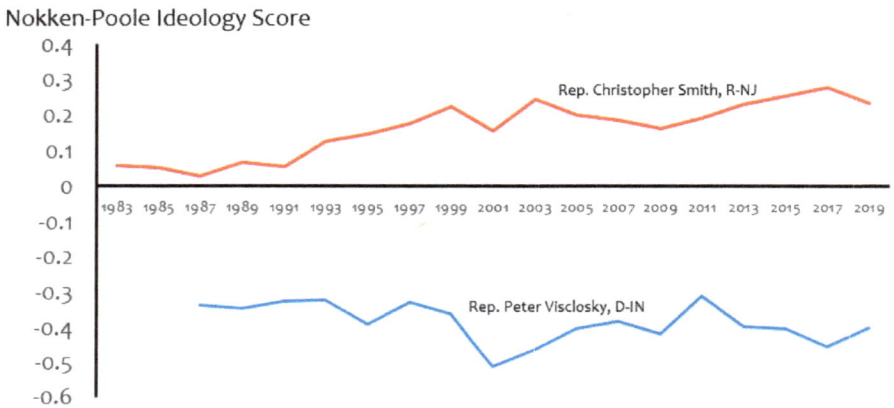

Figure 3. Early-1980s cohort examples, U.S. House of Representatives.

The Nokken–Poole ranges from the *Late 1980s Cohort* span from a low of 840 basis points (absolute value), which is nontrivial, to a high of 7760 basis points, which is quite remarkable. This latter range belongs to John Duncan, a Republican from Tennessee, while the former belongs to Nita Lowey, a Democrat from New York. While Duncan exhibits the least stable political ideology among Republicans in the *Late-1980s Cohort* for the U.S. House of Representatives, that position among Democrats belongs to Frank Pallone of New Jersey, whose political ideology swings 4840 basis points (absolute value) along the policy space in Figure 1. Figure 4 presents the Nokken–Poole time series for both Duncan and Pallone.

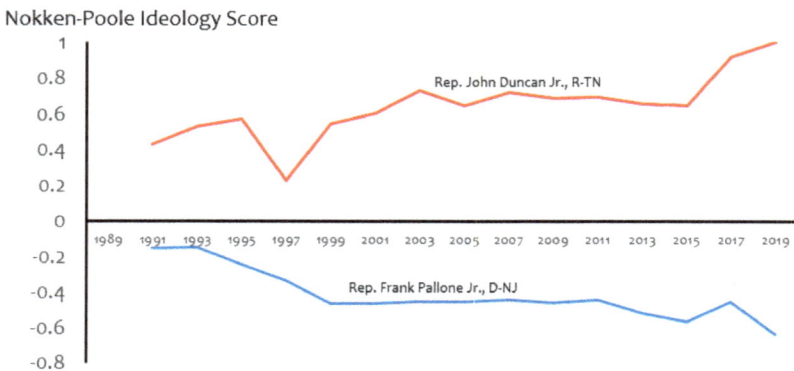

Figure 4. Late-1980s cohort examples, U.S. House of Representatives.

A comparison of Visclosky, from the *Early 1980s Cohort*, and Pallone, from the *Late 1980s Cohort*, illustrates some of the issues explored in this study. First, these two time series are good examples of how political ideology exhibits instability in the absolute sense. As stated previously, the political ideologies of these two Democratic Senators swing 1880 and 4840 basis points, respectively, across the policy space in Figure 1. If the time period of their voting activity is restricted to 1997 through 2001, Visclosky's political ideology again exhibits sizable instability in the absolute sense, as it changes by 1820 basis points. On the other hand, Pallone's political ideology is relatively stable in the absolute sense over that same time period, as it swings by only 20 basis points along the policy space. However, Pallone lies to the left of Visclosky along the policy space at the beginning of this brief period (i.e., 1997), whereas Visclosky lies to the left of Pallone by the end of the period (i.e., 2001). Thus, in this case a sizable shift in political ideology in the absolute sense led to a rearrangement of legislators along the policy space in Figure 1. Did Visclosky's constituents in Indiana anticipate such a sizable absolute shift in his political ideology over this brief period? More importantly, did these same constituents expect their congressman to move to the left of a Democratic legislator from New Jersey over this brief period of time, as occurred in this particular situation?[14]

The remaining portion of Table 2 presents statistical tests of the stability of political ideology among long-serving members of the U.S. House of Representatives. These tests estimate (by OLS) the specification in Equation (2) above. Estimates of b_1 for each legislator listed in Table 2 are presented under the column heading "$TREND_t$" in Table 2. The two columns to the right contain significance levels for each estimate and the number of observations in each case, respectively.[15] Overall, the results indicate that Democrats tend to become more liberal in their political ideology with the passage of time, while Republicans tend to become more conservative. Of the 12 long-serving Democrats listed in Table 2, nine (i.e., 75 percent) become more liberal, while three (i.e., 25 percent) became more conservative.[16] Of the nine long-serving Republicans listed in Table 2, six (i.e., about 67 percent) became more conservative, and three (i.e., about 33 percent) became more liberal over time. In terms of only the statistically significant coefficients, three of the five Republicans (i.e., 60 percent) became more conservative over time, while two (i.e., 40 percent) became more liberal. For Democrats, four of five (i.e., 80 percent) became more liberal, while one (i.e., 20 percent) became more conservative.[17]

In eight of the 10 cases where instability in political ideology is statistically significant, the legislator's political ideology changes, in one direction or the other, from 20 to 30 basis points per Congressional session.[18] This is noteworthy given that it indicates that over the course of a 20-year legislative career (i.e., 10 Congressional sessions), the political ideology of many U.S. Representatives swings, in one direction or the other, up to 800 basis points. Even more remarkable are the coefficient estimates for Duncan and Pallone, which indicate movements in political ideology of 320 and 130 basis points per Congressional session, respectively. As such, movements in political ideology cover 1600 and 650 basis points, respectively, over just five consecutive Congressional sessions (i.e., 10 years) served.

---

[14] U.S. President Donald Trump (R-NY) captured 57.2 percent of the popular vote in Indiana during the 2016 presidential election. His opponent, Hillary Clinton (D-NY), won 37.9 percent of the popular vote in Indiana. In New Jersey, on the other hand, Trump garnered only 41.8 percent of the popular vote, whereas Clinton carried the state with 55 percent of the popular vote. This result, among others, indicates that voters in Indiana prefer more conservative policies than do their counterparts in New Jersey.

[15] Given the presence of the lagged value of a legislator's Nokken–Poole score, the SAS statistical package recommends use of the Durbin *t* test statistic to test for autocorrelation.

[16] Autocorrelation is a problem in two of the nine cases of increasing liberalism among the long-serving Democrats in the U.S. House of Representatives.

[17] Autocorrelation is a problem in one of the four cases of a statistically significant increase in liberalism among the long-serving Democrats in the U.S. House of Representatives.

[18] Again, autocorrelation is a problem in one of these eight cases of a statistically significant trend among the long-serving lawmakers in the U.S. House of Representatives.

Table 3 presents the empirical results for members of the U.S. Senate. As indicated near the top of Table 3, the *Early Cohorts* subsample includes only one Senator—Patrick Leahy, a Democrat from Vermont. In his case, a noteworthy degree of instability of political ideology is exhibited by his Nokken–Poole range of 2540 basis points (absolute value). A graphical representation of the instability in Leahy's political ideology is presented in Figure 5.

Table 3. Political ideology in the U.S. Senate.

Name	$|NP_L-NP_S|$	$TREND_t$	*p*-Value	*n*	AC
Early Cohorts					
Leahy, Patrick	0.254	−0.005 ‡	0.038	21	yes
Late 1970s Cohort					
Cochran, Thad	0.156	0.006 *	0.001	19	no
Hatch, Orrin	0.239	−0.003	0.173	20	no
Early 1980s Cohort					
Grassley, Charles	0.390	0.015 *	0.001	18	no
Late 1980s Cohort					
McCain, John	0.289	0.003	0.258	15	yes

Notes: One-tailed *p*-values reported above. *(‡) denote the 0.01(0.05) level of significance. AC = autocorrelation. The null hypothesis of "no autocorrelation" is tested using the Durbin *t* test statistic.

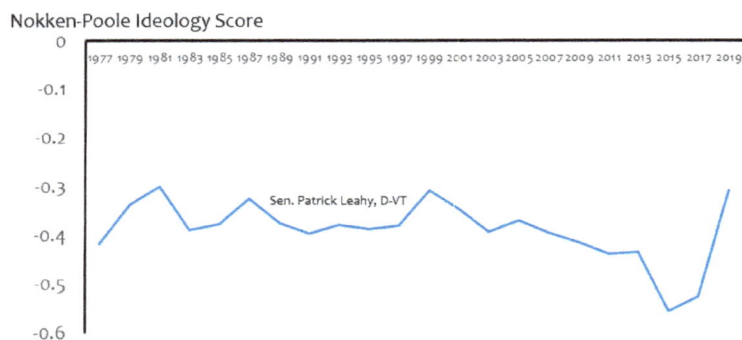

Figure 5. Early cohort example, U.S. Senate.

As with Table 2, the remaining portions of Table 3 present data on political ideology from the other cohorts in the U.S. Senate. In terms of the widest range, Charles Grassley, a Republican from Iowa who represents the *Early 1980s Cohort*, exhibits a political ideology range, using Nokken–Poole scores, of 3900 basis points. Next, Orrin Hatch, a Republican from Utah, leads the *Late 1970s Cohort* with a political ideology range of 2390 basis points, while the late John McCain, a Republican who represented Arizona, leads the *Late 1980s Cohort* with a political ideology range of 2890 basis points. Graphical representations of the instability of the political ideology of these three U.S. Senators are, beginning with the *Late 1970s Cohort* and proceeding to the *Late 1980s Cohort*, presented in Figures 6–8.

Nokken-Poole Ideology Score

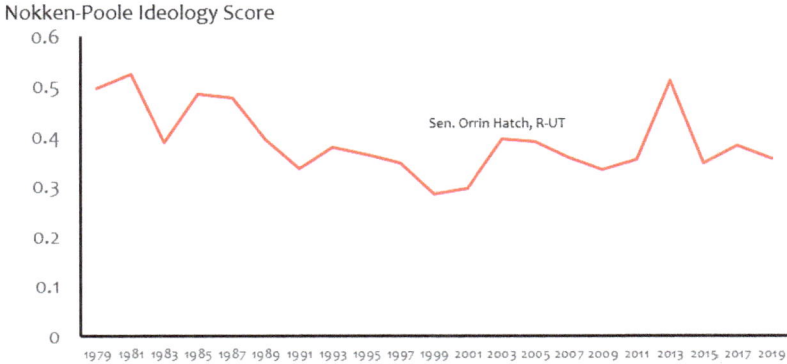

Figure 6. Late-1970s cohort example, U.S. Senate.

Nokken-Poole Ideology Score

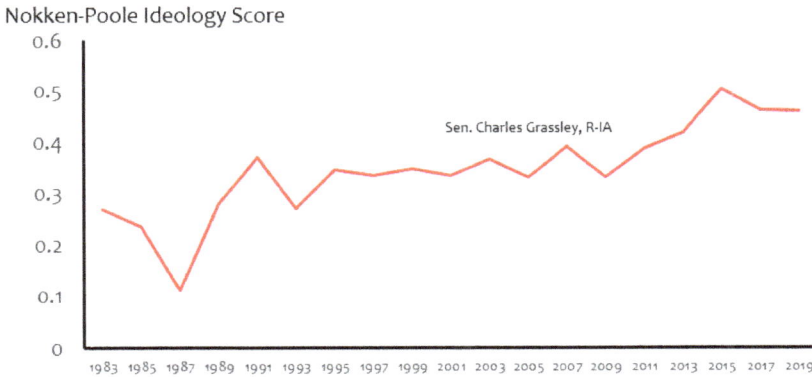

Figure 7. Early-1980s cohort example, U.S. Senate.

Nokken-Poole Ideology Score

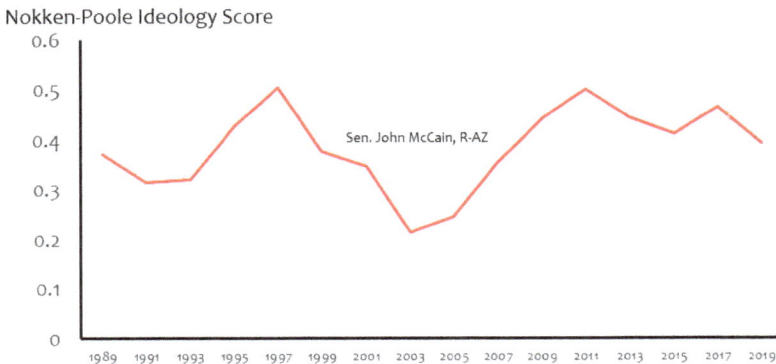

Figure 8. Late-1980s cohort example, U.S. Senate.

The remaining portion of Table 3 also presents statistical tests of the stability of political ideology among long-serving members of the U.S. Senate. These tests follow those discussed above for long-serving members of the U.S. House of Representatives. Overall, the results indicate that of the four long-serving Republicans listed in Table 3, three became more conservative and one became more liberal over time.[19] In terms of only the statistically significant coefficients, each of the two Republicans exhibiting instability in their political ideology became more conservative over time. Additionally, in one of the two cases where the legislator becomes more conservative, the legislator's political ideology changes by 60 basis points per Congressional session. Again, this is noteworthy given that it indicates that over the course of a 20-year legislative career (i.e., 10 Congressional sessions), the political ideologies of some U.S. Senators swing, in one direction or the other, up to 600 basis points. Even more remarkable, however, is the coefficient estimate for Grassley, which indicates a movement in political ideology of 150 basis points per Congressional session. At this rate, movement in one's political ideology would cover 1500 basis points over just five consecutive Congressional sessions (i.e., 10 years) served.

To provide a more general examination of the stability of political ideology of elected officials, Table 4 presents estimations of Equation (2) above using various pooled subsamples. The first two sets of results employ data from long-serving members of the U.S. House of Representatives from each of the two major political parties. As indicated there, both models are jointly significant and produce an R^2 of 0.811 or greater. The first model suggests that the typical Democrat enters the U.S. House with a Nokken–Poole score of −0.272, which is 2720 basis points to the left of center on the policy space in Figure 1. After that, he or she becomes more conservative over time, in this case at a rate of 10 basis points per Congressional session. However, this tendency or trend is not statistically significant at usual levels. Lastly, and as expected, past political ideology is positively and statistically significantly related to current political ideology.

Table 4. OLS results—pooled subsamples.

Variables	U.S. House Subsamples		U.S. Senate Subsample
	Democrats	**Republicans**	**Republicans**
constant	−0.272 *	0.090 *	0.144 *
	(−6.54)	(3.98)	(4.12)
$TREND_t$	0.001	0.002 ‡	0.003 †
	(0.99)	(2.12)	(1.78)
$IDEOL_{t-1}$	0.615 *	0.563 *	0.450 *
	(11.08)	(7.33)	(4.18)
Legislator Effects	yes	yes	yes
n	191	146	72
F-statistic	58.40 *	123.4 *	9.15 *
R^2	0.811	0.901	0.410

Notes: The numbers in parentheses above are *t*-values. *(‡)[†] denote the 0.01(0.05)[0.10] level of significance.

The second set of results cover the long-serving Republicans in the U.S. House of Representatives. As suggested by these results, the typical Republican enters the U.S. House of Representatives with a Nokken–Poole score of 0.090, which is 900 basis points to the right of center on the policy space in Figure 1. After that, he or she becomes more conservative over time, in this case at a rate of 20 basis points per Congressional session, a result that is statistically significant. Lastly, and again as expected, past political ideology is positively and statistically significantly related to current political ideology.

The final set of results presented in Table 4 employ data from long-serving Republicans in the U.S. Senate. As indicated in Table 4, this model is jointly significant and produces an R^2 of 0.410. In terms of the long-serving Republicans in the U.S. Senate, the results in Table 4 suggest that the typical

---

[19] Autocorrelation is a problem in one of the three cases of increasing conservatism among the long-serving Republicans in the U.S. Senate.

Republican enters the U.S. Senate with a Nokken–Poole score of 0.144, which is 1440 basis points to the right of center on the policy space in Figure 1. After that, he or she becomes more conservative over time, in this case at a rate of 30 basis points per Congressional session, a result that is again statistically significant.[20] The significance of the instability of legislators' political ideology over time in this and the previous case calls into question the alignment of Republicans' political ideologies to those of their constituencies.

5.2. Relevance and Limitations of the Findings

The main finding in our study—that the political ideology of federal legislators exhibits some instability over time—contributes to the economics literature in a number of ways. Among these, it extends seminal studies wherein economists examine the economics of information and its links to advertising, search and signaling (Stigler 1961; Darby and Karni 1973; Spence 1973; Nelson 1970, 1974). According to this foundational work, and the empirical studies that have emerged since, the quantity, quality and form of advertising and information provision are functions of goods (and buyer) characteristics, as well as relative prices (Ekelund et al. 1995; Mixon et al. 2009).[21] Nelson (1970, 1974) first suggested an analytical classification of goods with *search* and *experience* characteristics, wherein search (experience) goods are those for which judgments about the goods' attributes can (cannot) be made (at low cost) prior to purchase.[22] In the case of experience goods, such judgments are possible only after purchase. As such, goods and services can be placed on a continuum much like that presented above in Figure 1, although one where "search characteristics" and "experience characteristics" replace the "Liberal" and "Conservative" political ideology tags, respectively, at the two ends of the continuum.

The notion that the "legislative services" provided by representatives to their constituents lie somewhere along a search-experience characteristics continuum, using the categories in Nelson's (1974) analytical classification of goods and services, has been put forth in prior economics studies. As Mixon et al. (2009, p. 84) indicate, one point of view (e.g., Nelson 1976) holds that political services are more like search goods, given that candidates' records are available to the public, and thus a candidate's actual performance can be compared with his or her advertised performance. Another point of view asserts that political services are more like experience goods, given that it is difficult for voters to draw inferences about the future behavior of candidates (Telser 1976) and that that the costs of investigating candidates' political records can be high (Ferguson 1976).[23] The findings of this study, that the political ideologies of legislators exhibits instability over time, certainly reinforces the argument by Telser (1976) that it is difficult for voters to draw inferences about the future behavior of candidates for political office.

In terms of the relevance of our findings to political scientists, there is a line of argument in the political science literature that relates to the discussion above regarding goods/services typology. As noted in Mixon et al. (2005), Boudreaux (1996) points out that the plethora of issues facing voters, combined with the fact that voting opportunities (e.g., elections for national office) are, at best, infrequently presented to voters suggests that decisions made by voters in the political realm are likely to be relatively uninformed. As such, and contrary to Wittman (1995), these decisions are unlikely to promote efficient policies or outcomes.[24] Boudreaux's (1996) arguments are based in part

---

[20] As in the previous models, past political ideology is positively and statistically significantly related to current political ideology.
[21] Foundational empirical studies in this stream of the economics literature include Laband (1986, 1989, 1991), Ekelund et al. (1995) and Mixon (1995).
[22] Darby and Karni (1973) suggest a third classification of goods—credence goods—for which judgments about the good's attributes are prohibitively costly even after purchase.
[23] For examples of prior empirical work on this topic, see Crain and Goff (1988), Mixon (2002), Mixon and Upadhyaya (2002, 2003), Mixon et al. (2003a), Mixon et al. (2003b) and Mixon et al. (2009).
[24] Boudreaux (1996, pp. 117–18) points out that the typical national election involves perhaps thousands of highly aggregated issues—from abortion to school choice. Moreover, each voter has a maximum of nine national ballots to cast during a six-year span, suggesting that political decisions by voters, as opposed to market decisions by households/consumers, are invariably cluttered with "romance pollution" (see also Brennan and Lomasky 1993).

on Downs (1957), who asserts that if the voter does not pursue politics as a hobby, he or she will be badly informed. The phenomenon described above, which Downs (1957) termed "rational ignorance," leads voters to seek low-cost informational cues in choosing from among political candidates.[25] Within a framework asserting that political information is costly to acquire, seminal work by Kramer (1971) argues that voters support the incumbent if his or her *recent* political performance has been satisfactory on the basis of some *relatively simple* standard (e.g., real GDP growth).

Another research stream, based on early research by Lewis-Beck and Rice (1983), suggests that, *ceteris paribus*, voters prefer local candidates to more distant candidates in political contests. As Faith and Tollison (1983) point out, the advantage to voters of home grown candidates stems from the human capital advantage that local candidates have in the form of information about the political conditions/desires that exist in the home district.[26] In addition to this advantage, Kjar and Laband (2002) add that because it is costly to "fire" a representative for poor performance, voters will prefer local candidates with longstanding ties to the district. These candidates implicitly put more specific human and/or other types of capital at risk as a type of performance bond (Telser 1980; Klein and Leffler 1981; Shapiro 1983) than do candidates with lesser ties to a district (Kjar and Laband 2002, p. 144).[27] As in the case of how the findings in this study are situated within the academic literature on the economics of information, the suggestion from our results that the political ideologies of legislators exhibits instability over time creates difficulties for voters with regard to attempts to employ low-cost information cues, such as geographical proximity, at the polls. For example, our finding that a Democratic representative from Indiana became more liberal, over time, than his colleague from New Jersey likely caused some consternation among the Indiana electorate. A similar pattern in state-level politics in Indiana would devalue the practice of localism (in voting) in that state.

Although the findings presented in this study have particular relevance to both the economics and political science branches of the academic literature, our work is not without limitations, particularly in its use of political ideology scores. Our use of Nokken and Poole (2004) scores as a measure of political ideology follows what Jackson and Kingdon (1992, p. 805) refer to as the typical approach by economists to the study of legislators and legislatures, wherein the framing and passing of legislation is posed as a competition between a legislator's political ideology and the economic interests of his or her local constituency. Jackson and Kingdon (1992, p. 806) assert that commonly-used measures of ideological preferences, such as ADA scores or other compilations of roll call votes (e.g., Nokken–Poole scores), lead to a statistical bias that overestimates the influence of personal ideology and underestimates the relationship with other variables.[28] More specifically, they argue that the votes that constitute a political ideology score are affected by a number of systematic factors, such as interest group pressures, presidential agendas, committee activities, the persuasions of party leaders, and the consequences of the agenda-setting process (Jackson and Kingdon 1992, p. 813).

Jackson and Kingdon (1992, p. 815) support the use of ideological measures that are constructed independently of roll call votes in order to understand the impact of political ideology on the behavior of elected officials. Using such measures requires studying political ideology directly, as in the case of survey research and more intensive approaches (e.g., see Converse 1964; Inglehart 1988), or through analyses of the contents of the writings and speeches of politicians. As Jackson and Kingdon (1992,

---

[25] Cebula and Mixon (2012) point out that Downs's (1957) work forms the foundation of scholarly research on voter participation in the U.S. that focuses on whether or not the decision to vote, in general, is rational.

[26] Faith and Tollison (1983) and Kjar and Laband (2002) also add that the search costs associated with detecting the merits of home district candidates will generally be lower than those associated with discovery of the merits of more distant candidates.

[27] In other words, voters understand and appreciate the implied efficiency of casting ballots in favor of candidates who have much to lose locally from nonperformance in the legislative arena (Kjar and Laband 2002, p. 144). For a look at some of the empirical research on presidential elections from this stream of literature, see Lewis-Beck and Rice (1983), Rice and Macht (1987), Kjar and Laband (2002), Mixon and Tyrone (2004), Disarro et al. (2007), Mixon et al. (2008), Kahane (2009) and Mixon (2013, 2018).

[28] Jackson and Kingdon (1992, p. 813) assert that this issue is exacerbated in the case of a single dimension, as would occur when using League of Conservation Voters scores of political ideology to analyze voting on strip mining legislation.

p. 815) point out, there is a long tradition in political science of probing the beliefs, values and preferences of politicians (e.g., see Miller and Stokes 1963; Fenno 1978, 1986; Aberbach et al. 1981; Kingdon 1989). Acknowledgment of our study's limitations, at least in the ways stated by Jackson and Kingdon (1992), would point toward inclusion of regressors in our econometric model that capture the systematic factors referred to above that influence political ideology scores, or, alternatively, use of survey data and/or results from content analysis instead of traditional scores of political ideology. Perhaps future research, which we discuss in greater depth in the final section of the study, could delve into these and other issues.

6. Conclusions and Recommendations for Future Research

Given that previous public choice studies have shown that voters tend to vote for candidates from parties who are aligned with their own political ideologies, the present study addresses the important question: How stable is a legislator's political ideology over time? To address this particular question, we employ numerical scores of legislators' political ideology for long-serving members of the U.S. House of Representatives and the U.S. Senate. As indicated above, results from individual time-series estimations suggest that political ideology is unstable over time for a sizable portion of the members of both major political parties who serve in the U.S. Congress. These results run somewhat counter to those in early work by Jennings (1992), and in more recent research by Jewitt and Goren (2016). Additionally, analysis of the pooled data suggests that, after accounting for inertia in political ideology and individual legislator effects, Republican legislators become more conservative over time.

Taken individually, these sets of results generate additional research questions for public choice scholars to ponder. These begin with the recommendation that future research delve further into the apparent differences in the instability of political ideology by major political party in the U.S. Is the apparent difference between the instability in conservative political ideology and liberal political ideology one of a statistically significant nature, as indicated here? Or, would additional empirical analysis, using a larger data set than employed in this study, find a statistically significant degree of instability in the political ideologies of Democrats in the U.S. Congress?

Taken together, the results presented in this paper point toward deeper scientific study of the stability of political ideology in the legislative body. For example, future research could explore the correlates of political ideology, beginning with the demographics of legislators who comprise a particular legislative chamber. Panel data, using samples from the U.S. and elsewhere, might flesh out the important explanatory variables, such as gender, age, prior education and experience, to name a few, that shape political ideology and its stability. Moreover, empirical approaches that link the ideologies of legislators to those of their constituencies could explore whether shifts in the ideologies of legislators is aligned with shifts in electorate ideology, or whether a misalignment is occurring in this process. If ideology misalignment is indeed occurring, then further exploration into the type of echo chamber that a legislative body constitutes may point toward secondary constituencies that influence the political ideologies of elected officials. This line of inquiry could follow Mixon et al. (2009) by examining the role of campaign contributions plays in the importance of positioning along the traditional unidimensional policy space discussed in the public choice literature.

Author Contributions: F.G.M., research question, empirical model and estimation, original draft; C.S., literature review, original draft, editing; K.P.U., empirical model and estimation, editing.

Funding: This research received no external funding.

Acknowledgments: The authors thank two anonymous reviewers for many helpful comments on a prior version. The usual caveat applies.

Conflicts of Interest: The authors declare no conflicts of interest.

References

Aberbach, Joel D., Robert D. Putnam, and Bert A. Rockman. 1981. *Bureaucrats and Politicians in Western Democracies*. Cambridge: Harvard University Press.

Abramowitz, Alan I. 1994. Issue Evolution Reconsidered: Racial Attitudes and Partisanship in the U.S. Electorate. *American Journal of Political Science* 38: 1–24. [CrossRef]

Abramowitz, Alan I., and Kyle L. Saunders. 1998. Ideological Realignment in the U.S. Electorate. *Journal of Politics* 60: 634–52. [CrossRef]

Bartle, John. 2000. Political Awareness, Opinion Constraint and the Stability of Ideological Positions. *Political Studies* 48: 467–84. [CrossRef]

Berry, William D., Evan J. Ringquist, Richard C. Fording, and Russell L. Hanson. 1998. Measuring Citizen and Government Ideology in the American States, 1960–1993. *American Journal of Political Science* 42: 327–48. [CrossRef]

Berry, William D., Evan J. Ringquist, Richard C. Fording, and Russell L. Hanson. 2007. The Measurement and Stability of State Citizen Ideology. *State Politics & Policy Quarterly* 7: 111–32.

Boche, Adam, Jeffrey B. Lewis, Aaron Rudkin, and Luke Sonnet. 2018. The New Voteview.com: Preserving and Continuing Poole's Infrastructure for Scholars, Students and Observers of Congress. *Public Choice* 176: 17–32. [CrossRef]

Boudreaux, Donald J. 1996. Was Your High School Civics Teacher Right after All? *The Independent Review* 1: 111–28.

Brace, Paul, Kevin Arceneaux, Martin Johnson, and Stacy G. Ulbig. 2004. Does State Political Ideology Change over Time? *Political Research Quarterly* 57: 529–40.

Brennan, Geoffrey, and Loren Lomasky. 1993. *Democracy and Decision: The Pure Theory of Electoral Preference*. New York: Cambridge University Press.

Carmines, Edward G., and Geoffrey C. Layman. 1997. Issue Evolution in Postwar American Politics: Old Certainties and Fresh Tensions. In *Present Discontents: American Politics in the Very Late Twentieth Century*. Edited by Byron E. Shafer. Chatham: Chatham House.

Carmines, Edward G., and Harold W. Stanley. 1990. Ideological Realignment in the Contemporary South: Where have all the Conservatives Gone? In *The Disappearing South? Studies in Regional Change and Continuity*. Edited by Robert P. Steed, Laurence W. Moreland and Tod A. Baker. Tuscaloosa: University of Alabama Press.

Carmines, Edward G., and Harold W. Stanley. 1992. The Transformation of the New Deal Party System: Social Groups, Political Ideology, and Changing Partisanship among Northern Whites, 1972–1988. *Political Behavior* 14: 213–37. [CrossRef]

Carmines, Edward G., and James A. Stimson. 1989. *Issue Evolution: Race and the Transformation of American Politics*. Princeton: Princeton University Press.

Cebula, Richard J., and Franklin G. Mixon Jr. 2012. Dodging the Vote? Military Conscription and U.S. Voter Participation, 1948–2006. *Empirical Economics* 42: 325–43. [CrossRef]

Converse, Philip E. 1964. The Nature of Belief Systems in Mass Publics. In *Ideology and Discontent*. Edited by David E. Apter. New York: The Free Press of Glencoe.

Crain, W. Mark, and Brian L. Goff. 1988. *Televised Legislatures: Political Information Technology and Public Choice*. Boston: Kluwer Academic.

Darby, Michael R., and Edi Karni. 1973. Free Competition and the Optimal Amount of Fraud. *Journal of Law and Economics* 16: 67–88. [CrossRef]

Disarro, Brian, Jillian Barber, and Tom W. Rice. 2007. The Home State Effect in Presidential Elections: Advances in the Study of Localism. *Presidential Studies Quarterly* 37: 558–66. [CrossRef]

Downs, Anthony. 1957. *An Economic Theory of Democracy*. New York: Harper & Row.

Ekelund, Robert B., Jr., Franklin G. Mixon Jr., and Rand W. Ressler. 1995. Advertising and Information: An Empirical Study of Search, Experience and Credence Goods. *Journal of Economic Studies* 22: 33–43. [CrossRef]

Faith, Roger L., and Robert D. Tollison. 1983. Voter Search for Efficient Representation. *Research in Law and Economics* 5: 211–24.

Fenno, Richard F., Jr. 1978. *Home Style: House Members in their Districts*. Boston: Little and Brown.

Fenno, Richard F., Jr. 1986. Observation, Context, and Sequence in the Study of Politics. *American Political Science Review* 80: 3–16. [CrossRef]

Ferguson, James M. 1976. Political Information: Comment. *Journal of Law and Economics* 19: 341–46. [CrossRef]

Goren, Paul. 2005. Party Identification and Core Political Values. *American Journal of Political Science* 49: 881–96. [CrossRef]

Harring, Niklas, and Jacob Sohlberg. 2017. The Varying Effects of Left-Right Ideology on Support for the Environment: Evidence from a Swedish Survey Experiment. *Environmental Politics* 26: 278–300. [CrossRef]

Hotelling, Harold. 1929. Stability in Competition. *The Economic Journal* 39: 41–57. [CrossRef]

Inglehart, Ronald. 1988. The Renaissance of Political Culture. *American Political Science Review* 82: 1203–230. [CrossRef]

Jackson, John E., and John W. Kingdon. 1992. Ideology, Interest Group Scores, and Legislative Votes. *American Journal of Political Science* 36: 805–23. [CrossRef]

Jennings, M. Kent. 1992. Ideological Thinking among Mass Publics and Political Elites. *Public Opinion Quarterly* 56: 419–41. [CrossRef]

Jewitt, Caitlin E., and Paul Goren. 2016. Ideological Structure and Consistency in the Age of Polarization. *American Politics Research* 44: 81–105. [CrossRef]

Jost, John T., Christopher M. Federico, and Jaime L. Napier. 2009. Political Ideology: Its Structure, Functions, and Elective Affinities. *Annual Review of Psychology* 60: 307–37. [CrossRef]

Kahane, Leo H. 2009. It's the Economy, and then Some: Modeling the Presidential Vote with State Panel Data. *Public Choice* 139: 343–56. [CrossRef]

Kingdon, John D. 1989. *Congressmen's Voting Decisions*. Ann Arbor: University of Michigan Press.

Kjar, Scott A., and David N. Laband. 2002. On 'Home Grown-ness' in Politics: Evidence from the 1998 Election for Alabama's Third Congressional District. *Public Choice* 112: 143–50. [CrossRef]

Klein, Benjamin, and Keith B. Leffler. 1981. The Role of Market Forces in Assuring Contractual Performance. *Journal of Political Economy* 89: 615–41. [CrossRef]

Knoke, David. 1979. Stratification and the Dimensions of American Political Orientations. *American Journal of Political Science* 23: 772–91. [CrossRef]

Kramer, Gerald H. 1971. Short-Term Fluctuations in U.S. Voting Behavior, 1896–1964. *American Political Science Review* 65: 131–43. [CrossRef]

Krehbiel, Keith. 1998. *Pivotal Politics: A Theory of U.S. Lawmaking*. Chicago: University of Chicago Press.

Ksiazkiewicz, Aleksander, Steven Ludeke, and Robert Krueger. 2016. The Role of Cognitive Style in the Link between Genes and Political Ideology. *Political Psychology* 37: 761–76. [CrossRef]

Laband, David N. 1986. Advertising as Information: An Empirical Note. *Review of Economics and Statistics* 68: 517–21. [CrossRef]

Laband, David N. 1989. The Durability of Informational Signals and the Content of Advertising. *Journal of Advertising* 18: 13–18. [CrossRef]

Laband, David N. 1991. An Objective Measure of Search Versus Experience Goods. *Economic Inquiry* 29: 497–509. [CrossRef]

Layman, Geoffrey C., and Thomas M. Carsey. 2000. *Ideological Realignment in Contemporary American Politics: The Case of Party Activists*. Unpublished Manuscript.

Leach, Robert. 2015. *Political Ideology in Britain*. London: Palgrave Macmillan.

Lee, Robert D. 2013. *Religion and Politics in the Middle East: Identity, Ideology, Institutions, and Attitudes*. New York: Routledge.

Levine, Jeffrey, Edward G. Carmines, and Robert Huckfeldt. 1997. The Rise of Ideology in the Post-New Deal Party System, 1972–1992. *American Politics Quarterly* 25: 19–34. [CrossRef]

Lewis, Jeffrey B., Keith T. Poole, Howard Rosenthal, Adam Boche, Aaron Rudkin, and Luke Sonnet. 2018. Voteview: Congressional Roll-Call Votes Database. Available online: https://voteview.com/ (accessed on 1 May 2019).

Lewis-Beck, Michael S., and Tom W. Rice. 1983. Localism in Presidential Elections: The Home State Advantage. *American Journal of Political Science* 27: 548–56. [CrossRef]

Lupton, Robert N., William M. Myers, and Judd R. Thornton. 2015. Political Sophistication and the Dimensionality of Elite and Mass Attitudes, 1980–2004. *Journal of Politics* 77: 368–80.

Melville, Andrei. 2018. Russian Political Ideology. In *Russia: Strategy, Policy and Administration*. Edited by Irvin Studin. London: Palgrave Macmillan.

Miller, Warren E., and Donald E. Stokes. 1963. Constituency Influence in Congress. *American Political Science Review* 57: 45–56. [CrossRef]

Mixon, Franklin G., Jr. 1995. Advertising as Information: Further Evidence. *Southern Economic Journal* 61: 1213–18. [CrossRef]

Mixon, Franklin G., Jr. 2002. Does Legislative Television alter the Relationship between Voters and Politicians? *Rationality and Society* 14: 109–28. [CrossRef]

Mixon, Franklin G., Jr. 2013. Warm Springs Ran Deep: Friends-and-Neighbors Voting in the U.S. Presidential Elections of 1940 and 1944. *Journal of Politics and Law* 6: 105–15. [CrossRef]

Mixon, Franklin G., Jr. 2018. Glass Houses and Friends-and-Neighbors Voting: An Exploratory Analysis of the Impact of Political Scandal on Localism. *Economies* 6: 48. [CrossRef]

Mixon, Franklin G., Jr., and J. Matthew Tyrone. 2004. The 'Home Grown' Presidency: Empirical Evidence on Localism in Presidential Voting, 1972–2000. *Applied Economics* 36: 1745–49. [CrossRef]

Mixon, Franklin G., Jr., and Kamal P. Upadhyaya. 2002. Legislative Television as an Institutional Entry Barrier: The Impact of C-SPAN2 on Turnover in the U.S. Senate, 1946–1998. *Public Choice* 112: 433–48. [CrossRef]

Mixon, Franklin G., Jr., and Kamal P. Upadhyaya. 2003. *Legislative Television as Political Advertising: A Public Choice Approach*. New York: Universe.

Mixon, Franklin G., Jr., M. Troy Gibson, and Kamal P. Upadhyaya. 2003a. Has Legislative Television changed Legislator Behavior? C-SPAN2 and the Frequency of Senate Filibustering. *Public Choice* 115: 139–62. [CrossRef]

Mixon, Franklin G., Jr., Rand W. Ressler, and M. Troy Gibson. 2003b. Congressional Memberships as Political Advertising: Evidence from the U.S. Senate. *Southern Economic Journal* 70: 414–24. [CrossRef]

Mixon, Franklin G., Len J. Treviño, and Taisa C. Minto. 2005. Are Legislative TV and Campaign Finance Regulations Complementary Entry Barriers? Evidence from the USA. *Applied Economics* 37: 387–96. [CrossRef]

Mixon, Franklin G., Jr., Ernest W. King, and Matthew L. Lawing. 2008. Modeling the Impact of Localism in U.S. Presidential Elections. *Journal of Public Finance and Public Choice* 26: 3–18.

Mixon, Franklin G., Jr., Rand W. Ressler, and M. Troy Gibson. 2009. False Advertising and Experience Goods: The Case of Political Services in the U.S. Senate. *Public Choice* 138: 83–95. [CrossRef]

Naumann, Laura P., Verónica Benet-Martínez, and Penelope Espinoza. 2017. Correlates of Political Ideology among U. S.-Born Mexican Americans: Cultural Identification, Acculturation Attitudes, and Socioeconomic Attitudes. *Social Psychology and Personality Science* 8: 20–28. [CrossRef]

Nelson, Phillip. 1970. Information and Consumer Behavior. *Journal of Political Economy* 78: 311–29. [CrossRef]

Nelson, Phillip. 1974. Advertising as Information. *Journal of Political Economy* 82: 729–54. [CrossRef]

Nelson, Phillip. 1976. Political Information. *Journal of Law and Economics* 19: 315–36. [CrossRef]

Nokken, Timothy P., and Keith T. Poole. 2004. Congressional Party Defection in American History. *Legislative Studies Quarterly* 29: 545–68. [CrossRef]

Peña, Alejandro M. 2016. *Transnational Governance and South American Politics*. London: Palgrave Macmillan.

Petrocik, John R. 1996. Issue Ownership in Presidential Elections, with a 1980 Case Study. *American Journal of Political Science* 40: 825–50. [CrossRef]

Poole, Keith T., and Howard Rosenthal. 1997. *Congress: A Political-Economic History of Roll Call Voting*. New York: Oxford University Press.

Poole, Keith T., and Howard L. Rosenthal. 2000. *Voteview Manual*. Pittsburgh: Carnegie Mellon University.

Rice, Tom W., and Alisa A. Macht. 1987. Friends and Neighbors Voting in Statewide General Elections. *American Journal of Political Science* 31: 448–52. [CrossRef]

Sears, David O., and Carolyn L. Funk. 1999. Evidence of the Long-Term Persistence of Adults' Political Predispositions. *Journal of Politics* 61: 1–28. [CrossRef]

Seeberg, Henrik B. 2017. How Stable is Political Parties' Issue Ownership? A Cross-Time, Cross-National Analysis. *Political Studies* 65: 475–92. [CrossRef]

Shapiro, Carl. 1983. Premiums for High Quality Products as Returns to Reputation. *Quarterly Journal of Economics* 98: 659–79. [CrossRef]

Spence, Michael. 1973. Job Market Signalling. *Quarterly Journal of Economics* 87: 355–79. [CrossRef]

Stigler, George J. 1961. The Economics of Information. *Journal of Political Economy* 69: 213–25. [CrossRef]

Telser, Lester G. 1976. Political Information: Comment. *Journal of Law and Economics* 19: 337–40. [CrossRef]

Telser, Lester G. 1980. A Theory of Self-Enforcing Agreements. *Journal of Business* 53: 27–44. [CrossRef]

Wittman, Donald. 1995. *The Myth of the Democratic Failure*. Chicago: University of Chicago Press.

Wright, Gerald C., Robert S. Erikson, and John P. McIver. 1985. Measuring State Partisanship and Ideology with Survey Data. *Journal of Politics* 47: 469–89. [CrossRef]

![economies logo] *economies*

MDPI

Article

The Political Economy of Abandoned Mine Land Fund Disbursements

Jessi Troyan [1] and Joshua Hall [2,*]

[1]   Cardinal Institute for West Virginia Policy, Charleston, WV 25339, USA; jltroyan@gmail.com
[2]   West Virginia University, Chambers College of Business & Economics, Morgantown, WV 26506, USA
[*]   Correspondence: joshua.hall@mail.wvu.edu; Tel.: +1-304-293-7870

Received: 14 December 2018; Accepted: 4 January 2019; Published: 10 January 2019

Abstract: What factors determine federal spending on environmental goods? Is severity of the hazard the only metric of consideration, or do other factors play a vital role in explaining spending? This paper seeks to answer this question and to identify disbursement patterns within the context of the Abandoned Mine Land Fund (AMLF) program, a fund created as an aspect of the Surface Mining Control and Reclamation Act of 1977. We explore whether political factors, as well as environmental and health factors, have an explanatory role in disbursement of AMLF monies. The political factors examined include environmental interest group influence and legislator preferences and/or pressures to fund sites in their home states or districts. The results found here suggest that there exists a mix of public and private interests present in AMLF disbursement decisions during the overall span of the program, and that political influences have gained strength in the decision-making calculus in response to changes in the funding structure of the AMLF.

Keywords: public choice; public interest; seniority; mining; political economy

JEL Classification: D7; H5

---

1. Introduction

What are the determinants of federal spending on environmental goods? Is severity of the environmental hazard the only metric of consideration, or do other factors play a vital role in explaining how funding is disbursed? In this paper, we aim not only to provide answers to these questions, but also to illuminate disbursement patterns of monies from the Abandoned Mine Land Fund (AMLF) that go toward the reclamation of abandoned mine sites throughout the United States. Though the program itself is small, this analytical setting is interesting because of the limited scope of program objectives and the rigidly defined funding source (at least initially). This suggests that the execution of abandoned mine reclamation projects facilitated by the fund should be difficult to influence politically. Within this setting, we examine whether political factors, in addition to severity of abandoned mine site hazard and general abandoned mine site characteristics, influence the distribution of AMLF monies.

This project contributes firstly to the economic analysis of government activity. Broadly, there are two economic strands of thought regarding government action. The first is that government action is motivated primarily by the public interest. Congruent with this perspective, money from the AMLF would go toward sites that pose the most severe environmental risks to the general public. The other perspective sees government action as being subject to the influences of interest groups and politician self-interest. Orthogonal to the vision of a benevolent government, these concentrated interests are seen as the driving influences of fund disbursement. López and Leighton (2013) provide a good overview of both of these theories in their analysis of the role of ideas in political change.

Within the existing literature, little has been said specifically regarding the AMLF as an environmental remediation program. However, work has been done with respect to other similarly intended programs such as Superfund that parallels the questions asked in this paper. Barnett (1985) and Hird (1990, 1993, 1994) offer support for the public interest perspective with their findings that Superfund monies and efforts are allocated toward remediating the most severe sites The evidence in these works, however, is not strong enough to reject the hypothesis that there are *zero* pork-spending influences in Superfund allocations but does suggest that these influences are minor with respect to total disbursements.

Nonetheless, McNeil et al. (1988) find evidence for the pork-spending hypothesis with respect to tax implementation and subsequent spending. They found that evidence in EPA data that taxes for Superfund were often collected in certain areas, but the bulk of spending occurred elsewhere. Likewise, the theory of rationally self-interested politicians is likewise supported throughout other works. Stroup (1996) and Yandle (1992) argue that Superfund monies are sought by politicians to be brought back to their home constituencies. Tilton (1995) draws comparisons between Superfund and the AML program under the Surface Mining Control and Reclamation Act (SMCRA) in the ways each of these programs dealt with problems of past pollution and finds that AML fares better in terms of assigning responsibility for the past pollution and mitigating future production cost uncertainty associated with liability costs. Nonetheless, the scope of the analysis does not consider how political factors or pure environmental or human well-being concerns affect the execution of either of these pollution mitigation programs. The paper closest to ours in the Superfund literature is Stratmann (1998), who uses a political economy model similar to ours to look at the geographic disbursement of Superfund expenditures to separate out public interest and public choice influences.

We use this literature to inform our study of the Abandoned Mine Land Fund. In Section 2, we provide an overview of the history of the AMLF. We then discuss our theoretical framework in Section 3 and follow that up with information on our data in Section 4. Section 5 presents our empirical results, with Section 6 concluding.

2. History of the Abandoned Mine Land Fund

The AMLF was created as a part of SMCRA in 1977. Bamberger (1997) provides a nice overview of the history of the AMLF through 1997. Yonk et al. (2017) have a more recent overview of the history of SMCRA through a public choice lens. The overarching goal of SMCRA is to establish a federal standard for environmentally responsible surface mining, and restoration of the lands after mining has ceased to ensure mitigation of adverse environmental effects of this method of extraction. Due to lax enforcement of state mining regulations prior to the passing of SMCRA, many smaller sites were subject to "blast and grab" mining techniques where small, independent miners/mining operations, often referred to as wildcatters, would use whatever least cost method was at their disposal to expose and extract coal. Afterwards, they might simply leave the area thereafter with no attempt at reclamation. These practices resulted in degradation of land and environmental quality. While small sites characterized the abandoned mines, the prevalence of these sites was the main contributor to alarm.

Consistent with the broader goals of SMCRA, the objective of AMLF is to provide for a general funding pool to be allocated towards reclamation efforts of already existing abandoned mine sites, in addition to SMCRA's efforts of enforcing reclamation on present and future mine sites. As delineated within SMCRA, monies in AMLF may be used for purposes including, but not limited to, reclamation and restoration of abandoned coal surface mines, processing and disposal areas, sealing and filling of deep mine entries, land restoration to mitigate erosion and sedimentation, waterbed restoration, construction and operation of water treatment plants, pollution mitigation for burning coal refuse disposal, and control of coal mine subsidence.

The coffers of the AMLF are provided for via a fee levied on extracted coal as specified in section 403 of SMCRA:

> All operators of coal mining operations subject to the provisions of this Act shall pay to the Secretary of the Interior, for deposit in the fund, a reclamation fee of 35 cents per ton of coal produced by surface coal mining and 15 cents per ton of coal produced by underground

mining or 10 per centum of the value of the coal at the mine, as determined by the Secretary, whichever is less, except that the reclamation fee for lignite coal shall be at a rate of 2 per centum of the value of the coal at the mine, or 10 cents per ton, whichever is less.

These fees were initially slated to expire in 1992, but extensions have been passed by Congress to maintain the collection of fees, thereby continuing the reclamation of abandoned mine sites.

Out of the monies collected from domestic coal production fees, 50% of those collections are allocated to the states. The remaining half is allocated across three broad objectives and falls under federal discretion and the control of the Secretary of the Interior. Ten percent of these funds are marked for allocation into the Rural Abandoned Mine Program. Twenty percent of the funds are funneled into a pool that is used for supplemental grants going toward remediation of more hazardous sites. The remaining 20% can be described as a portmanteau pool where funds are used for emergency projects, federal administrative costs, projects in states without approved reclamation plans, and the Small Operator Assistance Program.

Currently, the Office of Surface Mining (OSM) has collected over $10.1 billion worth of fees toward the AMLF. Out of that total, over $7.6 billion has been distributed. Furthermore, OSM estimates that over $3 billion worth of high priority sites remain to be remediated. Back-of-the-envelope arithmetic suggests that the mission of OSM with respect to reclaiming abandoned mines is nearing its twilight. However, one should be careful to avoid the assumption that the volume and severity of abandoned mine sites exists in a static state. Instead, these should be considered in a dynamic light for reasons such as the potential future hazardous deterioration of presently stable underground mines.

In the nearly forty years since the passing of SMCRA and the creation of the AML reclamation program, various changes to SMCRA itself have been implemented and the funding structure of AMLF has likewise been altered. The first structural change relevant to this analysis is the enactment of the Abandoned Mine Reclamation Act (AMRA) of 1990 that provided for the accruement of interest on AMLF balances that were not appropriated. This marks the first codified instance in the lifespan of the program that incentivizes any change in allocation patterns. Specifically, this act provides the incentive to decrease general allocations and hold a balance in the AMLF from year to year in order to grow the fund absent additional taxes collected or to mitigate cycles in funding due to cyclical coal production.

The next major restructuring of reclamation funding occurred with the passing of the SMCRA Amendments Act of 2006. First, it incrementally reduces the taxes levied per ton of coal produced through September 2021. However, this rate reduction is offset by requirement of "Treasury payments to certified states and tribes in lieu of payments from AMLF." A further stipulation, requiring future AMLF allocations to be based upon historic coal production, also shifts the allocation patterns. The final restructurings of the AML program relevant to this study are tucked away within the passages of Public Law (PL) 112-141, the "Moving Ahead for Progress in the 21st Century Act," and PL 113-40, the "Helium Stewardship Act of 2013." In short, minutia within these bills cap the amount of money allocated to a given state or tribe out of the in-lieu Treasury funds established in the SMCRA Amendments Act annually at $15M and $28M, respectively.

3. Theoretical Framework

This paper's conceptual framework incorporates tenets of economic theories of regulation, bureaucracy, and interest group influences in order to provide a more cohesive and comprehensive explanation of the disbursement of AMLF monies. Within the economic theory of regulation, legislators maximize their acquisition of support from among competing constituencies. Theoretically and practically, this predicts that legislators do not adopt a corner solution with respect to helping one constituency versus another. Instead, in equilibrium, individual legislators make support trade-offs at the margin in order to attain the optimal amount of support. Within the context of AMLF decision making by politicians, the relevant constituencies to consider are interest groups who may provide financial electoral support and the general public responsible for vote counts. From this scenario, both the severity of environmental hazard posed by the abandoned mine site as well as the interest group strength possess important explanatory power regarding AMLF disbursements.

The equilibrium framework of regulation and interest groups implies that bureaucrats are politicians' pawns in executing legislation (Becker 1983; Peltzman 1976). Therefore, it logically follows that such models have no room for bureaucratic influence in policy decision-making. However, if the bureau has significant enough autonomy in pursuing its own interests, as the Office of Surface Mining, Reclamation and Enforcement generally does, the economic theory of bureaucracy must be introduced into this analysis in order to more accurately explain the patterns of AMLF disbursement.

Within the economics of bureaucracy, there are also multiple competing explanations of the autonomy and objectives of bureaucracies. One hypothesis suggests that bureaucrats pursue their own interests within the organization, and those interests do not consistently align with the law's intent (Niskanen 1971). McCubbins et al. (1989) put forth a hypothesis where bureaucrats and politicians have differing objectives, but that constraints such as budget appropriation, administrative rules, and oversight can effectively curb purely bureaucratically interested actions. Weingast and Moran (1983) suggest an even more constrained theory of bureaucratic action with their congressional control hypothesis.

Potentially more important than the theories of regulation and bureaucracy is the relationship between legislators and the implementation of the regulations they are responsible for enacting. Consistent with the public choice view that politicians act in their own self interest—substantively meaning they take actions that are likely to increase their chances of job security by means of re-election—politicians have a vested interest in securing funds for their respective states and/or districts. Doing so increases local aspects such as environmental quality, real estate values, and potential tourism revenues. Likewise, reclamation activities could be expected to provide positive employment effects in the area. While the employment effects may only be relevant in the short run, they also typically fall within the reelection timeframe, thereby further incentivizing politicians to secure this virtually 'free lunch' money. As such, this interaction suggests that senior politicians will be more effective in funneling AMLF allocations to their home regions.

From a policy perspective, it is important to know the extent to which political factors play a role in the distribution of public funds. This is especially true when politics is not supposed to play a role. If political influence can be identified, then perhaps a change can be made to political institutions to remove politics from the process. For example, Garrett and Sobel (2003) find that Federal Emergency Management Agency (FEMA) disaster expenditures are higher in states where their members of Congress serve on FEMA oversight committees. A post 9-11 reorganization of FEMA, however, removed this form of political influence according to Sobel et al. (2007). Similarly, Twight (1989) highlights how politics prevented the military from closing or realigning any domestic military bases from 1960 to 1988. Reforms in the late 1980s led to political factors no longer playing a role (Beaulier et al. 2011). By looking at all the institutional changes in the AMLF program over time in one paper, we provide insight into how institutional changes may have influenced the role of politics in the allocation of funding.

Furthermore, the nature of AMLF disbursements with respect to whether it more adequately can be described as a disguised welfare program, or general spending on environmental goods has important implications for how we predict funds to be allocated.

4. Data and Model Estimation

As described in the preceding section, the explanatory factors of AMLF disbursement are many. The theoretical underpinning suggests that funding of abandoned mine reclamation projects is a function of hazard severity, and the characteristics of legislators, interest groups, and bureaucratic agents. This general empirical model has been used to study agency dependency (Anderson and Potoski 2016), federal transportation disbursements, (Bilotkach 2018), airport funding under the Essential Air Service Act (Hall et al. 2015), federal disaster declarations and assistance (Husted and Nickerson 2014), NIH funding (Batinti 2016), antitrust enforcement (Dove and Dove 2014), and even disbursement of the swine flu vaccine (Ryan 2014). Such an empirical model will be used to explain and predict funding tendencies of projects that fall under the umbrella of AMLF reclamation objectives. The empirical model to be estimated is an ordinary least squares model that includes state and year fixed effects in order to account for unobserved variations in political and economic conditions throughout the span of the data set.

For policymakers not familiar with the methodology employed in these analyses, the goal is to estimate an empirical model that explains variation in AMLF funding. If done properly, we can isolate the effect of specific factors holding constant other variables that might influence AMLF funding. For example, a positive and statistically significant coefficient on whether a mine was an underground mine strongly suggests that underground mines receive higher levels of AMLF funding because policymakers believe they are more costly to remediate, other things being equal. Similarly, a positive and statistically significant coefficient on any variables measuring political influence suggests that political oversight of the AMLF influences the allocation of funds.

The equation we estimate is:

$$
\begin{aligned}
\text{AMLF Disbursements}_{i,t} = {} & \beta_0 + \beta_1 \text{HAppSen}_{i,t} + \beta_2 \text{SHAppSen}_{i,t} + \beta_3 \text{GreenIndex}_{i,t} + \beta_4 \text{Income}_{i,t} \\
& + \beta_5 \text{Private}_{i,t} + \beta_6 \text{State}_{i,t} + \beta_7 \text{Pri1}_{i,t} + \beta_8 \text{Pri2}_{i,t} \\
& + \beta_9 \text{Surface}_{i,t} + \beta_{10} \text{Underground}_{i,t} + \beta_{11} \text{Both}_{i,t} + \beta_{12} \text{Processing}_{i,t} \\
& + \gamma_i + \delta t + \sigma_{i,t}.
\end{aligned}
\tag{1}
$$

The primary dependent variable is the SMCRA-funded AMLF allocation towards reclamation of abandoned mine sites throughout years spanning from 1984 through 2013. These are presented in thousands of inflation-adjusted (1984) dollars. Additional regressions are estimated with the dependent variable as a standardized measurement of SMCRA-funded AMLF allocation per unit of area on a given site to address variation in the size of abandoned mine sites. The data is collected from the Office of Surface Mining Reclamation and Enforcement's Abandoned Mine Land Inventory System, e-AMLIS. This database consists of an inventory of land and water impacted by past mining endeavors. It is detailed to the extent of including information regarding location, type, and extent of damages as well as reclamation costs. Data is provided by the states managing their own abandoned mine problems or through the OSMRE office responsible for managing these cases where states do not bear that responsibility. In this analysis, only reclamation sites that have been funded to some extent by AMLF are included. However, there exist other abandoned mine sites within the database that have simply not been allocated funding or they have been completely reclaimed through private efforts and funding. Table 1 presents summary statistics for the entire sample.

Severity of the environmental hazard is measured by the priority status assigned to each abandoned mine site, per problem type, by OSMRE. There are five tiers of priority assigned to inventoried sites. Within this analysis, priority types are coded as dummy variables, so as to treat each level of hazard independently without assuming a linear scale in the degree of hazard. The most serious abandoned mine land problems are those that pose a threat to health, safety, and general welfare of people. These are assigned either Priority 1 or Priority 2 status, and are the only problems required by law to be inventoried. Within these top two priorities, there are seventeen different problem types accounted for—noted without respect to severity. Those problems that have only environmental impacts are classified as Priority 3 problems and are included in the inventory when reclamation on these sites is funded, in some proportion, out of AMLF. Priority 4 and 5 sites consist of lower severity coal related problems such as public facilities and development of public lands. These lower priority reclamation projects have fewer records kept on them, are less likely to receive AMLF monies, and are not included in this dataset. Intuitively, funding amounts are predicted to align with priority levels; the higher the priority, the greater the funding allocated. (As pointed out by an astute referee, this suggests that Priority 1 sites are more costly to reclaim. We are not aware of any data on the cost of reclamation per site type. Our intuition here is driven by the fact that the difference between Priority 1 and Priority 2 sites is that Priority 1 sites are categorized as such because they pose a higher threat to the health and safety of the general public. To us, this suggests higher costs related to the urgency of the reclamation project, in addition to the difficulty of remedying health hazards.) For purposes of this analysis, only Priority 1 and 2 sites are considered, and take a value of one if applicable and zero otherwise.

Table 1. Summary statistics for database of abandoned mine land sites, 1984–2013.

Variable	N	Mean	Std Dev	Min	Max
Private Ownership	35,528	66.822	46.192	0	100
State Ownership	34,021	4.062	18.455	0	100
House Appropriations Seniority	36,311	27.715	20.646	0	73
Senate Appropriations Seniority	36,311	7.407	9.653	0	51
Environmental Group Strength	36,314	7.132	2.694	3.400	13.10
Priority 1	36,314	0.208	0.406	0	1
Priority 2	36,314	0.590	0.492	0	1
Underground Site	36,314	0.397	0.489	0	1
Surface Site	36,314	0.345	0.475	0	1
Surface + UG Site	36,314	0.238	0.426	0	1
Processing Site	36,314	0.016	0.125	0	1
AMLF Allocation (1000)	36,314	108.793	352.075	0.0004	13,984
Per Capita (PC) Income (1000)	36,311	26.957	8.447	13.358	68.80
House Appropriations Member	36,311	0.882	0.323	0	1
Senate Appropriations Member	36,311	0.549	0.498	0	1

Along with priority designation, abandoned mine sites can be categorized by the type of mining that occurred on site that now requires reclamation. Here, there are four different mine site types accounted for in the e-AMLIS inventory—surface, underground, both, and processing. Presumably, project sites where only processing mining operations occurred would be predicted to receive larger AMLF allocations since the reclamation project is inherently more involved due to the fact that reclamation activities would predominantly involve cleaning up the chemicals involved in processing coal for use. Processing sites have a higher propensity for causing harm to general health, safety, and human well-being. Surface mines are predicted to receive smaller allocations than processing sites, but the largest allocations with respect to the other extraction sites. This is due to the physical nature of the reclamation project itself. Reclamation of abandoned surface mine sites would involve greater terrain restructuring, re-vegetation, and waterway cleaning and restoration. Purely underground abandoned mine sites would be predicted to have the smallest allocations due to the less involved nature of the reclamation project. In these cases, the reclamation process would be primarily characterized by mineshaft reinforcement to prevent cave-ins, and mine entry sealing to prevent, or at least reduce the risk of people entering abandoned deep mines. Finally, abandoned mine sites where both surface and underground mining occurred are predicted to receive AMLF allocations between the size of purely surface or underground sites receive since costs can be diffused across reclamation of both kinds of operations. In theory, the size of distribution on sites where both surface and underground mines occurred would be on a spectrum from pure surface to pure underground with the amount being a weighted average of the proportional combination of mine types. However, data to this extent of detail is unavailable. As such, the amounts predicted reflect an aggregated average of proportion. All four categories are considered in this analysis. Like the priority sites, the site characteristic variables are coded as dummy variables with a value of one corresponding to the relevant sites and zero otherwise.

Additional site specifics are accounted for by ownership characteristics of the land where the given abandoned mine site is located. By the e-AMLIS classifications, there are seven different possible categories of landowners, not all of which hold exclusive ownership rights to the given land area. The seven potential stakes are private, state, tribal, Bureau of Land Management, forest service, national park, and a catchall category of other federally owned lands. These ownership stakes are provided as percentages. Among these ownership stakes, we would expect that proportion of private ownership and size of AMLF disbursement will be inversely related. Conversely, higher proportions of state-owned lands on abandoned mine sites are likely to receive the greater AMLF allocations. The remaining five types of land ownership are not considered for purposes of this analysis due to the fact that they make up a miniscule proportion of abandoned mine site ownership on any given site and correspond to a relatively small number of mine sites in the data set. Nonetheless, each of these would be expected to exhibit similar allocation patterns as state-owned lands since they also fall under the broader category of publicly owned lands.

Characteristics of legislators are accounted for by seniority and membership on fiscally relevant congressional committees. The main variables included are cumulative seniority of members on the Senate Appropriations, and House Appropriations committees by year and by state. This data is collected from the respective committee's history websites. For all of these variables, a positive relationship is expected between committee seniority and AMLF allocations. Relatively higher positive relationships are expected for House Appropriations committee members' seniority since they represent a smaller constituency relative to senators.

Variables concerning interest group strength are collected from the 1991–1992 Green Index (Hall and Kerr 1991). Specifically, this index considers membership per 1000 state residents in environmental organizations, namely Greenpeace, the National Wildlife Federation, and the Sierra Club in 1990. Ideally, this index would be more current, perhaps updated annually. Nonetheless, this provides the most current and comprehensive measure of environmental interest group presence across states. This variable is predicted to have a positive influence on the AMLF allocation through the mechanism of these environmental interest groups pressuring representatives to secure funding for reclamation sites in their respective states. If politicians are self-interested, they have an incentive to respond to these vocal members of their constituency. Real state per capita income is included to account for constituent demand for environmental goods.

In addition to the broad inspection of how these factors influence the allocation of AML funds over the recorded lifespan of the program, each of the legal changes in the funding structure previously mentioned are considered, period-by-period to examine the extent to which these changes alter the respective public interest and political influences on AML reclamation funding.

The general predictions regarding these legal changes in the funding structure are simple and intuitive. At the outset of the program, the expectation is that AMLF distribution patterns follow the intentions of the program, to reclaim hazardous abandoned mine sites, without respect to outside political sway. When AML funding expands from being a purely fee-based pool such as with the passing of SMCRA '06, the political influences on allocation decisions will gain gravity. Likewise, as Treasury payments to states and tribes are capped, as is the case with the passage of PL 112-141, that same political influence on allocation decisions will at least wane, if not drop completely out of the distribution calculus.

For purposes of this analysis, abandoned mine sites on Indian Reservation lands are omitted due primarily to the inconsistencies associated with the political variables in question. Given that the reservations are viewed as sovereign entities within United States territory, there exist no measures of seniority within the House and Senate Appropriations committees or within the Green Index for these territories. The lack of a complete set measures render introduction of analysis of AMLF distribution patters on reservations problematic.

5. Empirical Results

Regression results are presented in Tables 2–6. In all tables, specifications (1) and (2) report results with AMLF allocations in inflation-adjusted dollars as the dependent variable, while (3) and (4) give these same results with respect to the funding-per-metric unit standardization as the dependent variable. All results are estimated using ordinary least squares (OLS). Specifications (1) and (3) do not include state and year fixed effects, while specifications (2) and (4) do include state and year fixed effects.

5.1. AMLF 1984–2013

Table 2 gives an overview of the AMLF distribution patterns over the entire scope of our data set—consisting of 33,947 mine site observations in specifications (1) and (2) and 33,313 observations in (3) and (4) over a nearly thirty-year span. Across all specifications, sites with a Priority 1 ranking are granted larger AMLF allocations. This can be seen in the positive and statistically significant coefficient on the variable Priority 1 in specifications (1), (2), (3), and (4). This result also holds with respect to site-only considerations for Priority 2 abandoned mine sites, though not in funding-per-unit estimations.

Table 2. The determinants of receiving AMLF site funding, 1984–2013.

Variable	(1)	(2)	(3)	(4)
House Appropriations Seniority	0.125	−1.208 ***	0.058	0.263 **
	(0.092)	(0.197)	(0.053)	(0.115)
Senate Appropriations Seniority	3.542 ***	−0.290	1.146 ***	1.217 ***
	(0.203)	(0.356)	(0.117)	(0.206)
Environmental Group Strength	2.639 ***	−29.644 *	−3.006 ***	−39.049 ***
	(0.785)	(16.630)	(0.451)	(10.894)
PC Income (1000)	0.376	−0.249	1.118 ***	1.373 *
	(0.255)	(1.383)	(0.147)	(0.804)
Private Ownership	−0.197 ***	−0.177 ***	−0.028	0.023
	(0.042)	(0.051)	(0.024)	(0.030)
State Ownership	0.582 ***	0.440 ***	0.520 ***	0.571 ***
	(0.106)	(0.111)	(0.061)	(0.065)
Priority 1	48.108 ***	69.563 ***	38.658 ***	39.596 ***
	(5.883)	(6.266)	(3.405)	(3.646)
Priority 2	72.863 ***	80.359 ***	19.313 ***	17.515 ***
	(4.700)	(4.832)	(2.717)	(2.811)
Surface Site	−10.978	28.915	−31.990 **	−4.532
	(27.547)	(27.872)	(16.042)	(16.322)
Underground (UG) Site	−59.629 **	−20.963	−6.573	15.199
	(27.449)	(27.677)	(15.987)	(16.211)
Surface + UG Site	2.272	46.466 *	−18.253	9.503
	(27.609)	(27.942)	(16.078)	(16.363)
Processing Site	43.544	89.884 ***	−11.778	6.480
	(30.910)	(31.189)	(17.959)	(18.233)
Constant	31.794	687.050 ***	20.547	670.500 ***
	(28.832)	(167.982)	(16.759)	(108.005)
State and Year Fixed Effects?	No	Yes	No	Yes
Observations	33,947	33,947	33,313	33,313
Adjusted R^2	0.028	0.059	0.016	0.033
Residual Std. Error	332.785	327.470	189.952	188.332
F Statistic	82.279 ***	33.092 ***	46.128 ***	18.065 ***

Notes: Dependent variable in specification (1) and (2) is per site AMLF allocations in inflation-adjusted dollars, while the dependent variable in specifications (3) and (4) is per site AMLF allocation per metric unit of the mine site. Numbers in parentheses are standard errors. *** $p < 0.01$, ** $p < 0.05$, and * $p < 0.1$.

Priority 2 sites are predicted to receive greater allocations in the site-only specifications. This may be largely accounted for by the fact that Priority 2 abandoned mine sites make up nearly 60% of the full data set, whereas Priority 1 sites make up only slightly more than 20% of the full data set. A snapshot of the distributive patterns suggests that holding other considerations constant, including state and year effects, an abandoned mine site with approved funding for reclamation is predicted to receive roughly $69,600 if it is categorized as a Priority 1 site, and $80,400 if Priority 2. In specifications where funding is considered on a per-unit basis and the underlying state and year effects are accounted for, sites with Priority 1 designation are predicted to receive $39,600 per unit of area to be reclaimed and Priority 2 sites are predicted to receive $17,500 per unit of area.

Contrary to initial predictions, the type of mine site being reclaimed has little bearing on the allocation received. Specification (2) suggests that an abandoned mine site will receive roughly $46,500 more in AMLF allocation if it was a combination mine site, and $89,900 more if a processing site. Specification (4) suggests that none of the site categories has an influence on monies received. Those virtually anomalous instances aside, there is no sound evidence that the type of mine itself abandoned factors into allocation decisions. It may instead be the case that mine site type is built into the priority designations, thereby rendering these details largely irrelevant.

Ownership characteristics do suggest a substantive relationship across the span of the data set. In all four specifications, percentages of state-owned lands displayed positive and statistically significant coefficients. These coefficients range a short span from 0.440 to 0.582, and seem to have a trivial influence on the AMLF allocations. However, one should bear in mind that, in such a case where abandoned mines are located on 100% state-owned lands, these results suggest that total allocations may be boosted by roughly $50,000 due to ownership stakes alone. For mines on privately owned lands, a negative and significant relationship is suggested when considering funding on per-site basis. By the same logic as before, a site on completely privately held land can expect to see an allocation roughly $18,000 smaller.

The influence that the cumulative seniority of House Appropriations committee members in a given state wields upon AMLF distributions is inconsistent, and weak across the twenty year span. The coefficient from specification (2), -1.208, suggests that an additional year of cumulative seniority decreases AMLF allocations by roughly $1200 to a given mine site, whereas the coefficient from specification (4), 0.263, suggests instead that an additional year of seniority increases the reclamation funding per metric unit on a mine site by roughly $260. While coefficients themselves are small, their real-world significance comes in the aggregation, as examples may illustrate. Suppose a site is granted AMLF monies in the given state and year where House Appropriations seniority is the maximum value, 78 years of cumulative seniority. Per the specifications in column 2, this suggests that a site would be granted around $95,000 less in funding. Taking a less extreme example, consider the average seniority in the set, 25 years. These preliminary regression results suggest that, on average, the seniority of the state's members on the House Appropriations committee contributes to a $30,000 decrease in expected AMLF monies. In the case of the positive coefficient gleaned from specification (4), the aggregated implications are again, quite substantial in their potential. By quick calculations, this result suggests that AMLF allocations can be boosted, on average, by roughly $6,600 per unit of area to be reclaimed at an abandoned mine site. The statistical significance is stronger on the negative coefficient, but, given that significance is suggested in opposite directions, it remains ambiguous whether this particular factor is influential, and in which direction if it is.

Unlike the similar measure for the House, the Senate Appropriations committee seniority is suggested to be influential on the size of AMLF allocations. In all but specification (2), this variable displays a positive, and statistically significant relationship on funding. Specifications (1), (3), and (4) display coefficients of 3.542, 1.146, and 1.217, respectively. Following the same logic as explained with the House variable, these estimates are more meaningful in their aggregates than their marginal values. In a given state with the maximum Senate Appropriations committee seniority (49 years), this influence potentially amounts to roughly $60,000–$175,000 boosts in allocations. While less striking when considering average seniority, the figures are still meaningful with $10,000–$28,000 estimated boosts per site-area-unit or sites broadly considered.

Interest group strength, as measured by the Green Index, exhibits strong evidence about the direction of influence on AMLF allocations. Specifications (1) through (4) give statistically significant estimates of 2.639, -29.644, -3.006, and -39.049 respectively. Considering the more explanatory second specification, this suggests that, for each additional unit increase in this index, a given mine site is expected to receive nearly $30,000 less in AMLF allocation. Considering the fourth specification, this estimate suggests that a one-unit increase on the Green Index for a given state leads to a nearly $40,000 decrease in AMLF allocation per metric unit area of mine site being reclaimed. While initial predictions consisted of the interest group variable having a positive influence on the amount of funding, it may more likely be the case, in light of these results, that environmental interest groups would actively dissuade their political representatives and the like from channeling federal money going towards abandoned mine reclamation projects and instead attempting to assign responsibility to other potentially responsible parties for bearing the burden of these costs.

Finally, the income variable provides some suggestion that the higher income states receive more funding, ceteris paribus. In specifications (3) and (4), the coefficient estimate for per capita income is positive and statistically significant. The overall trend suggests that, for each additional thousand dollars of per capita income a state has, a reclamation site in that state is expected to receive nearly an additional $1100 in AMLF allocation on a per-site basis, or nearly $1400 per unit area being reclaimed when underlying conditions for states and years are controlled for.

5.2. AMLF Inception through the Abandoned Mine Reclamation Act of 1990

Table 3 gives an overview of the AMLF distribution patterns over the scope of the data set spanning from its inception in 1977 to when the first major changes in the program were instituted, with the Abandoned Mine Reclamation Act of 1990. This subset consists of 1251 mine site observations in all four specifications.

Over this time span, the results subtly suggest that Priority 1 and Priority 2 sites are given larger allocations. This can be seen in the positive and statistically significant coefficients on Priority 1 (specifications (2) and (3)) and Priority 2 (specifications (2) and (4)). The per-size estimates in specification (2) suggest that Priority 1 sites receive allocations nearly $92,500 larger and that Priority 2 sites receive allocations slightly over $100,000 larger. Considering funding per unit reclaimed, specification (3) suggests that Priority 1 areas receive roughly $43,500 more per unit of area reclaimed, but the significance drops out upon the inclusion of fixed effects in (4). However, Priority 2 sites are estimated to receive slightly more than $28,000 per unit area reclaimed by the estimations in (4). Nonetheless, that such results are found only subject to certain regression specifications, suggests that Priority designations alone have little influence over the amounts of funding allocated to specific reclaimed abandoned mine sites.

Results here suggest that the type of mine site being reclaimed has bearing on the allocation received only along a per-site basis. Specifications (1) and (2) suggest that abandoned mine sites will receive smaller AMLF allocations across all four varieties of site. Considering specification (2) only, sites are estimated to receive approximately $571,000, $646,000, $590,000, and $624,000 less per surface, underground, combination, and processing sites, respectively. While the estimates found here seem amiss, much of that is likely explained by the considerably large constant terms estimated across the four specifications.

Ownership characteristics do not suggest a substantive relationship across the span of the data set. In all four specifications, percentages of either privately-owned and state-owned lands displayed no statistically significant coefficients.

The influence that the cumulative seniority of House Appropriations committee members in a given state wields upon AMLF distributions is inconsistent across the span. The specification (1) coefficient suggests that an additional year of cumulative seniority increases AMLF allocations by roughly $1300 dollars to a given mine site, whereas specification (2) suggests instead that an additional year of seniority decreases the reclamation funding per mine site by over $22,000. While the estimates from (1) and (2) suggest ambiguity due to the opposing signs, intuition supports the notion that the more accurate scenario is that seniority out of the House Appropriations committee has a negative relationship with AMLF disbursements. This logic is supported by the stronger statistical significance found in the second specification, as well as the underlying fact that the included fixed effects account for more unobservables across the states and years in question.

Table 3. The determinants of receiving AMLF site funding, 1984 to AMRA 1990.

Variable	(1)	(2)	(3)	(4)
House Appropriations Seniority	1.286 **	−22.043 ***	0.205	3.122
	(0.630)	(5.269)	(0.291)	(2.434)
Senate Appropriations Seniority	11.943 ***	21.700	4.110 ***	−29.318 ***
	(2.061)	(21.816)	(0.952)	(10.076)
Environmental Group Strength	32.068 ***	−595.784	9.727 ***	981.853 ***
	(7.693)	(672.184)	(3.555)	(310.454)
PC Income (1000)	−31.358 ***	−28.958	−8.330 **	−3.004
	(9.143)	(70.858)	(4.226)	(32.727)
Private Ownership	0.123	0.502	0.319	−0.001
	(0.545)	(1.011)	(0.252)	(0.467)
State Ownership	−7.970	17.618	0.533	18.726
	(26.385)	(31.478)	(12.194)	(14.539)
Priority 1	5.241	92.472 *	43.365 **	35.098
	(47.198)	(50.601)	(21.814)	(23.370)
Priority 2	19.267	100.015 ***	22.103	28.074 *
	(32.230)	(34.934)	(14.896)	(16.135)
Surface Site	−566.235 ***	−571.213 ***	−15.395	−11.594
	(152.366)	(151.885)	(70.418)	(70.150)
Underground Site	−653.969 ***	−645.920 ***	−13.370	−6.135
	(152.491)	(151.002)	(70.476)	(69.742)
Surface + UG Site	−566.665 ***	−589.889 ***	−21.545	−25.858
	(153.624)	(153.346)	(71.000)	(70.824)
Processing Site	−570.970 ***	−624.009 ***	−27.180	−6.102
	(179.303)	(178.099)	(82.868)	(82.257)
Constant	963.014 ***	3501.752	95.627	−3159.686 ***
	(205.085)	(2630.303)	(94.783)	(1214.831)
State and Year Fixed Effects?	No	Yes	No	Yes
Observations	1251	1251	1251	1251
Adjusted R^2	0.074	0.110	0.029	0.069
Residual Std. Error	364.857	357.627	168.625	165.174
F Statistic	9.306 ***	5.184 ***	4.164 ***	3.496 ***

Notes: Dependent variable in specification (1) and (2) is per site AMLF allocations in inflation-adjusted dollars, while the dependent variable in specifications (3) and (4) is per site AMLF allocation per metric unit of the mine site. Numbers in parentheses are standard errors. *** $p < 0.01$, ** $p < 0.05$, and * $p < 0.1$.

Like the similar measure for the House, Senate Appropriations committee seniority is suggested to be questionably influential on the size of AMLF allocations. In specifications (1) and (3), this variable displays a positive, and statistically significant relationship on funding, while (4) provides strong evidence to the contrary. Following the same logic as explained with the House variable, intuition suggests that the negative relationship found in (4) may be the best estimate, again due to the included state and year fixed effects.

Again interest group strength, as measured by the Green Index, exhibits strong evidence about the direction of influence on AMLF allocations. Only the second specification fails to give a statistically significant coefficient estimate. The first, third, and fourth specifications give statistically significant estimates of 32.068, 9.727, and 981.853, respectively. During this early time span in the existence of the program, it seems that environmental groups within are a more powerful force in getting resources allocated toward the reclamation of the environmental blights in their respective states.

Finally, the income variable mildly suggests that the allocation of AMLF monies to mine reclamation is more akin to an environmental welfare program. In specifications (1) and (3), the coefficient estimates for per capita income are negative and statistically significant. However, once fixed effects are included, significance disappears and renders the effect null. Loosely though, we can infer that states with relatively poorer populations require more financial assistance in order to address and reclaim their abandoned mine sites.

5.3. AMRA 1990 through SMCRA Amendments Act of 2006

In the span following the passage of the Abandoned Mine Reclamation Act of 1990 through the SMCRA Amendments Act of 2006, another subset of the data is considered in order to examine the changes in allocation influences in response to the legally changed structure of funding the program. This subsection corresponds to 8825 site observations in the first two specifications, and 8644 in the third and fourth. The results are presented in full in Table 4.

Table 4. The determinants of receiving AMLF site funding, AMRA 1990 to SMCRA 2006.

Variable	(1)	(2)	(3)	(4)
House Appropriations Seniority	0.192	−1.080 ***	0.214 **	0.587 ***
	(0.166)	(0.374)	(0.096)	(0.209)
Senate Appropriations Seniority	2.663 ***	1.039	0.793 ***	1.142 *
	(0.374)	(1.148)	(0.216)	(0.669)
Environmental Group Strength	4.893 ***	−26.744	−2.918 ***	−32.798 **
	(1.598)	(24.534)	(0.926)	(16.257)
PC Income (1000)	−1.441 **	−6.276	0.969 **	0.920
	(0.684)	(4.039)	(0.397)	(2.382)
Private Ownership	−0.102	−0.208 **	−0.146 ***	−0.161 ***
	(0.090)	(0.097)	(0.052)	(0.056)
State Ownership	0.411 **	0.022	0.356 ***	0.327 ***
	(0.181)	(0.188)	(0.105)	(0.110)
Priority 1	31.535 ***	46.081 ***	21.874 ***	21.361 ***
	(10.943)	(12.049)	(6.357)	(7.043)
Priority 2	48.244 ***	59.555 ***	3.328	2.987
	(8.719)	(9.076)	(5.063)	(5.315)
Surface Site	−16.452	61.068	−33.796	−6.548
	(45.974)	(47.303)	(26.615)	(27.616)
Underground Site	−60.204	9.170	−16.711	0.641
	(45.843)	(47.032)	(26.540)	(27.459)
Surface + UG Site	4.356	87.575 *	−30.271	−3.612
	(46.174)	(47.536)	(26.731)	(27.752)
Processing Site	20.138	111.172 **	−5.534	7.976
	(52.061)	(53.246)	(30.134)	(31.105)
Constant	81.696	610.762 **	52.290 *	370.194 **
	(50.677)	(249.445)	(29.316)	(161.342)
State and Year Fixed Effects?	No	Yes	No	Yes
Observations	8825	8825	8644	8644
Adjusted R²	0.020	0.047	0.009	0.017
Residual Std. Error	319.948	315.522	183.359	182.616
F Statistic	15.803 ***	9.306 ***	7.661 ***	3.904 ***

Notes: Dependent variable in specification (1) and (2) is per site AMLF allocations in inflation-adjusted dollars, while the dependent variable in specifications (3) and (4) is per site AMLF allocation per metric unit of the mine site. Numbers in parentheses are standard errors. *** $p < 0.01$, ** $p < 0.05$, and * $p < 0.1$.

Within this subset, the first thing that becomes clear is that, unlike the previous subset analyzed, little evidence is suggested that mine type is a significant determining factor in AMLF allocations. Only for combination mines or processing sites in specification (2) is there any statistically significant coefficient estimate produced by the regression results. On the per site basis, combination sites tend to receive roughly $87,500 more federal monies for reclamation efforts, while processing sites see slightly more than $111,000 additional funds. Certainly, the processing site estimates fall in line with initial predictions. However, in this subset of the data, much like the overall trend of AMLF allocations, mine type is a trivial detail in the funding considerations.

Hazard severity in this regression setup displays exactly the same characteristics with respect to statistical significance as it did in the overall dataset and results in Table 2. Priority 1 sites across all four specifications display evidence of positive and statistically significant relationships to funding amounts. Furthermore, the range in magnitude across the four specifications is roughly consistent. Additionally, the coefficient estimates for Priority 2 sites provide evidence that, with respect to site-only considerations, being deemed a Priority 2 status reclamation site is positively and statistically significantly related to larger AMLF allocations. Similar to the results and rationale in Table 2, the coefficient estimates on Priority 2 sites are larger in magnitude than that for Priority 1s, but are likely explained by the proportion of Priority 2 sites in this subsection of the data—again corresponding to roughly 60% Priority 2s and 20% Priority 1s.

Evidence for political influences in AMLF allocations reemerges in this timeframe. Across specifications (2) through (4), the seniority measures for the House Appropriations committee members display statistically significant relationships to AMLF distributions. Only for the House variable in specification (2) is this variable estimated to have a negative relationship. Overall, both of these variables positively influence AMLF allocations, with Senate Appropriations seniority being the stronger of the two influences with estimations of 2.663, 0.793, and 1.142 in specifications (1), (3), and (4), respectively. Significance is stronger, but magnitude smaller for House estimations in (1) through (4).

Furthermore, by this time period in the AML reclamation program, the significance of abandoned mine land location comes back into play—much as it did in the overall program estimates. In all but specification (2), a mine site is expected to receive greater funding allocations per percent proportion of site on state owned lands. The corresponding estimates in (1), (3), and (4) are consistent in magnitude at 0.411, 0.356, and 0.327 to suggest a stronger validity of the estimate. Likewise, across specifications (2) through (4), a site being on privately owned lands is associated with lesser amounts of funding. At any rate, evidence is strongly suggestive that abandoned mine sites on state owned lands are deemed a higher priority, in terms of AMLF monies, for reclamation.

Lastly, these estimates provide evidence again that reclamation funds are positively related to a state's per capita income. In specifications (1) through (3), positive and statistically significant coefficients are estimated for the relationship between state per capita income and the AMLF monies received.

Overall, the results in this subsection of the data suggest that a mix of hazard and political aspects influence the allocation of money out of the AMLF to abandoned mine sites. Political influences are stronger in this time span than overall, and during the time frames prior to amendments. Public interest influences are weaker in this roughly fifteen year period than they are overall, but stronger than the first seventeen years.

5.4. SMCRA Amendments Act of 2006 through PL 112-141

Passage of the SMCRA Amendments Act of 2006 marked the starkest change in funding composition of the broader AMLF. In short, this act broadened the scope of funding sources from being strictly coal-fee-funded to having a specific portion of its budget comprised of Treasury allocation. This time frame covers a roughly six-year span from late-2006 to mid-2012, consisting of 1716 observations in specifications (1) and (2) and 1687 in (3) and (4). Full results are presented in Table 5.

In this time frame, the strongest evidence for a public interest view of AMLF allocations is given with the estimates to Priority 1 and 2 sites. In all four specifications, Priority 1 sites are estimated to have positive and statistically significant relationships with the amount of funding granted to a site or per unit area of a site with coefficients of 66.949, 137.052, 47.340, and 55.932 in specifications (1) through (4), respectively. Paralleling the patterns in previous tables, Priority 2 sites have positive and statistically significant coefficients estimated in all four specifications, at 87.625, 112.395, 37.363, and 41.259, respectively. In the site-only considerations, the larger coefficients can be explained through the greater prevalence of Priority 2 sites within the data set. However, the predictions that Priority 1 sites would receive larger allocations comes into alignment when the funding is considered on a per-unit of area basis. This general result is borne throughout a number of alternate specifications.

Table 5. The determinants of receiving AMLF site funding, SMCRA 2006 through PL 112-141 (2012).

Variable	(1)	(2)	(3)	(4)
House Appropriations Seniority	−0.094	−0.225	0.137	0.055
	(0.617)	(1.364)	(0.336)	(0.740)
Senate Appropriations Seniority	1.537	0.504	0.885	−2.051
	(1.004)	(3.829)	(0.549)	(2.099)
Environmental Group Strength	−11.290	−70.951	−4.466	30.513
	(7.063)	(52.871)	(3.865)	(29.995)
PC Income (1000)	3.938	30.345	2.450	39.929 ***
	(3.484)	(19.960)	(1.907)	(10.816)
Private Ownership	0.467 *	0.386	0.191	0.229
	(0.258)	(0.269)	(0.141)	(0.147)
State Ownership	2.332 ***	2.204 ***	0.137	0.222
	(0.529)	(0.571)	(0.290)	(0.310)
Priority 1	66.949 **	137.052 ***	47.340 ***	55.932 ***
	(28.808)	(33.300)	(15.756)	(18.010)
Priority 2	87.625 ***	112.395 ***	37.363 ***	41.259 ***
	(23.888)	(24.887)	(13.061)	(13.468)
Surface Site	53.727	105.381	−32.629	−34.226
	(98.572)	(99.636)	(54.980)	(55.094)
Underground Site	20.915	19.310	19.339	5.504
	(97.638)	(96.958)	(54.467)	(53.678)
Surface + UG Site	79.253	120.324	−9.716	−11.065
	(98.433)	(98.645)	(54.891)	(54.545)
Processing Site	28.951	11.698	−12.473	−30.226
	(128.855)	(131.763)	(72.379)	(73.575)
Constant	−121.942	−428.162	−64.696	−2091.367 ***
	(151.155)	(1219.813)	(83.294)	(666.602)
State and Year Fixed Effects?	No	Yes	No	Yes
Observations	1716	1716	1687	1687
Adjusted R^2	0.021	0.048	0.014	0.054
Residual Std. Error	384.271	379.079	207.701	203.468
F Statistic	4.107 ***	3.088 ***	2.979 ***	3.332 ***

Notes: Dependent variable in specification (1) and (2) is per site AMLF allocations in inflation-adjusted dollars, while the dependent variable in specifications (3) and (4) is per site AMLF allocation per metric unit of the mine site. Numbers in parentheses are standard errors. *** $p < 0.01$, ** $p < 0.05$, and * $p < 0.1$.

None of the other political or economic variables bear consistent evidence of influencing allocation decisions throughout the main and alternative specifications in this shorter time period. Thus, it suggests that despite the changes to the funding structure of the program, the AML program hones its integrity.

5.5. PL 112-141 through PL 113-40

The final subsection of the dataset analyzed consists of the span between the passages of laws that capped the Treasury in-lieu payments to states for abandoned mine site reclamation projects. This specific set covers a roughly 18-month period from the July 2012 enactment of PL 112-141 to the enactment of PL 113-40 in the beginning of January 2014. There are 832 observations analyzed in specifications (1) and (2), and 816 in (3) and (4) in Table 6.

Within this 18-month time span, regression results suggest that the allocation pattern of AMLF monies maintains the originally intended purpose of the program as evidenced by the positive and statistically significant coefficient estimates given for Priority 1 and 2 sites across all specifications except (1) for Priority 1. In (2) and (4), where state and year fixed effects are taken into account, estimates suggest that a Priority 1 reclamation project is expected to receive roughly an additional $224,000 per site, or roughly $146,000 per unit area reclaimed. Priority 2 projects are estimated to receive roughly an additional $245,000 per site, or roughly $79,000 per unit area from AMLF allocations.

Table 6. The determinants of receiving AMLF site funding, PL 112-141 to PL 113-40.

Variable	(1)	(2)	(3)	(4)
House Appropriations Seniority	−6.191 *	−9.586	−3.056 **	45.847
	(3.224)	(61.732)	(1.527)	(29.571)
Senate Appropriations Seniority	5.301 **	1.664	2.028 *	0.161
	(2.268)	(4.219)	(1.078)	(2.027)
Environmental Group Strength	−2.147	−34.625	−5.658	151.990
	(10.854)	(205.311)	(5.178)	(98.403)
PC Income (1000)	7.622 *	11.931	3.373 *	9.696
	(3.952)	(12.588)	(1.905)	(6.039)
Private Ownership	0.434	−0.051	0.348	0.412
	(0.569)	(0.628)	(0.271)	(0.305)
State Ownership	1.927	1.093	0.079	0.100
	(1.808)	(1.845)	(0.879)	(0.908)
Priority 1	89.946	223.694 ***	123.174 ***	145.645 ***
	(70.781)	(82.097)	(33.687)	(39.776)
Priority 2	185.607 ***	244.542 ***	68.527 **	78.817 **
	(62.766)	(64.825)	(29.791)	(31.242)
Surface Site	245.520	324.284	120.021	161.992
	(363.392)	(363.093)	(171.561)	(173.803)
Underground Site	185.177	250.504	128.050	137.683
	(361.812)	(359.834)	(170.785)	(172.166)
Surface + UG Site	319.017	382.575	161.958	167.584
	(363.769)	(361.811)	(171.681)	(173.102)
Processing Site	1736.858 ***	2275.683 ***	206.145	240.879
	(411.611)	(425.240)	(194.294)	(203.458)
Constant	−593.614	−618.558	−270.164	−2090.760 **
	(414.049)	(2124.185)	(196.509)	(1016.938)
State and Year Fixed Effects?	No	Yes	No	Yes
Observations	832	832	816	816
Adjusted R^2	0.096	0.117	0.018	0.015
Residual Std. Error	609.675	602.616	287.271	287.738
F Statistic	8.389 ***	4.448 ***	2.243 ***	1.382 *

Notes: Dependent variable in specification (1) and (2) is per site AMLF allocations in inflation-adjusted dollars, while the dependent variable in specifications (3) and (4) is per site AMLF allocation per metric unit of the mine site. Numbers in parentheses are standard errors. *** $p < 0.01$, ** $p < 0.05$, and * $p < 0.1$.

Further bolstering the suggestion that AMLF distribution patterns returned to intended purposes are the estimates on the ownership characteristic, political, and economic variables. In none of the four specifications is there evidence that either private or state proportions of land ownership have any influence on funding decisions. With respect to seniority of House and Senate Appropriations committee members, there is evidence in specifications (1) and (3). However, when the state and year fixed effects are introduced into the specifications, all statistical significance drops from the coefficient estimates, thus suggesting that these influences are moot. A similar story can be told with respect to the estimates on the environmental interest group variable. Again, the pattern holds with respect to per capita income in a state; positive statistical significance is estimated on the coefficients in (1) and (3), but significance drops in (2) and (4) once the fixed effects are included.

Once again, there is little evidence in the general trend that mine site type is an influential factor in funding decisions. Out of the four mine types, only processing mines were estimated to receive larger AMLF allocations. Coefficient estimates were found to be positive and statistically significant only at the site level, at 1736.858 and 2275.683 in specifications (1) and (2), respectively. These estimates suggest that processing sites during the July 2012–December 2013 time frame received upwards of two million dollars in reclamation funding. However, when considering funding per unit area of a site, there is no discernible relationship to be found for any of the potential abandoned mine types.

6. Conclusions

This paper examines the question of what determines the size of disbursements from AMLF to support reclamation projects on abandoned mine sites. Specifically, it examines if the severity of environmental hazard is solely responsible for AMLF allocations and the magnitude thereof or whether other political and economic forces influence the federal funding of abandoned mine site reclamation.

Overall, the evidence suggests that funding for abandoned mine reclamation is a mixture of the products of public and political interests. With the exception of the 1984–1991 time span, sites designated as Priority 1 or 2 consistently are predicted to receive larger disbursements. However, in these time spans, political influences—especially through Senate Appropriations committee tenure and state-ownership of lands—wield consistently strong and significant weight on allocation decisions. This political influence is most pronounced in the years after the AMLF coffers are provided for with Treasury funds in addition to fees levied on domestically extracted coal. After the allocations out of Treasury funds are capped to states, the political influence wanes and the hazard level of sites again becomes the primary influential factor in funding receipts—further bolstering a public interest view of the AML program in total.

From a policy perspective, the biggest takeaway from our findings are that political institutions can be changed to remove politics. While the AML program, and the mission of reclaiming abandoned mine lands in total is but a small mission in the scope of federal activities, examination of the funding distribution trends in light of differing institutional contexts analyzed here shed light on how similar programs can be more effectively implemented under the federal umbrella. In short, a program with minimal scope of objectives and funded via taxes/fees—implying a hard budget constraint—limit the extent to which political influences can sway the decision-making calculus of monies allocated through the program—furthermore, supposing the introduction of a softer budget constraint through federal appropriations toward a given project in question, capping the distributions out of that portion of funding likewise limit the extent of political sway. In this sense, our finding contributes to similar papers in public choice showing how institutional reforms can reduce or remove the influence of politics (Beaulier et al. 2011; Hall and Williams 2012; Sobel et al. 2007).

Author Contributions: Writing—Original Draft, J.T.; Writing—Review and Editing, J.H.

Funding: This research received no external funding.

Acknowledgments: The authors acknowledge and appreciate the feedback of Thomas Stratmann.

Conflicts of Interest: The authors receive no funding for this paper. During his career, Joshua Hall has received funding from the Charles Koch Foundation, the Thomas Smith Foundation, the Alliance for Markets Solutions, the Institute for Humane Studies, Liberty Fund, and over 30 colleges and universities.

References

Anderson, Sarah E., and Matthew Potoski. 2016. Agency structure and the distribution of federal spending. *Journal of Public Administration Research and Theory* 26: 461–74. [CrossRef]

Bamberger, Robert. 1997. *The Abandoned Mine Land Fund: Grants Distribution and Issues.* Washington: Congressional Research Service.

Barnett, Harold C. 1985. The allocation of superfund, 1981–1983. *Land Economics* 61: 255–62. [CrossRef]

Batinti, Alberto. 2016. NIH biomedical funding: Evidence of executive dominance in swing-voter states during presidential elections. *Public Choice* 168: 239–63. [CrossRef]

Beaulier, Scott A., Joshua C. Hall, and Allen K. Lynch. 2011. The impact of political factors on military base closures. *Journal of Economic Policy Reform* 14: 333–42. [CrossRef]

Becker, Gary S. 1983. A theory of competition among pressure groups for political influence. *Quarterly Journal of Economics* 98: 371–400. [CrossRef]

Bilotkach, Volodymyr. 2018. Political economy of infrastructure investment: Evidence from the economic stimulus airport grants. *Economics of Transportation* 13: 27–35. [CrossRef]

Dove, John A., and Laura R. Dove. 2014. An examination of multistate antitrust enforcement by us state attorneys general. *Journal of Applied Economics & Policy* 32: 45–74.

Garrett, Thomas A., and Russell S. Sobel. 2003. The political economy of FEMA disaster payments. *Economic Inquiry* 41: 496–509. [CrossRef]

Hall, Bob, and Mary Lee Kerr. 1991. *1991–1992 Green Index: A State-by-State Guide to the Nation's Environmental Health*. Washington: Island Press.

Hall, Joshua, and Michael Williams. 2012. *A Process for Cleaning Up Federal Regulations: Insights from BRAC and the Dutch Administrative Burden Reduction Programme*. Arlington: Mercatus Center.

Hall, Joshua, Amanda Ross, and Christopher Yencha. 2015. The political economy of the essential air service program. *Public Choice* 165: 147–64. [CrossRef]

Hird, John A. 1990. Superfund expenditures and cleanup priorities: Distributive politics or the public interest? *Journal of Policy Analysis and Management* 9: 455–83. [CrossRef]

Hird, John A. 1993. Environmental policy and equity: The case of Superfund. *Journal of Policy Analysis and Management* 12: 323–43. [CrossRef]

Hird, John A. 1994. *Superfund: The Political Economy of Risk*. Baltimore: John Hopkins University Press.

Husted, Thomas, and David Nickerson. 2014. Political economy of presidential disaster declarations and federal disaster assistance. *Public Finance Review* 42: 35–57. [CrossRef]

López, Edward J., and Wayne A. Leighton. 2013. *Madmen, Intellectuals, and Academic Scribblers: The Economic Engine of Political Change*. Palo Alto: Stanford University Press.

McCubbins, Matthew D., Roger G. Noll, and Barry R. Weingast. 1989. Structure and process, politics and policy: Administrative arrangements and the political control of agencies. *Virginia Law Review* 75: 431–82. [CrossRef]

McNeil, Douglas W., Andrew W. Foshee, and Clark R. Burbee. 1988. Superfund taxes and expenditures: Regional redistributions. *Review of Regional Studies* 18: 4.

Niskanen, William A. 1971. *Bureaucracy and Representative Government*. Chicago: Aldine-Atherton.

Peltzman, Sam. 1976. Toward a more general theory of regulation. *Journal of Law and Economics* 19: 211–40. [CrossRef]

Ryan, Matt E. 2014. Allocating infection: The political economy of the swine flu (H1N1) vaccine. *Economic Inquiry* 52: 138–54. [CrossRef]

Sobel, Russell S., Christopher J. Coyne, and Peter T. Leeson. 2007. The political economy of FEMA: Did reorganization matter? *Journal of Public Finance and Public Choice* 17: 49–65.

Stratmann, Thomas. 1998. The politics of Superfund. In *Political Environmentalism: Going Behind the Green Curtain*. Edited by Terry L. Anderson. Palo Alto: Hoover Institution Press, pp. 239–62.

Stroup, Richard. 1996. *Superfund: The Shortcut That Failed*. Bozeman: Property and Environment Research Center.

Tilton, John E. 1995. Assigning the liability for past pollution: Lessons from the US mining industry. *Journal of Institutional and Theoretical Economics* 151: 139–54.

Twight, Charlotte. 1989. Institutional underpinnings of parochialism: The case of military base closures. *Cato Journal* 9: 73–106.

Weingast, Barry R., and Mark J. Moran. 1983. Bureaucratic discretion or congressional control? Regulatory policymaking by the Federal Trade Commission. *Journal of Political Economy* 91: 765–800. [CrossRef]

Yandle, Bruce. 1992. Environment and efficiency lovers. *Society* 29: 23–32. [CrossRef]

Yonk, Ryan, Arthur R. Wardle, and Josh Smith. 2017. *A Public Choice Exploration of the Surface Mining Control and Reclamation Act*. Logan: Strata.

economies

MDPI

Article

Political Entrepreneurs and Pork-Barrel Spending

J. Zachary Klingensmith

Penn State Erie, The Behrend College, Black School of Business, 4701 College Drive, Erie, PA 16563, USA;
jzk17@psu.edu

Received: 10 January 2019; Accepted: 20 February 2019; Published: 28 February 2019

Abstract: Pork-barrel spending is the use of federal money for localized projects that yield only a narrow geographic benefit. It is a commonly held belief that politicians use this spending to improve their chances of re-election. One way that an incumbent can increase their chances of re-election is through increased fundraising. Political entrepreneurs see this opportunity and attempt to benefit from these projects in exchange for campaign contributions. This paper investigates whether incumbents are able to use their position to bolster their campaign contributions. I find pork-barrel spending and political contributions to be positively related, but this effect is only present when the incumbent properly times the project. I also find that general federal appropriations do not have the same impact. This supports the claim that pork-barrel spending can be used as a currency in the marketplace for political capital.

Keywords: pork-barrel spending; campaign finance; incumbency advantage; elections

JEL Classification: D72; H50

1. Introduction

1.1. Advertising, Credit-Claiming, and Position-Taking

In his seminal work, *Congress: The Electoral Connection*, Mayhew (1974) claimed that members of Congress devote resources to three basic activities when seeking re-election. They can *advertise* through speeches, public openings, and campaign ads. They can *credit-claim* by showing off the positive things they have done for their constituents. This can include federal money appropriated to their district, or policies that have a net benefit for their voters. Finally, members of Congress can *take positions* by using their voting behavior to form a political platform.

Targeted expenditures, which are also called pork-barrel spending, allow incumbents to both *credit claim* and *advertise* simultaneously. They accomplish this through three channels. First, pork-barrel spending allows an incumbent to *advertise* by initiating pork-barrel projects that are visible and useful to the constituents. It is not surprising to see the legislator at the groundbreaking of a project or toting oversized scissors at a grand opening. Second, an incumbent can *credit-claim* if the pork-barrel spending results in improved economic conditions. If a constituent's life is improved through a pork-barrel project, that citizen is more likely to cast a vote for the incumbent. Third, an incumbent can increase their ability to *advertise* through campaign contributions. In this scenario, political entrepreneurs engage in rent-seeking behavior by making campaign contributions to incumbents in exchange for preferential treatment, including the funneling of pork-barrel money to prominent donors. For example, the owner of a concrete supplier may make a contribution to the incumbent's campaign, and in exchange, the donor receives a contract for a new sidewalk project in the district.

This paper focuses on the third channel. The main goal of this paper is to determine whether rent-seeking does in fact occur by estimating the effect that pork-barrel spending has on fundraising. While others have studied why politicians use pork-barrel spending, I use a novel approach to isolate one specific way that politicians use pork-barrel money to their benefit. To accomplish this goal, I test three hypotheses: first, whether pork-barrel spending has an impact on an incumbent's ability to fundraise, second, whether the timing of the pork-barrel appropriations matter, and third, whether general federal appropriations do not have the same impact on fundraising that pork-barrel spending does. If I can prove each hypothesis, then it provides evidence that political entrepreneurs are active in the political market for pork-barrel spending, and that incumbents are more than happy to go along with the process.

1.2. Political Entreprenurs and Rent-Seeking

A political entrepreneur is someone in the private sector that attempts to "change the direction and flow of politics" through the act of rent-seeking. Political entrepreneurs create inefficiencies in the market as they have "energies and talents that could be used elsewhere" (Schneider and Teske 1992). Instead of focusing their creative energies on enhancing the product or service they offer, they use that energy and capital in an attempt to change laws and encourage projects that would benefit their business.

By definition, those engaging in rent-seeking, including political entrepreneurs, attempt to redistribute gains to themselves in the absence of the creation of any new gains (Tullock 1967; Krueger 1974; Posner 1975; Tullock et al. 1980). Political entrepreneurs have an incentive to lobby for less regulations (or regulations that hurt competing industries) or for funding directed to projects that can benefit the entrepreneur, even at the expense of the population at large. Rent-seeking is viewed as "in-kind" where lobbyists use benefits such as fancy dinners and nice vacations to encourage beneficial legislative changes (Mixon et al. 1994). Additionally, lobbyists can attempt to spur legislative change through the use of indirect rent-seeking, where special-interest groups attempt to influence legislation "by holding demonstrations, purchasing billboard, radio, or television advertising, or by funding, publishing, and circulating policy-oriented journals and research (the type of activity usually done by public policy institutes)" (Sobel and Garrett 2002). While exchanging political favors for campaign contributions is not technically bribery, it is a form of in-kind rent-seeking. Past studies have shown that the effect of rent-seeking can be as large as 22% of gross national product. (Laband and Sophocleus 1988).

As is the case in the private market, the political entrepreneur must realize that a profit opportunity exists, and must be willing to take action as they would in a private market (Holcombe 2002; McCaffrey and Salerno 2011). The end result is a system of political capitalism where the political elite and the economic elite cooperate in a way that is mutually beneficial (Holcombe 2015). Therefore, both the politicians and the political entrepreneurs have motivation to work together while engaging in this rent-seeking behavior. For the politician, this creates a scenario where the politician may betray their political beliefs to gain political capital for future use (Lopez 2002). This can include "calling in favors", such as campaign donations, from those that have benefited from policies and projects made possible by the legislator.

1.3. Pork-Barrel Spending and Campaign Contributions

Pork-barrel spending is defined as federal appropriations used to fund localized projects that yield concentrated geographical benefits. There has been an abundant number of papers published attempting to identify why legislators are so motivated to use pork-barrel money. Only a handful are mentioned below. However, if pork-barrel spending can increase campaign contributions, that by itself is a sufficient reason to expend resources to seek it. A long series of studies have shown that campaign expenditures are directly related to success in an election (Dawson and Zinser 1976; Jacobson 1981, 1990; Palda 1973, 1975; Samuels 2002; Stratmann 2013; Welch 1974, 1976). This is even more important to incumbents facing a tight election. While campaign fundraising is typically more important to challengers, as they must overcome the incumbency bias (Jacobson 1990), political organizations are able to aid marginal incumbents from potentially damaging economic forces through additional campaign funding (Jacobson 1981). Therefore, political entrepreneurs may be able to identify incumbents in the greatest need, and more importantly, those most willing to cooperate in exchange for said campaign contributions.

Returning to the earlier theme of the paper, the use of pork-barrel spending would simultaneously allow a legislator to engage in two types of re-election activity: *credit-claiming* and *advertising*. When a legislator directs pork-barrel projects to those that return the favor through campaign contributions, they are engaging in *credit-claiming*. At the same time, those political contributions can be used for additional *advertisements* such as radio and television commercials.

The link between campaign contributions and corporate gains is largely anecdotal in the United States (Milyo 1999; Stratmann 1995); however, empirical evidence of this effect has been shown in other countries such as Brazil (Boas et al. 2014). For example, in 1993, individual members of the Brazilian congressional Joint Budget Committee accepted kickbacks of up to 3% of a project's value in compensation for their assistance in funding approval (Boas et al. 2014; Krieger et al. 1994). Even more recently, Andrade Gutierrez, one of the largest construction companies in Brazil, increased its contributions in municipal elections from nearly $75,000 to $37.1 million. At the same time, the company was awarded nearly $3 billion in construction contracts associated with the 2014 World Cup (Payne 2014). It should be noted that the Brazilian political system is often seen as an anomaly, and may not be directly comparable to the American political system. At the same time, the motivations that exist within the Brazilian political system are the same as those that exist in the American political system.

Pinpointing the relationship between corporate gains and fundraising in the United States has been problematic for many reasons. First, due to campaign finance laws, corporations can only donate money to political action committees (PACs), which then use the money to support a politician or issue. Records of contributions to PACs are less detailed than those that record donations to candidates, and therefore, it is difficult to measure corporate efforts to support incumbents. Moreover, the links between corporate gains and public policy is rarely obvious.

Although it tends to be difficult to link corporate profits to national programs, this problem is reduced for the case of targeted expenditures. Pork may be presumed to have the greatest effect on the profits of firms in the district receiving the expenditures. Potential donors benefit both from contracts to produce the services provided, necessary infrastructure for those projects, and indirectly through expenditures by firms and their employees in the district of interest.

Of course, legislators may also attempt to use general appropriations to their advantage. Federal aid programs are much larger than targeted expenditures. However, legislators have a more difficult time claiming credit for general government spending. This is not to say that a legislator that pioneered major changes to a national program cannot claim credit. Instead, voters are not likely to give credit to their legislator for an annual increase in Social Security benefits or additional highway spending. This is both because a single legislator's vote is rarely decisive, and because many general federal appropriations are formula-based, so individual legislators have very little control over the amount of money that each state receives. As a consequence, large federal programs are very difficult to change in a manner that generates state or district-specific benefits.

2. Methodology

2.1. The Model

Given the extensive research conducted on political fundraising and the effects of campaign spending, there has been surprisingly little research on the effects of pork-barrel spending on campaign contributions. Samuels (2002) found that increased pork-barrel spending leads to an increase in incumbent fundraising, all other things being equal, in the Brazilian political system. Then, the additional campaign contributions are used to increase the likelihood of re-election. However, his work does not address the mechanism through which pork-barrel spending increases prospects for electoral success. This paper attempts to address this by examining the link between pork-barrel spending and incumbent fundraising.

While Samuels (2002) posited that pork-barrel spending increases fundraising, Stratmann (2013) contended that fundraising tends to increase pork. My results suggest that Stratmann has misidentified the relationship. Specifically, I find that an increase in pork-barrel spending leads to more campaign contributions. One possibility for the difference is that Stratmann's work focuses on the House of Representatives, whereas my work focuses on the Senate. Senators have more direct influence over public policies, including the appropriation of pork-barrel monies, than members of the House. Their six-year terms allow senators to reap benefits that may take longer to develop compared to the two-year terms for representatives. Moreover, states are able to capture a larger percentage of the benefits of any given project compared to that of a congressional district. While projects in a congressional district may benefit a small handful of companies within the district, those benefits will spill over into neighboring districts through the effects of sub-contracting, commuting, and shopping across district boundaries. Therefore, the state is able to capture most of the benefits from a given pork-barrel project, compared to only a portion at the district level.

This study is not without limitations. There is one significant disadvantage associated with a state-level analysis as opposed to that of a district-level study. There are two senators per state elected at-large. Therefore, it is impossible to untangle the effort of each senator. Further, it is also impossible to separate the efforts of the senators from the efforts of representatives who also exerted energies to obtain the funding. This implies that the Samuels and Stratmann's framework can be applied at the state-level only after several modifications are adopted. A more thorough look at the two senator problem will be addressed later in this paper.

I use a fundraising model based on Samuels (2002), Krebs (2001), and Bonneau (2007) for the purposes of estimation. The Samuels (2002) model estimates the percentage of campaign finance in a Brazilian state based on factors such as previous electoral success, number of terms served, and party leadership. Krebs (2001) analyzed fundraising in city council elections, and Bonneau (2007) addressed the determinants of fundraising in state Supreme Court elections. While the last two papers are not conducted at the federal level, many of the determinants still apply, regardless of the level of government being discussed.

This study extends Samuels's (2002) paper and complements Stratmann's (2013) approach in the following ways. First, the present study focuses on United States Senate elections from 2004 to 2018, rather than a single election. For three years, it was possible to trace pork-barrel spending to the individual representative responsible for its appropriation. Due to changes in reporting rules and a moratorium on pork-barrel spending starting in 2011, data can no longer be collected at the district level. Therefore, in order to examine a longer time period, the state level must be used. While there is an effort to use machine learning to allow artificial intelligence to identify pork-barrel spending deep within spending bills[1], that type of data is not currently available.

Second, unlike the Samuels (2002) paper, this paper focused on the United States. As mentioned, there are major differences between the American and Brazilian political systems, especially with respect to the acceptance of financial kickbacks. However, incumbents face the same pressures to utilize whatever means necessary (and legal) in order to be re-elected.

Finally, this study focuses on the Senate, unlike the work of Krebs (2001), Bonneau (2007), and Stratmann (2013), which examine other levels of government. If a linkage between campaign fundraising and pork-barrel spending is found, then it is entirely plausible that this is evidence of pork-barrel spending being used as political capital. This would reinforce the idea of pork-barrel spending being used for both *advertising* and *credit-claiming*.

---

[1]   https://dssg.uchicago.edu/2014/12/04/using-data-for-a-more-transparent-government/.

The general model that I use is as presented follows:

$$fundraising = \beta_0 + \beta_i \cdot pork + \beta_j \cdot electoral\ variables + \beta_k \cdot year + \epsilon$$

where *fundraising* is one of the two dependent variables used to measure the incumbent's ability to fundraise, *pork* is one of the variations of federal appropriations, *electoral variables* are control variables concerned with the political attributed of the incumbent, *year* are time variables, and ϵ is the error term. I discuss each type of variable in more depth below.

2.2. Fundraising Data

There are two dependent variables used in this study.

2.2.1. Incumbent Fundraising (in Millions of Dollars)

The first dependent variable is the total amount of money raised by the incumbent in millions of dollars during the election cycle as in Krebs (2001) and Bonneau (2007). This data is collected from the Center for Responsive Politics' Open Secrets.

2.2.2. Share of Fundraising

The second dependent variable is the share of fundraising is the percentage of the overall fundraising the incumbent accounted for in their specific race. For example, if the incumbent raised $7 million and the challenger raised $3 million, then the incumbent would have a 70% share of the fundraising, as they raised $7 million of the $10 million total raised in that specific electoral battle. Both Samuels (2002) and Stratmann (2013) used the share of fundraising variable. The share of fundraising has several advantages over the total fundraising variable. First, population does not matter when the share of fundraising is used, as it is simply a percentage of total fundraising. In addition, price level differences do not matter. Since the spending in Senate campaigns can vary drastically, the fundraising advantage variable allows for a more straightforward comparison of Senate races. The fundraising data are also collected from the Center for Responsive Politics' *Open Secrets*.

2.3. Pork-Barrel and Appropriations Spending Data

Data on the incumbent was collected for all senators vying for re-election from 2004–2018. Pork-barrel spending data is collected in two ways: aggregated by election cycle and disaggregated by the year within the election cycle.

2.3.1. Total Pork-Barrel Spending

Data on pork-barrel spending are taken from the Citizens against Government Waste (CAGW) dataset. The first variable measures the total amount of pork-barrel spending appropriated by the Senator's state during their six-year term. The data are presented in millions of dollars. I hypothesize that there will be a positive correlation between fundraising and pork-barrel spending. One potential issue is that if the timing of pork-barrel spending matters, then the relationship may be ambiguous.

2.3.2. Pork-Barrel Spending by Year

I also use a set of annual pork-barrel spending variables. The pork-barrel spending appropriated to a state is linked to electoral cycles, rather than years per se. For instance, if a Senator was up for re-election in 2008, I compute the amount of pork-barrel spending that went to the state from 2003–2008, both annually and in aggregate. This allows for a determination as to whether the timing of pork-barrel spending impacts campaign contributions. Specifically, I test to determine whether the pork-barrel spending appropriated in election years impacts fundraising. Since Senate terms are six years long, data from 1999–2018 is used. Since it is impossible to distinguish between the individual efforts of each senator, the total amount of pork-barrel spending appropriated by the state is used. Due to the inability to disaggregate, it is likely that free riding is occurring within the Senate (Rogers 2002). As mentioned earlier, even though a district-level study would yield stronger results, there are 20 years of pork barrel spending data available at the state level, but only three years of data at the district level.

To help illustrate the election cycles, I graph the average amount of pork-barrel spending from each "year to election" in Figure 1. In Figure 1 below, it is apparent that pork-barrel spending follows a political election cycle, as it spikes every two years, which corresponds with the Senate elections. I have included two different iterations of the data on the figure below. The bars on the left are the average pork-barrel appropriations from 1999–2018, whereas the bars on the right are the average pork-barrel spending from 1999–2010. The reason for this distinction is a 2011 Congressional moratorium on pork-barrel spending. The amount of pork-barrel spending has fallen drastically. The total pork-barrel spending by year is shown in Figure 2. The effect of the moratorium is apparent starting in 2011.

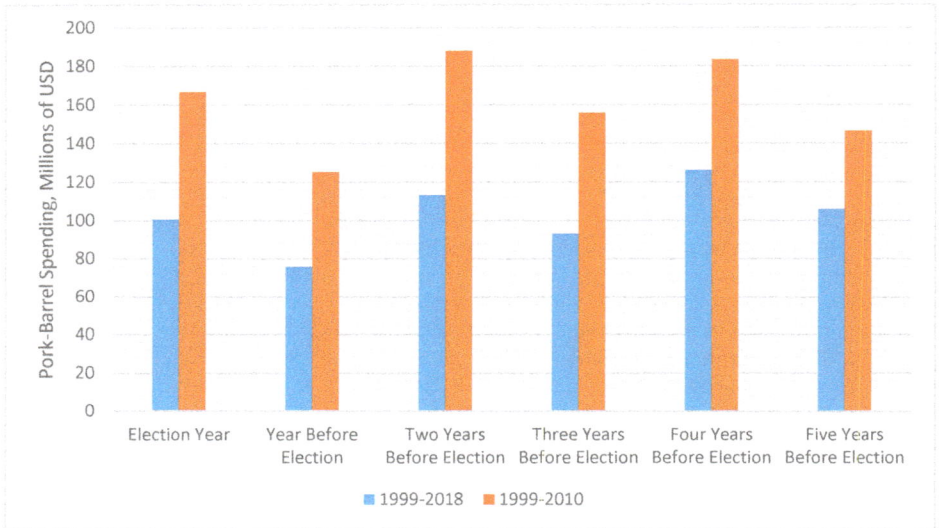

Figure 1. Pork-Barrel Spending by Year.

Various estimations have shown that pork-barrel spending appropriations in non-election years have no statistical impact. Therefore, for the purposes of this study, I use the pork-barrel spending appropriated in years with Senate elections. It is expected that there is both a "what have you done for me lately" attitude from both parties, in addition to some degree of interference being picked up due to the specification of the variable. Again, it is problematic that state-level data is being used as opposed to district-level data, as it is impossible to disaggregate the efforts of the two Senators. However, district-level data is not available for more than three years.

To determine whether and to what degree pork-barrel appropriations impact fundraising, two series of estimates are undertaken for each dependent variable. First, aggregated pork-barrel spending and the other control variables are used to estimate the total amount of funds raised by the incumbent. Next, the possibility of an electoral cycle in pork and pork-induced donations are estimated using annual data for the three election years during each senator's term. The inclusion of annual values also explores whether timing is important when considering the effects of pork-barrel spending on future fundraising.

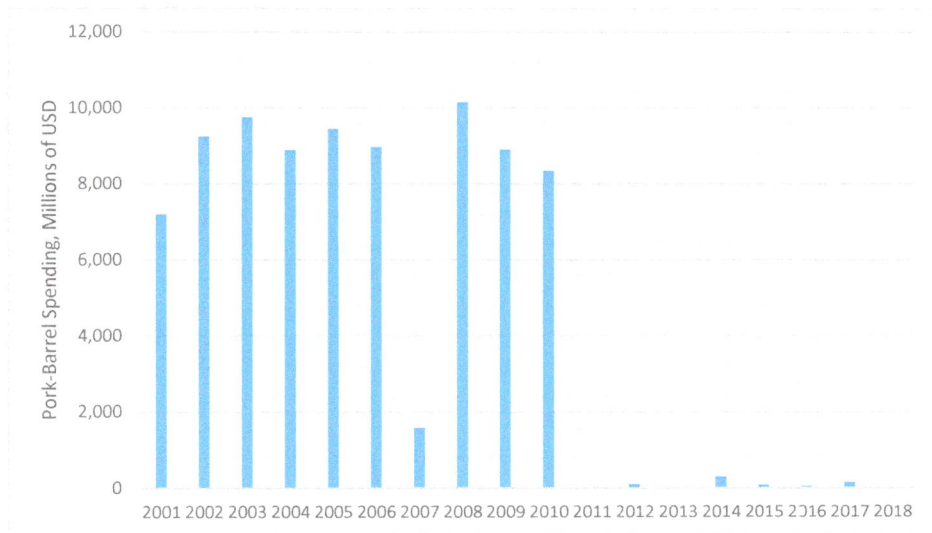

Figure 2. Pork-Barrel Spending by Year.

2.3.3. Federal Aid

In order to assess differences between the impacts of pork-barrel spending and general appropriations on fundraising, I use a federal aid variable from the United States (US) Census. This variable measures the amount of federal aid appropriated to each state. The federal aid is calculated by federal outlays to states from a variety of federal agencies. The data are collected from the United States Census Statistical Abstracts of the United States, and specifically from the section titled "Federal Aid to State and Local Governments—Selected Programs by State". The Federal Aid variable does not include Social Security or Medicare. In addition, I removed Medicaid spending, since it is also formula-based. As was the case with pork-barrel spending, two forms of this variable are used. The first is the aggregate federal appropriations in billions of dollars during the Senator's six-year term. The second is the annual, disaggregated federal appropriation in the years prior to an incumbent's re-election year. Unfortunately, due to budget cuts, the US Census no longer collects these data. As a result, the regressions that use federal appropriation data are restricted to 2004–2010.

It should not be surprising that federal aid can also be used by political entrepreneurs to manipulate the political process. Even though I hypothesize that pork-barrel spending will have a more intense impact on the ability to fundraise, past research has found federal aid being used for political reasons as well. For example, one study found that states can move their caucus/primary dates in order to obtain additional federal grants by making their primary/caucus more important (Mixon and Hobson 2001).

By using the appropriations variable in addition to the pork-barrel spending variables, I am able to determine whether general appropriation spending has the same impact on fundraising as pork-barrel spending. If pork-barrel spending is shown to be more effective, then the estimates provide an explanation for the attraction to pork-barrel spending.

2.4. Characteristics of the Incumbent

Characteristics of individual senators were also collected. I only use incumbents who served a full term. Therefore, senators who were appointed during the previous term or won a special election are not included, as they did not have the full six years to obtain funding. From 2004–2018, 196 incumbents met these criteria, and were included. The descriptive statistics and the sources for the dataset are shown in Table 1.

2.4.1. Challenger Fundraising

When an incumbent feels challenged, they must increase their efforts to fundraise. One way to determine the competiveness of the election is by considering how much the challenger fundraised. Similar to the other fundraising data, the amount the challenger fundraised comes from *Open Secrets*. I hypothesize that the more the challenger fundraised, the more vulnerable the incumbent was, and thus, the more the incumbent would need to fundraise to stave off the added competition.

2.4.2. Cash-on-Hand

The amount of cash-on-hand is included since it can influence the need to fundraise. I hypothesize that an incumbent with more cash-on-hand will need less campaign contributions.

2.4.3. Performance in Previous Senate Election

The percent of the vote received in the previous election is used to gauge the vulnerability of the candidate. These data are collected from the Federal Election Commission (FEC). Candidates that win elections by large margins do not need to raise large amounts of money, since they are not vulnerable. For example, Robert C. Byrd never received less than 60% of the vote in a general election. At the same time, because he was never vulnerable, he didn't need to exert resources or energy on serious fundraising. The most that Byrd ever needed to raise was $5 million in his bid for re-election in 2006 (with many years needing $1 million or less.) Since his passing, the same seat has required more than $10 million in campaign financing. On the other hand, nearly $125 million was raised during the Cruz/O'Rourke Senate election battle in 2018. Therefore, I hypothesize a negative relationship between past performance and incumbent fundraising.

2.4.4. Number of Terms Served

This variable counts the number of full terms served by the incumbent in the United States Senate. Similar to the previous variable, this variable measures the vulnerability of the seat. Senators that have held the seat for a longer period of time often have more name recognition. Therefore, I hypothesize a negative relationship between the number of terms served and campaign fundraising. It is possible that the relationship will not be as strong, since there is often a push to "drain the swamp" and "stop career politicians", which could be a detriment to longer-serving Senators.

2.4.5. Democrat

This is a binary variable that has a value of one if the incumbent is a Democrat. This variable measures the impact of the incumbent's party on the incumbent's ability to fundraise. Historically, the Republican Party is thought to be connected to the super rich, and more likely to obtain campaign funds. However, in my dataset, the average raised by the Democrat is $13.53 million per election, compared to $10.77 million per election raised by Republicans. Therefore, I anticipate a positive relationship between the Democrat variable and campaign fundraising.

2.4.6. Do the Senators Belong to the Same Party?

The next variable is another binary variable that has a value of one if the two senators belong to the same party. If a state is red or blue, the two senators can work together under the party name to advance their own re-election campaigns. On the other hand, senators may have a tougher time in a purple state, since they may also need to compete against the state's other senator. In addition, Senators in purple states are more likely to be vulnerable, as there is less voter allegiance to a single party. Therefore, I hypothesize a positive relationship between the same party variable and campaign fundraising.

2.4.7. Female

The final incumbent characteristic variable is a binary variable with a value of one if the incumbent is female. There has also been some debate over whether or not females have greater difficulty in raising funds due to the historical male-dominated environment of the United States political system (Uhlaner and Schlozman 1986). More recent research has suggested that those differences may have been eliminated over the past few decades with sex no longer having an impact on electability (Hayes and Lawless 2015). The only issue that seems to remain is that news coverage still tends to rely on male experts, which could lead to a bias against females (Freedman and Fico 2005). Therefore, I hypothesize a positive relationship between the female variable and incumbent fundraising, because females may need additional fundraising to overcome the remaining bias.

2.5. Time Variables

The final set of variables are time-based binary variables ranging from 2004 to 2016 (with 2018 being the omitted year). These variables are meant to measure any idiosyncratic differences between different election cycles.

Table 1. Descriptive Statistics for State-Level Regression.

Variable	Source	Obs.	Mean	St. Dev.	Min	Max
Dependent Variables						
Incumbent Fundraising (millions of $)	OpenSecrets	196	12.25	8.47	1.7	51.57
Fundraising Advantage (in %)	OpenSecrets	196	78.59	19.28	17.33	100
Explanatory Variables						
Challenger Fundraising (millions of $)	OpenSecrets	196	5.97	10.68	0	85
Cash-on-Hand (millions of dollars)	OpenSecrets	196	1.68	2.68	0	17.16
Total Pork-Barrel Funding (millions of $)	CAGW	196	613.99	697.59	0	3640.2
Pork-Barrel Funding during Election Year	CAGW	196	100.43	142.23	0	733.63
Pork-Barrel Funding Two Years Prior	CAGW	196	113.05	140.26	0	671.8
Pork-Barrel Funding Four Years Prior	CAGW	196	126.04	144.46	0	733.63
Total Federal Aid (Billions of $)	Census	101	40.21	55.96	1.1	296.4
Federal Aid during Election Year	Census	101	9.59	12.04	1.2	66.6
Federal Aid Two Years Prior	Census	101	8.43	10.51	1.1	53.8
Federal Aid Four Years Prior	Census	101	7.42	9.12	0.9	46
% of Vote in Previous General Election	FEC	196	60.06	9.41	36.08	100
Number of Terms in Current Office	Congress	196	2.33	1.60	1	8
Are Senators from Same Party? *	Congress	196	0.709	0.455	0	1
Female *	Congress	196	0.209	0.408	0	1
Democrat *	Congress	196	0.536	0.5	0	1

* Variables marked with an asterisk are binary variables.

3. Results

3.1. Results

The first regression used a pooled ordinary least squares regression (OLS) approach to estimate total fundraising. The second estimate utilized the yearly pork-barrel appropriations during the election year and two years prior in lieu of the total, six-year pork-barrel appropriations. Regressions three and four replicated the first two regressions using the share of fundraising variable in place of the total fundraising variable.

Next, the same four regressions were repeated using federal aid to states instead of pork-barrel appropriations. Regression five used the six-year federal outlays, while regression six replaced the aggregate appropriation with annual outlays during the election year and two year prior in order to explore the possibility of an electoral cycle in the effects of state appropriations on overall fundraising.

Finally, regressions seven and eight replicated regressions five and six using the share of fundraising variable in place of the total fundraising variable.

Unlike the work of Samuels (2002) and Stratmann (2013), the present study includes federal elections from 2004 to 2018 instead of a single election cycle. Therefore, panel estimation techniques can be used. Each of the eight regressions above were repeated using a fixed-effect panel approach as well.

3.2. OLS Estimates of Fundraising with Pork-Barrel Spending

Table 2 displays the results of the pooled OLS estimates of both total fundraising (regressions one to two) and share of fundraising (regressions three to four), including both the aggregate pork-barrel appropriations and the yearly pork-barrel appropriations. For regressions one and two, the challenger fundraising variable is both significant and positively correlated with pork-barrel spending in their states. In addition, cash-on-hand and the log of the population are all significant and correlated with incumbent fundraising.

Most of the variables behaved as expected. For example, pork-barrel spending appropriated during the election year has a positive and statistically significant relationship with the total amount of money fundraised. At the same time, no such relationship occurs between pork-barrel spending and the incumbent's share of fundraising. One possible explanation is that an incumbent reacts to the degree of threat from the challenger. For instance, an incumbent with a low likelihood of being unseated does not need to worry about fundraising. Yet, they are likely to control a large percentage of the total fundraising, as a weak challenger is not able to fundraise. On the other hand, in a highly competitive race, the incumbent may have to use pork-barrel spending to increase total fundraising. However, even with the additional fundraising, the share is unaffected due to the higher fundraising level by the challenger.

The female variable is statistically significant and positively related to total fundraising. As discussed earlier, female performance is elections have become essentially equalized with male performance, but there is still evidence of barriers to overcome in terms of public perception.

Regressions three and four used the share of fundraising as the dependent variable. The time effects were not included, because we do not have to control for things such as price levels. In addition, challenger fundraising is not included, since it is already part of the share of the fundraising variable. As was the case with the first two regressions, the cash-on-hand variable is significant. Unlike the first set of regressions, the previous general election performance is positively correlated with share of fundraising. This again makes sense, as a relatively unchallenged incumbent will not need to fundraise (explaining the negative relationship between total fundraising and past election performance), but does not have a serious challenger. The end result is an incumbent with a low-level of total fundraising, but a high percentage of the total fundraising share.

The 'same party' variable is positive and significant. This shows that when both senators belong to the same party, the incumbent up for election enjoys a larger share of the total fundraising. This again makes sense in terms of the competitiveness of the seat. If both senators belong to the same party, it is likely that the state is either a deeper red or blue, indicating a greater degree of safety. When senators serve in a purple state, they tend to be far more vulnerable.

3.3. OLS Estimates of Fundraising with Federal Appropriations

The next four regressions replicate the first four, this time using federal aid to states as opposed to the more specific pork-barrel spending. As discussed, due to a reduction in federal funding, the US Census stopped collecting the federal outlay data after 2010. Therefore, these regressions cover the Senatorial general elections from 2004–2010. The results are displayed in Table 3. For each of the regressions, the control variables behave in much the same way as they did in regressions one to four, so I will not repeat the results. The main difference between pork-barrel spending and federal aid is that there is no significant relationship between federal aid and fundraising other than the federal aid appropriated during the election year, which is actually negatively correlated with total fundraising. These results support the hypothesis that general federal appropriations do not have the same impact on fundraising. Even when federal spending such as Social Security, Medicare, and Medicaid are excluded, there is still no discernable linkage between federal aid spending and fundraising.

Table 2. Pooled OLS Regressions using Federal Aid to States (Regressions One to Four).

Dependent Variable	Total Fundraising (mil $)		Share of Fundraising (%)	
Variable	(1)	(2)	(3)	(4)
Challenger Fundraising (in Millions of $)	0.414 *** (0.047)	0.401 *** (0.046)		
Cash on Hand (in Millions of $)	1.013 *** (0.180)	0.919 *** (0.181)	2.377 *** (0.468)	2.357 *** (0.473)
Total Pork Spending (in Millions of $)	−0.000 (0.001)		−0.001 (0.002)	
Pork in Election Year (in Millions of $)		0.017 ** (0.008)		0.008 (0.015)
Pork Two Years Prior (in Millions of $)		−0.008 (0.009)		−0.003 (0.020)
Pork Four Years Prior (in Millions of $)		0.002 (0.007)		−0.015 (0.016)
Previous Election Share	−0.235 *** (0.058)	−0.231 *** (0.057)	0.330 ** (0.154)	0.317 ** (0.155)
Terms	0.050 (0.330)	−0.049 (0.328)	1.227 (0.873)	1.342 (0.885)
Senators in Same Party?	−0.830 (1.047)	−1.230 (1.044)	7.699 *** (2.766)	8.082 *** (2.817)
Female	3.267 *** (1.179)	2.820 ** (1.203)	0.367 (3.130)	1.062 (3.189)
Democrat	1.239 (0.989)	1.185 (0.977)	−0.793 (2.539)	−0.636 (2.556)
2004 Election	−2.083 (1.803)	−4.067 * (2.075)		
2006 Election	−0.663 (1.749)	−2.983 (1.988)		
2008 Election	−0.159 (1.797)	−2.626 (2.013)		
2010 Election	−0.952 (1.870)	−2.447 (2.103)		
2012 Election	−0.579 (1.985)	0.642 (2.548)		
2014 Election	1.069 (1.832)	0.451 (1.977)		
2016 Election	0.564 (1.797)	0.403 (1.777)		
Constant	21.743 *** (3.656)	22.371 *** (3.603)	47.503 *** (8.727)	48.167 *** (8.733)
Observations	196	196	196	196
R-squared	0.494	0.514	0.256	0.262
F-statistic	11.71 ***	11.06 ***	9.25 ***	7.35 ***

Dependent Variables
Regressions One to Two: Total Fundraising by Incumbent (in millions of $)
Regressions Three to Four: Percentage of Fundraising by Incumbent

Standard errors in parentheses: *** = 1%, ** = 5%, * = 10% significance level.

Table 3. Pooled OLS Regressions using Federal Aid to States (Regressions Five to Eight).

Dependent Variable	Total Fundraising (Mil $)		Share of Fundraising (%)	
Variable	(5)	(6)	(7)	(8)
Challenger Fundraising	0.763 ***	0.723 ***		
(in Millions of $)	(0.098)	(0.085)		
Cash on Hand	1.060 ***	0.671 ***	2.331 ***	2.510 ***
(in Millions of $)	(0.200)	(0.189)	(0.610)	(0.663)
Total Aid Spending	0.014		−0.499	
(in Millions of $)	(0.011)		(0.033)	
Aid in Election Year		−0.925 ***		−0.354
(in Millions of $)		(0.299)		(0.915)
Aid Two Years Prior		0.738		1.117
(in Millions of $)		(0.586)		(1.891)
Aid Four Years Prior		0.671		−1.107
(in Millions of $)		(0.619)		(1.995)
Previous Election Share	−0.147 **	−0.103 *	0.282	0.299
	(0.071)	(0.061)	(0.221)	(0.226)
Terms	−0.033	0.061	−0.393	−0.543
	(0.380)	(0.330)	(1.205)	(1.225)
Senators in Same Party?	2.104	1.215	10.043 **	9.806 **
	(1.375)	(1.187)	(4.263)	(4.337)
Female	1.113	−0.666	−6.574	−6.871
	(1.514)	(1.330)	(4.771)	(4.895)
Democrat	0.770	0.302	3.040	3.686
	(1.122)	(0.983)	(3.554)	(3.623)
2004 Election	−0.774	−1.786		
	(1.580)	(1.527)		
2006 Election	−0.178	−2.985 *		
	(1.526)	(1.600)		
2008 Election	0.915	−1.156		
	(1.568)	(1.530)		
Constant	11.750 ***	10.650	54.353 ***	53.467
	(4.233)	(3.652)	(12.216)	(12.462)
Observations	101	101	101	101
R-squared	0.579	0.693	0.260	0.258
F-statistic	11.11 ***	15.12	4.66 ***	3.52 ***

Dependent Variables
Regressions Five to Six: Total Fundraising by Incumbent (in millions of $)
Regressions Seven to Eight: Percentage of Fundraising by Incumbent

Standard Errors in Parentheses: *** = 1%, ** = 5%, * = 10% significance level.

This first set of results supports the three hypotheses laid out earlier. First, pork-barrel spending can be used to advertise and credit-claim, as it was shown to positively impact an incumbent's ability to fundraise. Second, that the timing of the pork-barrel appropriations matter, as pork-barrel spending appropriated during the election year had the largest impact. Third, general federal appropriations does not have the same impact on fundraising that pork-barrel spending does, which demonstrates that targeted expenditures is a potential tool that has powers that general aid spending does not.

3.4. Panel Estimates of Fundraising with Pork-Barrel Spending

Even though the pooled OLS results support the three hypotheses regarding the impact that pork-barrel spending and appropriation spending have on fundraising, a panel approach was used as a robustness check. I repeated the previous eight regressions using panel estimates. I continued to use the election year binary variables in order to control for the election year. For example, the years after the 2008 financial crisis would be associated with increased targeted and general spending, but donors may have had less income from which to make donations.

Table 4 gives the estimates for regressions nine to 12. The results are similar to the estimates from regressions one to four, with only minor differences. First of all, the control variables in all four cases continued to behave similarly to the pooled OLS regressions. Again, challenger fundraising, service in the House of Representatives, the number of terms served, and being female are all significant and positively correlated with total fundraising. Second, the regressions utilizing the total incumbent fundraising variable continued to provide more robust results.

Table 4. Panel Regressions using Pork-Barrel Spending (Regressions Nine to 12).

Dependent Variable	Total Fundraising (Mil $)		Share of Fundraising (%)	
Variable	(9)	(10)	(11)	(12)
Challenger Fundraising (in Millions of $)	0.319 *** (0.044)	0.302 *** (0.044)		
Cash on Hand (in Millions of $)	0.793 *** (0.259)	0.632 ** (0.262)	2.880 *** (0.786)	2.666 (0.794)
Total Pork Spending (in Millions of $)	0.002 ** (0.001)		0.002 (0.002)	
Pork in Election Year (in Millions of $)		0.017 ** (0.007)		0.008 (0.015)
Pork Two Years Prior (in Millions of $)		−0.006 (0.009)		0.011 (0.022)
Pork Four Years Prior (in Millions of $)		−0.005 (0.006)		−0.015 (0.013)
Previous Election Share	−0.185 *** (0.056)	−0.194 *** (0.056)	0.035 (0.181)	0.028 (0.183)
Terms	0.285 (0.337)	0.530 * (0.334)	0.728 (1.048)	1.031 (1.041)
Senators in Same Party?	−1.050 (1.178)	−1.380 (1.180)	7.110 * (3.728)	6.368 (3.797)
Female	4.813 *** (1.355)	4.562 *** (1.359)	3.515 (4.306)	3.252 (4.351)
Democrat	1.321 (1.308)	0.729 (1.290)	6.880* (3.910)	6.903 (3.907)
2004 Election	−3.971 ** (1.587)	−5.752 *** (2.003)		
2006 Election	−2.442 * (1.432)	−3.842 ** (1.894)		
2008 Election	−0.209 (1.609)	−1.994 (2.050)		
2010 Election	−1.256 (1.675)	−2.102 (2.107)		
2012 Election	−1.804 (1.658)	0.179 (2.339)		
2014 Election	1.199 (1.701)	1.440 (1.874)		
2016 Election	−1.339 (1.618)	−1.889 (1.623)		
Constant	18.689 *** (3.539)	20.903 *** (3.470)	59.141 *** (10.728)	60.969 (10.562)
Observations	196	196	196	196
R-squared	0.497	0.507	0.198	0.167
F-statistic	8.62 ***	7.81 ***	3.56 ***	2.81 ***

Dependent Variables
Regressions Nine 10: Total Fundraising by Incumbent (in Millions of $)
Regressions 11 to 12: Percentage of Fundraising by Incumbent

Standard Errors in Parentheses: *** = 1%, ** = 5%, * = 10% Significance Level.

Again, pork-barrel spending influences fundraising, but only when properly timed. Specifically, when $1 million worth of pork-barrel money is brought into the state during the senator's election year, the senator is able to increase their fundraising by $17,000; that is, an additional dollar of fundraising costs around $60 worth of pork-barrel money. A key difference between the panel results and pooled OLS results is that total pork-barrel spending is significant and positively correlated with total fundraising. This indicates that pork-barrel spending throughout a senator's entire term does have a net positive effect on their fundraising. Additionally, pork-barrel spending continues to influence the percent of fundraising by the incumbent, but only when properly timed.

3.5. Panel Estimates of Fundraising with Federal Aid

I continue the analysis by repeating the four fundraising regressions with a fixed-effects panel estimation. Recall that this set of regressions utilized the federal aid variables instead of the pork-barrel spending variables.

Table 5 gives the estimates for regressions 13 to 16. Again, the results are similar to the estimates from regressions five to eight. The main difference is that the results are not as robust as the pooled OLS estimates.

Table 5. Panel Regressions using Federal Aid (Regressions 13–16).

Dependent Variable	Total Fundraising (Mil $)		Share of Fundraising (%)	
Variable	(13)	(14)	(15)	(16)
Challenger Fundraising (in Millions of $)	0.651 *** (0.110)	0.665 *** (0.090)		
Cash on Hand (in Millions of $)	0.270 (0.342)	0.145 (0.282)	3.379 *** (1.268)	3.267 ** (1.284)
Total Aid Spending (in Millions of $)	−0.008 (0.026)		−0.022 (0.099)	
Aid in Election Year (in Millions of $)		−1.737 *** (0.242)		−0.661 (1.042)
Aid Two Years Prior (in Millions of $)		1.081 (0.851)		0.190 (4.064)
Aid Four Years Prior (in Millions of $)		0.385 (0.665)		−0.393 (2.964)
Previous Election Share	−0.141 (0.010)	−0.079 (0.081)	−0.223 (0.399)	−0.123 (0.410)
Terms	0.596 (0.500)	0.545 (0.406)	−0.168 (1.978)	−0.084 (2.005)
Senators in Same Party?	3.237 (2.492)	2.748 (2.026)	8.823 (9.973)	7.597 (10.166)
Female	4.334 * (2.370)	3.807 ** (1.901)	−13.179 (9.268)	−13.632 (9.102)
Democrat	−1.906 (2.133)	−1.649 (1.733)	7.020 (8.075)	6.904 (8.245)
2004 Election	−1.251 (1.486)	−3.005 ** (1.480)		
2006 Election	−0.197 (1.668)	−3.883 ** (1.598)		
2008 Election	1.690 (1.550)	−1.005 (1.514)		
Constant	12.236** (5.857)	10.174* (5.863)	81.996 *** (22.321)	83.693 *** (26.403)
Observations	101	101	101	101
R-squared	0.598	0.749	0.181	0.200
F-statistic	5.55 ***	8.97 ***	1.41	1.19

Dependent Variables
Regressions 13 to 14: Total Fundraising by Incumbent (in millions of $)
Regressions 15 to 16: Percentage of Fundraising by Incumbent

Standard Errors in Parentheses: *** = 1%, ** = 5%, * = 10% Significance Level.

4. Discussion

Overall, the above results support the three hypotheses stated at the beginning of the paper. First, pork-barrel spending can have a positive and significant impact on fundraising. Second, the timing of the pork-barrel spending matters. To be specific, only pork-barrel spending in the election year seems to have an impact on campaign contributions. Third, the relationship between federal aid to states and incumbent fundraising is ambiguous; however, it is clear that the amount of fundraising per dollar of pork-barrel spending is far greater than the amount of fundraising per dollar of federal aid. This suggests that legislators should prefer pork-barrel spending over general appropriations for their states, possibly because the former is more visible and easier to take credit for. It would be difficult for a single senator to claim credit for a change in the entire Women, Infant, and Children (WIC) system (unless they were actually responsible for a major change, but this is rare). However, a senator could claim credit for a new highway, park, museum, or federal building in their state. This also lends support to universalism hypothesis of Weingast (1994), which stated that politicians are likely to work together on targeted spending bills, because it is in their respective fundraising interests to do so. This shows that pork-barrel spending is used as a source of political capital for both politicians and political entrepreneurs.

There are several variables that were not included in this study. First, some studies use per-capita measures. This is problematic for several reasons. First, it does not allow for a simple interpretation of the estimates. Instead of being able to estimate the number of dollars needed to increase fundraising by $1, all of the values are based on the size of the population. More importantly, estimates of per capita campaign spending are very weak.

Another possible change that could be made is to compare similar spending types. For example, I could have compared the impact of pork-barrel spending when included in a transportation omnibus bill compared to the impact of federal spending by the Department of Transportation. As previously mentioned, senators have much less control over the amount of money spent by executive agencies of the government. Therefore, incumbents can use pork-barrel spending to steer money to projects that they believe will provide a greater personal benefit.

5. Conclusions

We again return to the work of (Mayhew 1974) and the tools utilized by members of Congress to win re-election. This paper has demonstrated that incumbent senators can use their position to appropriate targeted expenditures in return for political contributions. This allows senators to engage in both *credit-claiming* and *advertising*. By taking credit for the pork-barrel money, they can use the subsequent campaign donations to enhance the amount of advertising possible, further increasing the likelihood of being re-elected. This also leads credence to the idea that political entrepreneurs are able to manipulate incumbents, especially those in vulnerable seats. They can accomplish this by rewarding incumbents with campaign dollars for targeted expenditures that directly benefit the political entrepreneurs.

By extending past research by Krebs (2001), Samuels (2002), Bonneau (2007), and Stratmann (2013), I was able to model and estimate an incumbent senator's ability to fundraise for re-election. The main novelty of the above estimates was the use of disaggregated pork-barrel appropriations. This furthers the existing literature pertaining to the motivation that incumbents have to use a type of funding that is often said to be inefficient.

In addition, the results are robust, as similar estimates are obtained using pooled OLS estimates and fixed-effect panel estimates. The results also suggest that state federal appropriations may increase fundraising by senators, although less so than targeted expenditures. This supports the hypothesis that legislators prefer to use pork-barrel spending, all other things being equal, because the results are more visible, easier to take credit for, and easier to direct to certain parties. Finally, as discussed earlier, there is evidence that pork-barrel spending is used as political capital.

This evidence also supports the claim that pork-barrel spending is used as a currency in the world of political capitalism. Incumbents steer federal money to states and districts to support localized projects. These projects directly benefit the particular businesses that win contracts associated with the appropriation. The business owners then reward the incumbents with campaign donations, which can be used to bolster their likelihood of re-election.

Funding: This research received no external funding.

Conflicts of Interest: The author declares no conflict of interest.

References

Boas, Taylor, Daniel Hidalgo, and Neal Richardson. 2014. The spoils of victory: Campaign donations and government contracts in Brazil. *The Journal of Politics* 76: 415–29. [CrossRef]

Bonneau, Chris. 2007. Campaign fundraising in state supreme court elections. *Social Science Quarterly* 88: 68–85. [CrossRef]

Dawson, Paul, and James Zinser. 1976. Political finance and participation in congressional elections. *The Annals of the American Academy of Political and Social Science* 425: 59–73. [CrossRef]

Freedman, Eric, and Frederick Fico. 2005. Male and Female Sources in Newspaper Coverage of Male and Female Candidates in Open Races for Governor in 2002. *Mass Communication and Society* 8: 257–72. [CrossRef]

Hayes, Danny, and Jennifer Lawless. 2015. A Non-Gendered Lens? Media, Voters, and Female Candidates in Contemporary Congressional Elections. *Perspective on Politics* 13: 95–118. [CrossRef]

Holcombe, Randall. 2002. Political entrepreneurship and the democratic allocation of economic resources. *The Review of Austrian Economics* 15: 143–59. [CrossRef]

Holcombe, Randall. 2015. Political capitalism. *Cato Journal* 35: 41–66.

Jacobson, Gary. 1981. *Strategy and Choice in Congressional Elections*. New Haven: Yale University Press.

Jacobson, Gary. 1990. The Effects of Campaign Spending in House Elections: New Evidence for Old Arguments. *American Journal of Political Science* 34: 334–62. [CrossRef]

Krebs, Timothy. 2001. Political experience and fundraising in city council elections. *Social Science Quarterly* 82: 536–51. [CrossRef]

Krieger, Gustavo, Fernando Rodrigues, and Elvis Bonassa. 1994. *Os donos do Congresso: A farsa na CPI do Orcamento*. Sao Paulo: Editora Atica.

Krueger, Anne. 1974. The Political Economy of the Rent-Seeking Society. *American Economic Review* 64: 291–303.

Laband, David, and John Sophocleus. 1988. The social cost of rent-seeking: First estimates. *Public Choice* 58: 269–75. [CrossRef]

Lopez, Edward. 2002. The legislator as political entrepreneur: Investment in political capital. *The Review of Austrian Economics* 15: 211–28. [CrossRef]

Mayhew, David. 1974. *Congress: The Electoral Connection*. New Haven: Yale University Press.

McCaffrey, Matthew, and Joseph Salerno. 2011. A theory of political entrepreneurship. *Modern Economy* 2: 552–60. [CrossRef]

Milyo, Jeffrey. 1999. The political economics of campaign finance. *The Independent Review* 3: 537–457.

Mixon, Franklin, and David Hobson. 2001. Intergovernmental grants and the positioning of presidential primaries and caucuses: Empirical evidence from the 1992, 1996, and 2000 election cycles. *Contemporary Economic Policy* 19: 27–38. [CrossRef]

Mixon, Franklin, David Laband, and Robert Ekelund. 1994. Rent seeking and hidden in-kind resource distortion: Some empirical evidence. *Public Choice* 78: 171–75. [CrossRef]

Palda, Kristian. 1973. Does advertising influence votes? An analysis of the 1966 and 1970 Quebec elections. *Canadian Journal of Political Science* 6: 638–55. [CrossRef]

Palda, Kristian. 1975. The Effect of Expenditures on Political Success. *Journal of Law and Economics* 18: 745–71. [CrossRef]

Payne, Marissa. 2014. Five sad and shocking facts about World Cup corruption in Brazil. *The Washington Post*, May 12.

Posner, Richard. 1975. The social costs of monopoly and regulations. *Journal of Political Economy* 83: 807–27. [CrossRef]

Rogers, James. 2002. Free Riding in State Legislatures. *Public Choice* 113: 59–76. [CrossRef]

Samuels, David. 2002. Pork barreling is not credit claiming of advertising: Campaign finance and the sources of the personal vote in Brazil. *The Journal of Politics* 64: 845–63. [CrossRef]

Schneider, Mark, and Paul Teske. 1992. Toward a theory of the political entrepreneur: Evidence from local government. *American Political Science Review* 85: 737–47. [CrossRef]

Sobel, Russell, and Thomas Garrett. 2002. On the measurement of rent seeking and its social opportunity cost. *Public Choice* 112: 115–36. [CrossRef]

Stratmann, Tomas. 1995. Some talk: Money in politics. A (partial) review of the literature. *Public Choice* 124: 135–56. [CrossRef]

Stratmann, Tomas. 2013. The effects of earmarks on the likelihood of reelection. *European Journal of Political Economy* 32: 341–55. [CrossRef]

Tullock, Gordon. 1967. The welfare costs of tariffs, monopolies, and theft. *Western Economic Journal* 5: 224–32. [CrossRef]

Tullock, Gordon, James Buchanan, and Robert Tollison. 1980. *Efficient Rent-Seeking in Toward a Theory of the Rent-Seeking Society*. College Station: Texas A&M Press, pp. 97–112.

Uhlaner, Carole, and Kay Schlozman. 1986. Candidate gender and congressional campaign receipts. *The Journal of Politics* 48: 30–50. [CrossRef]

Weingast, Barry. 1994. Reflections on Distributive Politics and Universalism. *Political Research Quarterly* 47: 319–27. [CrossRef]

Welch, William. 1974. The economics of campaign funds. *Public Choice* 20: 83–97. [CrossRef]

Welch, William. 1976. The effectiveness of expenditures in state legislative races. *American Politics Quarterly* 4: 333–56. [CrossRef]

economies

MDPI

Article

The Public Choice of Public Stadium Financing: Evidence from San Diego Referenda

Candon Johnson and Joshua Hall *

Center for Free Enterprise, West Virginia University, Morgantown, WV 26506, USA; cjohns77@mix.wvu.edu
* Correspondence: joshua.hall@mail.wvu.edu; Tel.: +1-304-293-7870

Received: 4 January 2019; Accepted: 19 March 2019; Published: 21 March 2019

Abstract: Local politicians and team owners frequently argue that the public financing of stadiums is important for local economic development. The sports economics literature, however, has largely found that new professional sport facilities do not generate any new net economic activity. We provide context to this literature by exploring the public choice in the public financing of stadiums. In 2016, San Diego had two ballot measures related to the San Diego Chargers. Measure C would allow officials to raise hotel taxes to pay for a new downtown stadium for the Chargers. Measure D would also raise hotel taxes, but explicitly prevented any money being spent on the Chargers. Both measures failed to receive 50% of the votes cast. We find that zip codes with a higher voter turnout were more likely to vote against both measures, highlighting the importance of the timing of referenda in limiting the ability of clearly defined groups, such as Chargers fans, to have a large influence on the voting outcome. Meanwhile, areas with more Trump voters were more likely to support higher taxes for the purpose of building the Chargers a new stadium.

Keywords: voting behavior; National Football League; Donald Trump

JEL Classification: D72; Z20

---

1. Introduction

Professional sports stadiums have been largely publicly funded in recent decades (Humphreys 2019). The public funding of stadiums is a topic of interest among economists and are of policy relevance, due to the large costs associated with building stadiums (Matheson 2019). The rationalization for public funding generally appears under the guise of economic growth, such as economic expansion and job creation. This growth does not appear, suggesting that the ability for professional sports to be a catalyst of economic growth has been overstated (Baade 1996). While professional sports are not an engine of economic growth, support for professional sports additionally comes from the potential social impacts. As stated in (Rosentraub 1996, p. 29), "Sports is too important a part of Western society for us to think that cities can exist without the teams and the events which define essential dimensions of our society and life." The public funding of stadiums has been partly responsible for stadiums returning to the city center, after decades of being located in suburban areas (Chapin 1999). The San Diego Chargers attempted to construct a stadium in downtown San Diego by securing public funding, through referenda included on the ballot during the 2016 US presidential election.

Professional sport stadiums are largely publicly funded infrastructure projects that benefit the owners and players, while providing no economic benefits to taxpayers (Baade 1996). The public funding of stadium construction, combined with the lack of evidence in favor of net economic benefits (Coates and Humphreys 2003a, 2003b, 2008), raises an important question: Why do voters support or reject public financing of professional sports stadiums? We provide insight into this question using a public choice analysis of votes on public financing for a new football stadium for the San Diego Chargers.

In 2016, on the same ballot as the US presidential election, the city of San Diego had two ballot measures related to the financing of a new convention center in San Diego and whether the San Diego Chargers of the National Football League would receive financing for a new stadium (Bonesteel 2016). These measures were known as Measure C and Measure D (San Diego Registrar of Voters 2018). Measure C was a downtown stadium initiative that would have raised the hotel occupancy tax by six percentage points, primarily to fund a new convention center and a stadium for the Chargers (Garrick 2016). Measure D was a response to Measure C being placed on the ballot (McSwain 2016). While Measure D would have raised hotel taxes to possibly fund a new convention center, it was only only by five percentage points (Showley 2016). The biggest difference, however, was that Measure D explicitly prevented any public money being used for the construction of professional sports facilities (Anderson 2016). Both measures failed at the ballot box, with both measures receiving under 45 percent 'yes' votes (Bonesteel 2016).

These two separate ballot measures, presented to San Diego voters at the same time, provide a unique opportunity to better understand voter preferences with respect to public financing of sports stadiums. In doing so, we contribute to the scholarly understanding of voter support for public financing of sports stadiums (Ahlfeldt and Maennig 2012; Brown and Paul 1999; Coates and Wicker 2015; Friedman and Mason 2004). Our findings highlight the importance of the public choice literature on electoral timing (Anzia 2011; Dunne et al. 1997; Holcombe and Kenny 2008; Meredith 2009), given that we find that a higher voter turnout is associated with fewer 'yes' votes. Having these referenda on the ballot at the same time as a Presidential election almost certainly reduced the likelihood of getting a majority of cast votes for either measure.

Our brief empirical paper proceeds as follows. Section 2 provides additional information on the San Diego ballot measures. Section 3 discusses our data and empirical approach, which builds off the public choice and sports economics literature on referendums. We present our empirical results in Section 4 and conclude in Section 5.

2. The San Diego Referenda

Founded in 1960, the Chargers played in Los Angeles for one season before moving to San Diego (Nunn and Rosentraub 1997). The team began playing in Qualcomm Stadium, now called the San Diego County Credit Union Stadium, in 1967 (Peach 2004). With an aging stadium, ranked among the worst in the NFL (Chase 2015), the Chargers pushed for a new stadium in San Diego. During the 2016 US presidential election, two measures appeared on the ballot regarding a new stadium for the San Diego Chargers (Schrotenboer 2016).

Measure C provided funding for a new stadium in downtown San Diego by raising the transient occupancy (i.e., hotel) tax six percentage points, from 10.5 to 16.5, with five-sixths of the fund being used for the new convention center and stadium (Schrotenboer 2016). A two percentage point assessment, which hotels charge to fund a tourism marketing district, would be eliminated (Lewis 2015). One-sixth of the tax increase would be placed into an existing San Diego Tourism and Marketing Fund. The tax increase would be decreased to three percentage points if the construction of the new stadium was not completed within two years, following the last home game in Qualcomm Stadium, or if all city bonds are re-paid, among other reasons. The stadium would seat 65,000 and be expandable to 75,000; the convention center would contain over 300,000 square feet of meeting space (Hazinski and Cotte 2016). The measure would fund $1.15 of $1.8 billion of the cost of stadium initiative for land acquisition, construction of the convention center, and construction of the integrated joint use portion. The remaining $650 million would be allotted to the construction of the stadium, being privately funded by the Chargers. In addition to the $650 million contribution, the Chargers would be required to give a 30-year commitment to play in the stadium, thus committing to the city of San Diego (Nelson 2016).

Arguments given in favor of Measure C included: No new taxes imposed on San Diego residents, the city overseeing the stadiums design, construction, and operations, and jobs will be created (Nelson 2016). The amount of jobs created were claimed to include 17,000 during construction, as well as 3000 permanent jobs (Sklar 2016). Arguments against included: Taxes should be used for other purposes, worsening San Diego's parking and traffic situation, and hurting tourism in San Diego (Hazinski and Cotte 2016). Sports have been shown to worsen traffic conditions, and the new stadium would be moving into an already congested area (Humphreys and Pyun 2018). Also, large conventions, such as the San Diego Comic-Con, were opposed to the measure (Cate et al. 2016). The Comic-Con preferred an expansion of the current convention center in San Diego, instead of a new convention center in a different area of San Diego.

Measure D would utilize an increase in transient occupancy taxes to fund a downtown convention center, but not a stadium, prohibiting the use of public funds on construction of a new stadium without a public vote (Anderson 2016). Hotels with 30 or more rooms, recreational vehicle parks, and campgrounds would see an increase of five percentage points, while hotels with fewer than 30 rooms would see an increase of 3.5 percentage points (San Diego City Attorney 2016). The measure would also allow for the sale of Qualcomm Stadium to one or more colleges or universities in San Diego, or the San Diego River Conservancy. While a stadium was not to be funded by the measure, it would allow for a sports facility to be combined with the convention center. It could also permit a new facility to be built in Mission Valley, the area where Qualcomm Stadium was located.

Ultimately, both measures failed to convince a majority of voters that they should be passed. Measure C garnered only 44% support and Measure D also failed, with only 41% support (Garrick 2016). Across the city, however, there were very different vote totals, suggesting that some concerns (such as traffic) might have been more salient for some voters than others. With the measures failing, the Chargers found another option by moving to Los Angeles, beginning in the 2017 NFL season (Pelissero 2017). Following the completion of the Los Angeles Stadium at Hollywood park, the Chargers and Rams will share the privately-funded venue (Chavez 2018).

3. Data and Empirical Approach

To better understand why San Diego voters vetoed both measures related to the San Diego Chargers (and a new convention center), we employ an empirical median voter model (Holcombe 1989). This model has been used extensively, in the sports economics literature, to better understand the factors influencing public support for stadium financing and mega-events, such as the Olympics. For example, Ahlfeldt and Maennig (2012) showed that voting in Munich, Germany for an Allianz Arena exhibited a Not In My Backyard (NIMBY) character, where voters further away from the stadium construction site were more supportive. Coates and Humphreys (2006) and Horn et al. (2015) showed that voters in closer proximity to the stadium site were more supportive of the stadium being built. Coates and Wicker (2015) found that areas with high rates of unemployment tended to be in favor of putting in a bid for the Olympics.

As is typical in empirical median voter models (Hall and Karadas 2018; Matti and Zhou 2017), a linear regression is used with the percentage of voters that voted yes as the dependent variable. Measures C and D both had similar voting outcomes in aggregate, but are different at the sub-city level. The linear model estimated is:

$$VoterSupport_i = \beta_1 Population_i + \beta_2 Voting_i + e_i, \tag{1}$$

where the dependent variable *VoterSupport* can represent the percentage of 'yes' votes on Measure C, percentage of 'yes' votes on Measure D, or the difference between support for Measure C and Measure

D. Vote data was retrieved from San Diego Registrar of Voters (2018) at the voting precinct level, and aggregated up to the zip code level using precinct maps from the County of San Diego.[1]

Population includes various demographic characteristics representing the preferences of the median voter. These variables were chosen based on the previous literature and concerns raised in public debate over the measures. Variables include per capita income; population (log); median home value; the percentage of the population that is foreign-born, white, and male; a dummy variable, equal to one if the zip code contained the proposed stadium/convention center or was adjacent to it; and average commute time.

All demographic data was obtained from the American Community Survey (ACS 2011–2015 five-year data profiles) at the zip code level. Per capita income, median home value, and population are used to control for zip code size and income differences. Foreign-born population is included, due to San Diego's proximity to the border between Mexico and the United States, and potential preference differences for professional football versus other sports, such as soccer. The motivation for average commute time comes from the work of Humphreys and Pyun (2018) on congestion, related to professional baseball games. Proximity is used because of its usage in similar research on stadium finance voting and the potential externalities related to living near a professional sports stadium (Coates and Humphreys 2006). Percentage of the population that is white and male provide further demographic controls, possibly related to preferences for professional football. The correlation between more % male and proximity to the proposed stadium is 0.52.

Voting includes the percentage of voters who voted for Donald Trump in the presidential election and voter turnout rate, both from the same time as Measures C and D. These two additional variables, from San Diego Registrar of Voters (2018), were added to address voter preferences and engagement. The percentage of the votes for Donald Trump in the presidential election is included to control for any possible partisan views on public financing of sports stadiums. The variation on this variable across zip codes ranges from 9.41% to 46.72%. Voter turnout—that is, the percentage of registered voters that voted in the election—is added to deal with differences in voter engagement and interest across zip codes. Voter turnout is correlated with per capita income at 0.76. Voter turnout can be important, due to the fact that low turnout can lead to a greater special interest influence (Dunne et al. 1997; Meredith 2009). Summary statistics are shown in Table 1.

Table 1. Summary Statistics.

	Mean	Std. Dev.	Min	Max
Percent Voted Yes on Measure C	43.90	6.19	32.90	55.90
Percent Voted Yes on Measure D	41.18	5.22	33.66	51.72
Difference Between Measure C & D Support	2.72	6.74	−10.68	17.91
Per Capita Income (000s)	38.54	16.40	12.11	79.00
Proximity	0.21	0.41	0.00	1.00
Population (log)	10.21	0.74	7.31	11.09
Percent of Population that is Foreign-born	24.67	9.97	6.10	45.00
Commute Time	23.31	2.58	19.20	28.30
Median Home Value (000s)	544.32	244.30	253.20	1200.00
Percent of Population that is White	67.23	16.89	22.40	91.40
Percent of Population that is Male	50.27	2.97	45.30	59.20
Percent Voted for Donald Trump	28.08	9.97	9.41	46.72
Voter Turnout Rate	80.65	6.45	63.63	89.86
Observations	34			

---

[1] Voting precincts do not perfectly map onto zip code boundaries, but very few precincts spanned multiple zip codes, thus measurement error is minimized.

4. Empirical Results

Table 2 presents the results of our ordinary least-squares regressions, with percentage of 'yes' votes on Measure C as the dependent variable. The regressions are broken into three important parts. In column (1), the baseline results include population characteristics. Characteristics include population, median home value, per capita income, and the percentage of the population that is male, white, or foreign-born. This baseline reveals no significant results for any of the population characteristics at conventional levels. Proximity and commute time are added in column (2). Average commute time appears as a positive and significant variable. This is surprising, as traffic congestion was cited as a reason to oppose the measure, and Humphreys and Pyun (2018) showed that congestion is increased by professional sports. More congestion would presumably increase average commute time, but perhaps areas with longer commute times preferred to see the stadium located downtown and not elsewhere in the city.

Table 2. Regression Results: Percent Voted Yes on Measure C.

Variable	(1)	(2)	(3)
Population (log)	−1.56725	−1.37962	−0.18548
	(−0.98)	(−1.00)	(−0.20)
Percent of Population that is Foreign-born	0.25765	0.11438	0.10184
	(1.80)	(0.87)	(1.01)
Percent of Population that is White	−0.01542	−0.00323	0.12049 *
	(−0.19)	(−0.04)	(2.38)
Percent of Population that is Male	−0.00089	0.58415	0.53991
	(−0.00)	(1.48)	(1.69)
Median Home Value (000s)	−0.00665	−0.00653	−0.00781
	(−0.58)	(−0.65)	(−1.16)
Per Capita Income (000s)	0.00239	0.02519	0.14425
	(0.01)	(0.17)	(1.13)
Proximity		−3.33682	−1.91676
		(−1.30)	(−1.14)
Commute Time		1.33486 **	0.98432 **
		(3.18)	(3.29)
Percent Voted for Donald Trump			0.46407 ***
			(5.62)
Voter Turnout Rate			−0.92239 **
			(−3.75)
Observations	34	34	34
R^2	0.303	0.516	0.817

Notes: *: $p < 0.1$; **: $p < 0.05$; ***: $p < 0.01$. *t* statistics in parentheses. Constant included, but not reported.

In the final column of Table 2, variables regarding political affiliation and voter turnout rate are added. Each voting variable is significant, with zip codes with higher support for Trump being more likely to support Measure C. A higher voter turnout rate was associated with less support of Measure C.

Support for Measure D was tested using the same process as Measure C, with results being displayed in Table 3. The baseline results for Measure D support indicate that the percent of the population that is foreign-born and the percent male are significant and positive, while per capita income is significant and negative. These results hold when adding proximity and commute time in column (2), but lose significance when adding voting variables. Upon adding the voting variable in column (3), voting on Measure D is very different; with the only similarity being that zip codes with higher voter turnout were less likely to vote for the measure. Areas with more Trump voters were less likely to vote in support of Measure D, all other things being equal. This is surprising, given that Measure D was colloquially known as the "Citizens' plan" for its seemingly pro-taxpayer provisions and constraints on public financing of stadium construction, especially as compared to Measure C. However, Measure D still involved a tax increase and expansion of the convention center, which are two of the reasons why it was opposed by the San Diego County Taxpayers Association.

When compared to voting on Measure C, our results suggest that Trump voters were against tax increases for these public projects; but, if taxes were going to be raised, they wanted the Chargers to be part of the deal. That is why it is important to remember that these coefficients represent the effect of the variable holding everything else constant and one of the biggest differences between Measure C and Measure D was the restriction on public funding of sports stadiums without explicit voter approval through a referendum. The final interesting thing to note from the vote on Measure D is that proximity to the expanded convention center/home of the Chargers under Measure C is negatively related to voting 'yes' on Measure D.

Table 3. Regression Results: Percent Voted Yes on Measure D.

	(1)	(2)	(3)
Population (log)	−0.621	−0.547	−0.504
	(−0.73)	(−0.64)	(−1.22)
Percent of Population that is Foreign-born	0.257 **	0.217 *	0.038
	(3.36)	(2.68)	(0.86)
Percent of Population that is White	0.049	0.049	−0.011
	(1.11)	(1.10)	(−0.51)
Percent of Population that is Male	0.602 **	0.719 **	0.072
	(3.06)	(2.95)	(0.51)
Median Home Value (000s)	0.001	0.001	−0.005
	(0.21)	(0.18)	(−1.76)
Per Capita Income (000s)	−0.213 *	−0.201 *	0.020
	(−2.31)	(−2.15)	(0.35)
Proximity		−0.322	−1.677 *
		(−0.20)	(−2.24)
Commute Time		0.372	0.125
		(1.43)	(0.93)
Percent Voted for Donald Trump			−0.316 ***
			(−8.57)
Voter Turnout Rate			−0.258 *
			(−2.36)
Observations	34	34	34
R^2	0.719	0.740	0.949

Notes: *: $p < 0.1$; **: $p < 0.05$; ***: $p < 0.01$. t statistics in parentheses. Constant included, but not reported.

With results differing between support for Measure C and Measure D, the within-zip code difference between voting on Measures C and D is tested. The difference between support for Measures C and D possibly captures fans of the San Diego Chargers. The results shown in Table 4 indicate that areas with longer commute times had a greater differential (votes for Measure C higher than Measure D).

Given that the reversion level was the Chargers possibly staying in Qualcomm, instead of leaving for Los Angeles, this could reflect that many suburban commuters did not want to commute downtown to attend Chargers games. Areas with a higher percentage of white voters had a preference for Measure C over D, all other things being equal. Trump voters overwhelmingly preferred C to D. Finally, zip codes with a higher voter turnout saw the difference between votes on Measure C and D shrink. Given the negative coefficients on voter turnout in the Measure C and Measure D specifications, this finding seems to confirm that higher voter turnout is bad for publicly-funded stadiums. This is consistent with the literature on low voter turnout being better for clearly-defined groups, such as Chargers fans (Anzia 2011; Dunne et al. 1997; Meredith 2009).

Table 4. Regression Results: Difference Between Measure C and Measure D.

	(1)	(2)	(3)
Population (log)	−0.946	−0.832	0.319
	(−0.50)	(−0.45)	(0.38)
Percent of Population that is Foreign-born	0.000	−0.103	0.064
	(0.00)	(−0.59)	(0.69)
Percent of Population that is White	−0.064	−0.052	0.132 **
	(−0.66)	(−0.54)	(2.86)
Percent of Population that is Male	−0.603	−0.135	0.467
	(−1.38)	(−0.26)	(1.60)
Median Home Value (000s)	−0.008	−0.008	−0.003
	(−0.58)	(−0.57)	(−0.41)
Per Capita Income (000s)	0.215	0.226	0.125
	(1.05)	(1.12)	(1.07)
Proximity		−3.015	−0.240
		(−0.88)	(−0.16)
Commute Time		0.963	0.860 **
		(1.72)	(3.15)
Percent Voted for Donald Trump			0.780 ***
			(10.37)
Voter Turnout Rate			−0.664 **
			(−2.97)
Observations	34	34	34
R^2	0.172	0.272	0.872

Notes: **: $p < 0.05$; ***: $p < 0.01$. *t* statistics in parentheses. Constant included, but not reported.

The results in Table 4 highlight the importance of the timing of the referenda. Had the referenda been included in an election that induced a lower voter turnout rate than the 2016 US presidential election, San Diego Chargers fans could have dictated the outcome of the results.

5. Conclusions

The San Diego Chargers are now the Los Angeles Chargers. This is, in no small part, due to the failure of the Chargers to secure public financing for a new stadium in downtown San Diego through Measure C. Using zip code-level voting data, we find that areas with more Trump voters were in favor of public subsidies for the Chargers. When looking at the vote on Measure D which prevented public funding from going to sports stadiums, we find that Trump voters were against higher taxes for only an expanded convention center.

Our other important finding is the importance of voter turnout. Zip codes with higher turnout were less likely to vote for Measures C and D. Dunne et al. (1997), among others, showed how low voter turnout enhanced the ability of special interests to get their preferred policies passed at the ballot box. Our results are consistent with this literature and highlight how the timing of these measures—that is, being at the same time as a Presidential election—likely depressed the percentage voting in favor of each measure. Given that Measure C required the approval of two-thirds of the voters to become law (a requirement in California for tax increases that have a specific use), the higher voter turnout likely influenced the outcome. In other settings, however, the timing of stadium funding referenda might matter for the eventual outcome.

Author Contributions: Writing—original draft, C.J.; Writing—review & editing, J.H.

Funding: This research received no external funding.

Conflicts of Interest: The authors receive no funding for this paper. During his career, Joshua Hall has received funding from the Charles Koch Foundation, the Thomas Smith Foundation, the Alliance for Markets Solutions, the Institute for Humane Studies, Liberty Fund, and over 30 colleges and universities. Candon Johnson has received funding from the Institute for Humane Studies through the Hayek Fund.

References

Ahlfeldt, Gabriel, and Wolfgang Maennig. 2012. Voting on a NIMBY facility: Proximity cost of an "iconic" stadium. *Urban Affairs Review* 48: 205–37. [CrossRef]

Anderson, Erik. 2016. Measure D: Citizens' plan coming up short. *KBPS*, November 9.

Anzia, Sarah F. 2011. Election timing and the electoral influence of interest groups. *Journal of Politics* 73: 412–27. [CrossRef]

Baade, Robert A. 1996. Professional sports as catalysts for metropolitan economic development. *Journal of Urban Affairs* 18: 1–17. [CrossRef]

Bonesteel, Matt. 2016. Chargers' stadium vote fails miserably, clouding future in San Diego. *San Diego Union-Tribune*, November 9.

Brown, Clyde, and David M. Paul. 1999. Local organized interests and the 1996 Cincinnati sports stadia tax referendum. *Journal of Sport and Social Issues* 23: 218–37. [CrossRef]

Cate, Chris, April Boling, and Julie Meier Wright. 2016. How a Chargers stadium jeopardizes San Diego Comic-Con. *San Diego Union-Tribune*, August 25.

Chapin, Tim. 1999. The political economy of sports facility location: An end-of-the-century review and assessment. *Marquette Sports LJ* 10: 361.

Chase, Chris. 2015. Ranking the best and worst NFL stadiums, from no. 1 (Lambeau) to 31 (Soldier). *USA Today*, October 16.

Chavez, Chris. 2018. Report: Rams, Chargers stadium to cost almost $5 billion. *Sports Illustrated*, March 27.

Coates, Dennis, and Brad R. Humphreys. 2003a. The effect of professional sports on earnings and employment in the services and retail sectors in us cities. *Regional Science and Urban Economics* 33: 175–98. [CrossRef]

Coates, Dennis, and Brad R. Humphreys. 2003b. Professional sports facilities, franchises and urban economic development. *Public Finance and Management* 3: 335–57.

Coates, Dennis, and Brad R. Humphreys. 2006. Proximity benefits and voting on stadium and arena subsidies. *Journal of Urban Economics* 59: 285–99. [CrossRef]

Coates, Dennis, and Brad R. Humphreys. 2008. Do economists reach a conclusion on subsidies for sports franchises, stadiums, and mega-events? *Econ Journal Watch* 5: 294–315.

Coates, Dennis, and Pamela Wicker. 2015. Why were voters against the 2022 Munich Winter Olympics in a referendum? *International Journal of Sport Finance* 10: 267.

Dunne, Stephanie, W Robert Reed, and James Wilbanks. 1997. Endogenizing the median voter: Public choice goes to school. *Public Choice* 93: 99–118. [CrossRef]

Friedman, Michael T., and Daniel S. Mason. 2004. A stakeholder approach to understanding economic development decision making: Public subsidies for professional sport facilities. *Economic Development Quarterly* 18: 236–54. [CrossRef]

Garrick, David. 2016. SD stadium measures both trailing badly. *San Diego Union-Tribune*, November 9.

Hall, Joshua C., and Serkan Karadas. 2018. Tuition increases Geaux away? Evidence from voting on Louisiana's amendment 2. *Applied Economics Letters* 25: 924–27. [CrossRef]

Hazinski, Thomas, and Jorge Cotte. 2016. *Report on Proposed Joint Development of a Stadium–Convention Center: Chargers Stadium–Convention Center*. Chicago: HVS Convention, Sports & Entertainment Facilities Consulting.

Holcombe, Randall G. 1989. The median voter model in public choice theory. *Public Choice* 61: 115–25. [CrossRef]

Holcombe, Randall G., and Lawrence W. Kenny. 2008. Does restricting choice in referenda enable governments to spend more? *Public Choice* 136: 87–101. [CrossRef]

Horn, Brady P., Michael Cantor, and Rodney Fort. 2015. Proximity and voting for professional sporting stadiums: The pattern of support for the Seahawk stadium referendum. *Contemporary Economic Policy* 33: 678–88. [CrossRef]

Humphreys, Brad. 2019. Should the construction of new professional sports facilities be subsidized? *Journal of Policy Analysis & Management* 38: 264–70.

Humphreys, Brad R., and Hyunwoong Pyun. 2018. Professional sporting events and traffic: Evidence from US cities. *Journal of Regional Science* 58: 869–86. [CrossRef]

Lewis, Scott. 2015. The genius of–and the problem with–the Briggs hotel-tax overhaul. *Voice of San Diego*, November 10.

Matheson, Victor. 2019. Is there a case for subsidizing sports stadiums? *Journal of Policy Analysis & Management* 38: 271–77.

Matti, Joshua, and Yang Zhou. 2017. The political economy of Brexit: Explaining the vote. *Applied Economics Letters* 24: 1131–34. [CrossRef]

McSwain, Dan. 2016. San Diego hoteliers find a little to like, plenty to hate with Measure D. *San Diego Union-Tribune*, November 4.

Meredith, Marc. 2009. The strategic timing of direct democracy. *Economics & Politics* 21: 159–77.

Nelson, Kevin. 2016. Measure C goes to the ballot for a major vote. *The Vista (University of Central Oklahoma)*, October 6.

Nunn, Samuel, and Mark S. Rosentraub. 1997. Sports wars: Suburbs and center cities in a zero-sum game. *Journal of Sport and Social Issues* 21: 65–82. [CrossRef]

Peach, James. 2004. Thorstein veblen, ty cobb, and the evolution of an institution. *Journal of Economic Issues* 38: 326–37. [CrossRef]

Pelissero, Tom. 2017. Awkward spot, awkward solution for Chargers in LA move. *USA Today*, January 12.

Rosentraub, Mark S. 1996. Does the emperor have new clothes? A reply to robert j. baade. *Journal of Urban Affairs* 18: 23–31. [CrossRef]

San Diego City Attorney. 2016. *City's Attorney's Impartial Analysis and Fiscal Impact Statement*. San Diego: San Diego Registrar of Voters.

San Diego Registrar of Voters. 2018. *Election Results*. San Diego: San Diego Registrar of Voters.

Schrotenboer, Brent. 2016. Stadium vote may define Chargers' future; two-thirds needed to raise hotel tax, but getting a majority would bode well. *USA Today*, November 8.

Showley, Roger. 2016. Taxpayers group opposes Briggs hotel-tax hike. *San Diego Union Tribune*, August 23.

Sklar, Debbie. 2016. Stadium ballot arguments focus on jobs, future events, tourism and priorities. *Times of San Diego*, August 26.

economies MDPI

Article

Glass Houses and Friends-and-Neighbors Voting: An Exploratory Analysis of the Impact of Political Scandal on Localism

Franklin G. Mixon, Jr.

Center for Economic Education, Columbus State University, Columbus, GA 31907, USA;
mixon_franklin@columbusstate.edu

Received: 4 July 2018; Accepted: 27 August 2018; Published: 3 September 2018

Abstract: The 2017 U.S. Senate Special Election in Alabama, which was decided on 12 December 2017, was one of the most contentious and scandal-laden political campaigns in recent memory. The Republican candidate, Roy Moore, gained notoriety during the 2017 campaign when a number of women alleged to national media that as teenagers they were subject to sexual advances by Moore, who was then in his early 30s and serving as a local assistant district attorney. The process and results of this particular election provide the heretofore unexamined impact of political scandal on localism or friends-and-neighbors voting in political contests. Based on data from the 2017 special election in Alabama, econometric results presented here suggest that a candidate who is embroiled in political scandal suffers an erosion in the usual friends-and-neighbors effect on his or her local vote share. In this particular case, the scandal hanging over Moore eroded all of the friends-and-neighbors effect that would have been expected (e.g., about five percentage points) in his home county, as well as about 40% of the advantage Moore had at home over his opponent in terms of constituent political ideology.

Keywords: friends-and-neighbors voting; localism in elections; reputation capital; political scandal

JEL Classification: D70; D72

1. Introduction

The 2017 U.S. Senate Special Election in Alabama, which was decided on 12 December 2017, encompassed one of the most contentious and scandal-laden political campaigns in recent memory. The election was won by the Democratic candidate, Doug Jones, a lawyer from Birmingham. Jones defeated Roy Moore, the Republican candidate from Gadsden, who had previously served as Chief Justice of the Alabama Supreme Court. Given the political intrigue that accompanied the campaign, during which Moore faced accusations of sexual improprieties, the process and results of this particular 2017 election provide an opportunity to explore the impact of political scandal on friends-and-neighbors voting (or localism) in election contests. More specifically, the present study fills a void in the public choice literature on localism (e.g., see Lewis-Beck and Rice 1983; Rice and Macht 1987; Kjar and Laband 2002; Disarro et al. 2007; Mixon 2013) by exploring how political scandal impacts the friends-and-neighbors advantage that typically accrues to local candidates in situations not involving political scandal.

Aside from the possibility that political scandal does not impact friends-and-neighbors voting, scandals, such as that faced by Moore, may lead to intensified support for the local candidate, as his or her constituents refuse to believe accusations of scandal and instead rally behind the candidate. On the other hand, local constituents may find allegations of scandal credible, and as a result they may opt to support the local candidate's rival in an effort to mitigate the higher expected agency costs from electing an untrustworthy representative. Results from a decomposition approach presented in this study suggest that the latter effect prevailed in the 2017 U.S. Senate Special Election in Alabama, as the political scandal that hung over Moore during the final weeks of the campaign eroded all the friends-and-neighbors effect that would have been expected (e.g., about five percentage points) in his home county. Moreover, in this case, the harshness of the political scandal reduced, by about 40%, the advantage Moore had at home over his opponent in terms of constituent political ideology.

2. Conceptual Framework and Prior Literature

Before turning to the empirical results mentioned above, this section of the study provides both a conceptual framework for studying the impact of political scandal on friends-and-neighbors voting and a review of prior studies on localism in elections. The conceptual framework includes a brief discussion of the agency costs of representative democracy, while the review of prior studies focuses on the stream of literature that includes estimates of the friends-and-neighbors effect in electoral contests in the U.S.

2.1. Conceptual Framework

As Kjar and Laband (2002) assert, voters reduce the agency costs of representative democracy simply by electing family members into office or by voting for individuals who have lived for many years in their respective political jurisdictions.[1] Home grown candidates offer an advantage to voters as they have relatively larger endowments of human capital in the form of information about the conditions of the local political jurisdiction and of the electorate's desires than do more distant candidates (Faith and Tollison 1983; Kjar and Laband 2002).[2] Moreover, voters face lower search costs with regard to the discovery of candidates' attributes in the case of local candidates. Lastly, given that "firing" representatives is costly, if not impossible (e.g., see Mixon 2000), voters will rationally prefer candidates with longstanding ties to the district as these candidates implicitly put more human and other capital at risk as a Klein and Leffler (1981) type of performance bond than do non-local candidates with fewer ties to the political jurisdiction (Kjar and Laband 2002). As Kjar and Laband (2002) assert, voters understand and appreciate the implied efficiency of casting their ballots in favor of a candidate who has much to lose locally from nonperformance in his or her capacity as an elected official.

In terms of political scandal, such as that faced by Moore in 2017, it may be the case that a candidate's friends and neighbors are unfazed by the allegations, and the effect of localism in this situation is similar to that in elections that are untainted by political scandal. Alternatively, the candidate's constituents may be unwilling to believe the allegations and, in response to the scandal, intensify their support for the local candidate. Thus, in this case, the scandal augments the traditional friends-and-neighbors effect. Lastly, it is also possible that the candidate's constituents do believe the allegations and that they respond by rallying behind his or her political opponent in an attempt to either punish the candidate, in the case of an incumbent, for betraying their trust, or to prevent the candidate, in the case of a challenger, from reaching a position from which to cause them to suffer political harm and/or to engage in costly monitoring efforts (i.e., to be exposed to agency costs).

2.2. Prior Literature

Academic research on localism in politics began with the pioneering work of Key and Heard (1949), and extends to a series of more recent empirical studies. In the first of these, Lewis-Beck and Rice (1983) find, using data from U.S. presidential elections from 1884 through to 1980, that candidates receive four percentage points more support from voters in their home states than they do in other states. Later, Rice and Macht (1987) come close to replicating this result in their analysis of U.S. gubernatorial

---

[1] See Sass (1992) for an excellent discussion of the costs associated with constitutional choice in representative democracy.
[2] Alternatively, problems associated with asymmetric information are not as severe for friends and neighbors (i.e., local constituents) as they are for more distant constituents.

and Senate elections from 1976 through to 1982, as county-level data in that study suggest a friends-and-neighbors voting effect of about 3.7 percentage points. These two early studies laid the foundation for a twenty-first century renaissance in the academic literature on friends-and-neighbors voting that includes the study by Kjar and Laband (2002). These authors examined election returns from the 1998 election for Alabama's Third Congressional District, finding a friends-and-neighbors voting effect ranging from 8.2 to 12.4 percentage points of the overall vote share. These numbers are larger than that found in Lewis-Beck and Rice (1983), and likely reflect a greater "closeness" between the candidates and constituencies associated with elections in U.S. Congressional districts vis-à-vis those held statewide.

As indicated in Table 1, the study by Kjar and Laband (2002) is followed by a series of studies of U.S. presidential elections.[3] Mixon and Tyrone (2004), for example, find, in their examination of U.S. presidential elections from 1972 through to 2000, a friends-and-neighbors voting effect ranging from 5.2 to 6.7 percentage points, while Disarro et al. (2007) present a percentage point estimate of 5.1 in their analysis of election returns data from 1880 through to 2004. Additional analyses of U.S. presidential elections from 1972 through to 2004 by Mixon et al. (2008) and Kahane (2009) produce percentage point estimates of the home state effect ranging from 4.9 to 7.7, and from 2.4 to 9.3, respectively. Lastly, Mixon (2013) takes a novel approach to the subject by exploring home grown-ness in the 1940 and 1944 presidential elections using countywide returns from Georgia, where incumbent U.S. President Franklin D. Roosevelt spent significant portions of his time in Warm Springs seeking warm water therapy for polio. That study finds that in Meriwether County, where Warm Springs is located, and in its bordering counties, Roosevelt's vote share was about 7.8 percentage points greater than it was in Georgia's other counties.

Table 1. Friends-and-neighbors effect estimates from prior studies.

Study	Subject	Friends-and-Neighbors Effect [a]
Lewis-Beck and Rice (1983)	U.S. Presidential Elections, 1884–1980	4.0
Rice and Macht (1987)	U.S. Gubernatorial and Senate Elections, 1976–1982	3.7
Kjar and Laband (2002)	Alabama's 3rd Congressional District, 1998	8.2–12.4
Mixon and Tyrone (2004)	U.S. Presidential Elections, 1972–2000	5.2–6.7
Disarro et al. (2007)	U.S. Presidential Elections, 1880–2004	5.1
Kahane (2009)	U.S. Presidential Elections, 1972–2004	2.4–9.3
Mixon et al. (2008)	U.S. Presidential Elections, 1972–2004	4.9–7.7
Mixon (2013)	U.S. Presidential Elections, 1940–1944	7.8

[a] Friends-and neighbors effect is measured in percentage points.

The current study follows Mixon (2013) in extending the literature on friends-and-neighbors voting by analyzing election returns from a statewide race—that of the 2017 U.S. Senate Special Election in Alabama—pitting Republican candidate, Roy Moore, against Democratic candidate, Doug Jones. Of interest here is the intense national focus on the scandal in Moore's personal life, including various allegations of sexual misconduct, which, in some cases, involved a minor. One would expect that the electoral boost from friends-and-neighbors support, or localism, is eroded by political scandal, as some, if not many, of a candidate's local political supporters abandon him or her in response to their concerns related to facing higher agency costs. Thus, if one takes the friends-and-neighbors effect estimated by Mixon et al. (2008) of five percentage points (see Table 1) as a baseline, one would expect political scandal would reduce that to something less than five percentage points. Quantifying this expected erosion is the aim of this study. Before turning to this analysis, the next section of the study offers a primer on the scandalous nature of this particular political contest.

---

[3] As the current study tests elements of friends and neighbors voting in a U.S. election, this particular section focuses only on empirical studies that examine U.S. elections.

3. Alabama's 2017 U.S. Senate Special Election: A Primer

Shortly after taking the oath as U.S. Attorney General in 2017, Alabamian, Jeff Sessions', U.S. Senate seat was turned over to Alabama Attorney General, Luther Strange, and preliminary discussions began regarding a special election to replace Sessions on a permanent basis (Smilowitz 2017). That decision was made by Alabama's Republican Governor, Kay Ivey, in late April of 2017 when 12 December 2017 was chosen as the date for the special election (Andone 2017). Less than one week after Ivey's announcement, Roy Moore, a resident of Etowah County and Chief Justice of Alabama's Supreme Court, resigned from his position and announced his intention to compete against Strange, who, in December of 2016, stated his desire to permanently replace Sessions, even before being nominated to hold the position on a temporary basis (Cason 2016, 2017).[4]

The Republican contest garnered national attention throughout the period leading up to the primary election in September of 2017. That process culminated in an election-eve rally in Alabama, and Moore's victory in the Republican primary (Borchers 2017). Any celebration by Moore and his campaign team was short-lived, however, as Leigh Corfman, a 53 year old customer service representative at a payday loan business, alleged to national media in early November 2017 that as a 14 year old she met Moore, who was in his early 30s and working as a local assistant district attorney, for the first time outside of a courtroom in Etowah County, Alabama. That meeting prompted what Corfman alleged was initiation by Moore of a sexual encounter (McCrummen et al. 2017). Corfman's was not the only allegation of such behavior, as three other women, who were between the ages of 16 and 18 at the time Moore was in his early 30s, told *The Washington Post* during the weeks leading up to Corfman's allegation that they too had been pursued by Moore (McCrummen et al. 2017).

By 5 December 2017, one week before the special election, at least nine women had accused Moore of inappropriate sexual behavior (Quinn 2017), causing Moore's candidacy to unravel. That trend continued through to 12 December 2017, when Doug Jones, a resident of Jefferson County and an Alabama attorney who had (relatively) quietly won the Democratic primary, defeated Moore in the general election by almost 22,000 votes, taking 50.8% of the major party vote share in a Republican-leaning state. On 28 December 2017, Ivey certified the special election results, nullifying a legal challenge by Moore, who had not conceded the race (Blinder 2017).

4. Econometric Model and Estimation Results

4.1. Econometric Model

This study takes an approach to modeling friends-and-neighbors voting that is similar to that in the series of studies, beginning with Kjar and Laband (2002), presented in Table 1. As such, the specification below:

$$\text{Moore Vote Share}_i = \alpha + \beta_1 \log \text{Per Capita Income}_i + \beta_2 \% \text{ College Graduate}_i + \beta_3 \% \text{Poverty}_i + \beta_4 \% \text{ Black}_i + \beta_5 \text{Electorate Ideology}_i + \beta_6 \text{Moore Home}_i + \varepsilon_i, \tag{1}$$

where the dependent variable, *Moore Vote Share*$_i$, is equal to the two-party vote share (percent) in Alabama county *i* captured by the Republican candidate, Roy Moore. This specification is proposed as a foundation for a decomposition approach that is discussed later in the study. Among the regressors in (1) are four demographic variables—log *Per Capita Income*$_i$, % *College Graduate*$_i$, % *Poverty*$_i$, and % *Black*$_i$. The first of these is the natural logarithm of per capita income in the county, *i*, the second is the percent county *i*'s population holding a college degree, while the third is the percent of county *i*'s population living at or below the poverty level. Given the Democratic Party's traditional affiliation with working

---

[4] That nomination process was further contested when, in mid-May of 2017, U.S. Representative Mo Brooks announced his candidacy (Hrynkiw 2017).

class voters, estimates of β_1, β_2, and β_3 are expected to be negatively signed. Support for Democratic candidates among black voters is also traditionally high, and more so in the case of this particular election given that a victory by Moore would be seen to further advance U.S. President Donald Trump's political agenda. As such, *Black$_i$*, which is the percent of county *i*'s population that is accounted for by black residents, is expected to retain a negatively-signed parameter estimate.

Next, as a measure of political leaning of the constituents of the county, *i*, *Electorate Ideology$_i$* is included on the right-hand side of (1). This variable is equal to the 2016 countywide vote share (percent) for incumbent U.S. Senator, Richard Shelby, a Republican, and it serves as a baseline for how conservative the voters are in a given county, *i*. As such, it is expected that the parameter estimate for β_5 will be positive as conservative Alabamians are more likely to support Moore, ceteris paribus. Finally, *Moore Home$_i$* is a dummy variable equal to 1 if county, *i*, represents Moore's home county, and 0 otherwise. As indicated earlier, the estimate for β_6 will be greater than zero if local constituents are unfazed by the allegations of scandal, or if they are unwilling to believe such allegations and, in response, intensify their support for Moore. This study posits, however, that the allegations were of such an extreme nature (i.e., inappropriate, and perhaps illegal, sexual behavior) that they were believed by a large portion of the local constituency, who became distrustful of Moore and concerned about the additional agency costs he might impose on them as a U.S. Representative. These concerns, coupled with the smaller gap on a unidimensional ideological spectrum between Republicans and Democrats in a state, such as Alabama (as opposed to states, such as New York or California), it is expected that the estimate of β_6 will be negative, as local constituents turn to Jones.

4.2. Estimation Results

To estimate (1), data from Alabama's 67 counties are collected.[5] Summary statistics (i.e., means and standard deviations) are presented in Table 2. Although not included, the mean of *Moore Vote Share$_i$* is 54.9, with a standard deviation of 19.2. In terms of the regressors, the average income across the 67 Alabama's counties is about $40,000, approximately 16.5% of each county's population holds a college degree, while about 22% of the typical county's residents live at or beneath the poverty level. Additionally, about 28.5% of the typical county's population is accounted for by black residents. Based on the political ideology variable, the state's voters lean conservative in national elections. As indicated in Table 2, the typical countywide election in 2016 produced about a 65% vote share for the Republican candidate, Richard Shelby.

Table 2. Summary statistics and Pearson correlation coefficients.

Variables	Means [S.D.]	% College Graduate	% Poverty	% Black	Electorate Ideology
log *Per Capita Income*	10.6 [0.2]	+0.633	−0.898	−0.644	+0.608
% College Graduate	16.7 [7.0]	•	−0.418	−0.041	−0.035
% Poverty	22.0 [6.6]	•	•	+0.807	−0.788
% Black	28.6 [22.3]	•	•	•	−0.974
Electorate Ideology	64.7 [18.4]	•	•	•	•

5 Demographic data are collected from us-places.com, alabamapossible.org and al.com. Elections results are collected from al.com and *The New York Times*.

Pearson correlation coefficients are also presented in Table 2. These indicate that the variable log *Per Capita Income* is relatively highly correlated with each of the other four regressors included in the table, and that *Electorate Ideology* is relatively highly correlated with three of the other four regressors. Additionally, two variables—% *Poverty* and % *Black*—display a strongly positive association. As such, OLS estimation of (1) above is likely to exhibit some of the negative effects (e.g., incorrectly signed regression coefficients and/or insignificant regression coefficients) of multicollinearity.

To explore the potential impact of collinearity among some of the variables, Table 3 presents OLS estimation results from three separate restricted specifications of the model in (1) above. Version (1), which includes only log *Per Capita Income*, % *Poverty*, % *Black*, and *Moore Home*, is jointly significant at the 0.01 level, while it produces an R^2 of 0.909. In this case, log *Per Capita Income* is negatively signed and significant, as expected, while both % *Poverty* and % *Black* retain negatively-signed coefficient estimates, as expected, with the latter reaching statistical significance.[6] The insignificance of at least one of these two variables, which in this case is % *Poverty*, is unsurprising given the relatively large Pearson correlation coefficient between them of +0.807. Lastly, the variable, *Moore Home*, is negatively-signed and significant, representing a departure from prior studies discussed above and summarized in Table 1. The result suggests that Moore's vote share in his home county is about 5.2 percentage points lower than that in the other Alabama counties, ceteris paribus.

Table 3. Summary of OLS results.

Regressors	(1)	(2)	(3)	(4)
constant	350.3 * (4.13)	93.61 * (23.50)	−11.32 * (−6.92)	−4.093 (−0.11)
log *Per Capita Income*	−25.04 * (−3.31)			−1.595 (−0.50)
% *College Graduate*		−0.719 * (−7.22)		−0.301 * (−3.65)
% *Poverty*	−0.215 (−0.71)	−0.213 (−1.17)		0.247 (1.77)
% *Black*	−0.908 * (−17.22)	−0.769 * (−14.57)		0.041 (0.90)
Electorate Ideology			1.025 * (42.09)	1.149 * (17.69)
Moore Home	−5.231 * (−5.80)	−5.899 * (−7.85)	−2.985 * (−5.66)	−2.765 * (−8.74)
F-statistic	155.4 *	227.7 *	718.5 *	690.6 *
R^2	0.909	0.936	0.957	0.986

Notes: The numbers in parentheses below the parameter estimates above are robust *t*-ratios (White 1980). * denotes the 0.05 level of significance.

Version (2) of Table 3 substitutes % *College Graduate* for log *Per Capita Income*.[7] Here, % *College Graduate* is negatively signed and significant, as expected, while the results for % *Poverty*, % *Black*, and *Moore Home* are similar to those found in version (1) of Table 3. The third restricted specification, which is presented in version (3) of Table 3, includes only *Constituent Ideology* and *Moore Home*, thus, creating a "political model" (versus the demographic-oriented models in version 1 and 2 of Table 3)

---

[6] The coefficient estimate attached to % *Black* suggests that a four percentage point increase in the percent of a county's population comprised of black residents leads to a 3.5 percentage point decrease, ceteris paribus, in Moore's vote share in that county.

[7] The Pearson correlation coefficient between these two variables is +0.633. This specification is jointly significant at the 0.01 level, while it produces an R^2 of 0.936.

of voting in this 2017 special election.[8] In this case, the positively-signed and statistically significant parameter estimate attached to *Constituent Ideology* suggests that Moore benefited, ceteris paribus, from the conservative preferences of the local constituency. Also, in this case, the size of the parameter estimate attached to *Moore Home* of −2.985 is about one-half of that (in absolute value) found in either version (1) or version (2).

Lastly, the results from the unrestricted specification in (1) are found in the final column of Table 3. This version is jointly significant at the 0.01 level, while it produces an R^2 of 0.985, which is quite remarkable for the cross-section data employed here. In terms of individual results, although the result for *Electorate Ideology* is similar to that in version 3, % *Poverty* and % *Black* are, unexpectedly, positively related to *Moore Vote Share*, although neither is significant. Given that the variance inflation factor (VIF) for % *Black* is slightly above 20, which is the reported threshold for a problematic degree of multicollinearity in Belsley et al. (1980), multicollinearity plays a role in producing these counterintuitive results.[9] Next, log *Per Capita Income* is negatively signed, as expected, but not statistically significant. The Pearson correlation coefficients shown in Table 2 suggest that this result is impacted to some degree by multicollinearity. Finally, the coefficient estimate for *Moore Home* is, at −2.765, similar to that found in version 3, and again runs counter to findings from prior research that are summarized in Table 1.

4.3. A Decomposition Approach

The foundational regressions above inform a decomposition of the vote share differences based on county classification (i.e., Moore home vs. other counties) into "explained" and "unexplained" portions. This approach employs a technique often used by labor economists in identifying the effect of gender or race discrimination on wages (see Kitagawa 1955; Blinder 1973; Oaxaca 1973; Oaxaca and Ransom 1999). First, the vote share for Moore in his home of Etowah County is compared to the mean of Moore's vote shares in the remaining 66 countywide election contests. In this case, Moore garnered 59.9% of the Etowah County vote, while he captured an average of 54.8% of the total from Alabama's other countywide election contests. As indicated in Table 4, the difference here of 5.1 percentage points (i.e., 59.9 minus 54.8) represents the total effect, and it is statistically significant.

Table 4. Decomposition results.

Moore Vote Share				
Home County	**Non-Home Counties**	**Total Effect**	**Endowment Effect**	**Residual Effect**
59.9	54.8	5.1 * ($p = 0.037$)	8.3	−3.2 [†]

Notes: * denotes the 0.05 level of significance. [†] denotes that the observation-specific nature of the variable, Moore Home, prevented stochastic treatment of the residual effect.

The "explained" portion of the total effect is referred to as the endowment effect. To estimate its magnitude, *Moore Vote Share$_i$* is regressed on % *College Graduate$_i$* and *Electoral Ideology$_i$* using a sub-sample of the data excluding Etowah County (i.e., Moore's home county).[10] OLS results are provided below:

$$\text{Moore Vote Share} = -3.539 - 0.443\% \text{ College Graduate} + 1.019 \text{ Electoral Ideology,} \tag{2}$$
$$(-2.56) \ (-10.01) \qquad\qquad\qquad (54.14)$$

---

[8] This specification is jointly significant at the 0.01 level, while it produces an R^2 of 0.957.
[9] Kennedy (2008) states that harmful multicollinearity is likely present for VIF greater than 10. Even this rule of thumb applies only to estimates for % *Black* and *Electorate Ideology*.
[10] This parsimonious specification is employed to avoid the incorrectly-signed estimates associated with % *Poverty* and % *Black*.

where the numbers in parentheses are *t*-ratios. This restricted specification is jointly significant and produces an R^2 of 0.984. Substituting the mean values of the regressors from the 66 counties in the sub-sample, this model predicts that Moore would have garnered an average of 54.9% of vote totals in these 66 individual countywide election contests. When mean values of the regressors from Etowah County are substituted, the model predicts that Moore would have captured 63.2% of his home county's vote had he been viewed by Etowah County's voters in a way comparable to how he was viewed by voters in the 66 sub-sample counties.

As indicated in Table 4, the difference between these two estimates, referred to as the "explained portion" or *the endowment effect*, is 8.3 percentage points (i.e., 63.2 minus 54.9), suggesting that endowment advantages accruing to Moore in Etowah County predict he should have performed 8.3 percentage points better in Etowah County than he did in the 66 remaining counties. The remaining difference represents the "unexplained" portion of the total effect and is referred to as the residual effect. In this case, Moore's performance at home exceeded his performance elsewhere by fewer percentage points (i.e., 5.1 percentage points) than would have been predicted (i.e., 8.3 percentage points) by differences in the endowments (regressors) included in (2) above. Thus, as indicated in Table 4, the residual effect in this case is −3.2 percentage points.[11]

To provide greater context for the estimate of the residual effect, Mixon et al. (2008) use the residual effect from a decomposition approach to estimate a "friends and neighbors" benefit of five percentage points. Using that study as a benchmark, and assuming the Moore-Jones contest were free of scandal, one might have expected that Moore's performance in Etowah County would have exceeded, by five percentage points, what the endowment effect would have predicted. Recalling that the endowment effect suggests that Moore would have performed 8.3 percentage points better at home than elsewhere simply as a result of the difference between his home county's endowments and those of the other counties, then, with the "friends and neighbors" bonus, one would expect Moore's performance in Etowah County to have been 13.3 percentage points better than elsewhere. Instead, Moore's actual home county vote share exceeded that of Jones by only 5.1 percentage points (i.e., the total effect). As such, the political scandal that hampered Moore's candidacy not only erased all of the expected "friends and neighbors" effect (of, perhaps, five percentage points), but it also eroded some of the benefit that should have accrued to Moore as a result of the difference between his home county's endowments and those of the other counties (i.e., the endowment effect).

The decomposition approach suggests that Moore's constituents did believe the allegations that arose during the final weeks of the election, and that they responded by switching their political support to Moore's opponent. Etowah County voters may have decided to pursue this course to prevent Moore from reaching a position, such as that of U.S. Representative, from which to cause them to suffer political harm and/or to engage in costly monitoring efforts (i.e., to be exposed to higher agency costs). This particular election involved a relatively moderate Democratic candidate in Doug Jones, which perhaps explains the intensity of the local electorate's reversal, which erased all of the friends-and-neighbors effect and a portion of the endowment effect. In cases involving scandal where the candidates' platforms exhibit more extreme bimodality (i.e., they are not as closely associated as in a state such as Alabama), complete erosion of the benefits of localism may not occur. In any case, the exploration of the impact of political scandal on friends-and-neighbors voting undertaken in this study indicates that this genre of the public choice literature is perhaps under-theorized, thus, opening up avenues for future research.

---

[11] Treating the residual effect stochastically, as is done with the total effect, requires subtracting the SSE from an OLS regression of (2) using the full sample from the SSE from an OLS regression of (2) using the full sample that also includes *Moore Home* and interaction terms involving *Moore Home* and the other two regressors, % *College Graduate* and *Electoral Ideology*. In this particular case, however, stochastic treatment of the residual effect was prevented by estimation issues associated with the observation-specific nature of *Moore Home*.

5. Concluding Comments

The 2017 U.S. Senate Special Election in Alabama—a contest between Democratic candidate, Doug Jones, a lawyer from Birmingham, and Roy Moore, the Republican candidate from Gadsden who had previously served as Chief Justice of the Alabama Supreme Court—was one of the most scandal-laden political contests in American history. During the last few months of the campaign, a number of women alleged to national media that as teenagers (as young as 14) they were subjected to sexual advances by Moore, who was then in his early 30s and working as an assistant district attorney. With only one week left in the fall 2017 campaign, the number of such accusers stood at nine, as Moore was living in a proverbial glass house while his campaign for the U.S. was unraveling.

This study addresses a void in the literature in this regard by presenting an econometric exploration of the countywide vote shares from this particular election, suggesting that the usual friends-and-neighbors, or localism, advantage that accrues to the local candidate in an election is eroded when that candidate is embroiled in political scandal. In fact, results from a decomposition approach presented in this study suggest not only that all the usual friends-and-neighbors effect is lost due to the presence of a major political scandal, but that almost one-half of the benefit of political ideology alignment that is expected to accrue to the local candidate is also eroded due to the scandal. That Jones eventually defeated Moore in the 2017 special election, even in Republican-leaning Alabama, attests to the deleterious effects of a scandal-induced erosion in friends-and-neighbors voting as a way of mitigating the agency costs faced by a constituency in a representative democracy.

Funding: This research received no external funding.

Conflicts of Interest: The author declares no conflicts of interest.

References

Andone, Dakin. 2017. Alabama to Hold Special Election to Replace Sessions in Senate. *CNN Politics*. April 21. Available online: https://www.cnn.com/2017/04/20/politics/alabama-special-election-us-senate/index.html (accessed on 29 August 2018).

Belsley, David A., Edwin Kuh, and Roy E. Welsch. 1980. *Regression Diagnostics: Identifying Influential Data and Sources of Collinearity*. New York: John Wiley & Sons.

Blinder, Alan S. 1973. Wage Discrimination: Reduced Form and Structural Estimates. *Journal of Human Resources* 8: 436–55. [CrossRef]

Blinder, Alan. 2017. Alabama Certifies Jones Win, Brushing Aside Challenge from Roy Moore. *The New York Times*, December 28.

Borchers, Callum. 2017. Bannon Beat Trump in Alabama (Kind of). *The Washington Post*, September 27.

Cason, Mike. 2016. Luther Strange Announces he is Running for Sessions' Seat. *al.com*, December 6.

Cason, Mike. 2017. Roy Moore Running for Senate, Resigns from Supreme Court to Challenge Luther Strange. *al.com*, April 26.

Disarro, Brian, Jillian Barber, and Tom W. Rice. 2007. The Home State Effect in Presidential Elections: Advances in the Study of Localism. *Presidential Studies Quarterly* 37: 558–66. [CrossRef]

Faith, Roger L., and Robert D. Tollison. 1983. Voter Search for Efficient Representation. *Research in Law and Economics* 5: 211–24.

Hrynkiw, Ivana. 2017. U.S. Rep. Mo Brooks Announces Candidacy for Senate, will Speak Across Alabama Monday. *al.com*, May 15.

Kahane, Leo H. 2009. It's the Economy, and then Some: Modeling the Presidential Vote with State Panel Data. *Public Choice* 139: 343–56. [CrossRef]

Kennedy, Peter. 2008. *A Guide to Econometrics*. Malden: Blackwell Publishing.

Key, Valdimer Orlando, and Alexander Heard. 1949. *Southern Politics in State and Nation*. Knoxville: Alfred A. Knopf.

Kitagawa, Evelyn M. 1955. Components of a Difference between Two Rates. *Journal of the American Statistical Association* 50: 1168–94.

Kjar, Scott A., and David N. Laband. 2002. On 'Home-Growness' in Politics: Evidence from the 1998 Election for Alabama's Third Congressional District. *Public Choice* 112: 143–50. [CrossRef]

Klein, Benjamin, and Keith B. Leffler. 1981. The Role of Market Forces in Assuring Contractual Performance. *Journal of Political Economy* 89: 615–41. [CrossRef]

Lewis-Beck, Michael S., and Tom W. Rice. 1983. Localism in Presidential Elections: The Home State Advantage. *American Journal of Political Science* 27: 548–56. [CrossRef]

McCrummen, Stephanie, Beth Reinhard, and Alice Crites. 2017. Woman Says Roy Moore Initiated Sexual Encounter when She was 14, He was 32. *The Washington Post*, November 9.

Mixon, Franklin G., Jr. 2000. The control of politicians within a constitutional framework: The case of state-level recall provisions. *Applied Economics* 32: 81–89. [CrossRef]

Mixon, Franklin G., Jr. 2013. Warm Springs Ran Deep: Friends-and-Neighbors Voting in the U.S. Presidential Elections of 1940 and 1944. *Journal of Politics and Law* 6: 105–15. [CrossRef]

Mixon, Franklin G., Jr., E.W. King, and M.L. Lawing. 2008. Modeling the Impact of Localism in U.S. Presidential Elections. *Journal of Public Finance and Public Choice* 26: 3–18.

Oaxaca, Ronald. 1973. Male-Female Wage Differentials in Urban Labor Markets. *International Economic Review* 14: 693–709. [CrossRef]

Oaxaca, Ronald L., and Michael R. Ransom. 1999. Identification in Detailed Wage Decompositions. *Review of Economics and Statistics* 81: 154–57. [CrossRef]

Quinn, Melissa. 2017. Roy Moore Spokeswoman: Voters must Remember there are Women who have not Accused the Judge of Any Sexual Misconduct. *Washington Examiner*, December 5.

Rice, Tom W., and Alisa A. Macht. 1987. Friends and Neighbors Voting in Statewide General Elections. *American Journal of Political Science* 31: 448–52. [CrossRef]

Sass, Tim R. 1992. Constitutional Choice in Representative Democracies. *Public Choice* 74: 405–24.

Smilowitz, Elliot. 2017. Alabama Attorney General Appointed to Sessions's Senate Seat. *The Hill*. February 9. Available online: http://thehill.com/homenews/senate/318660-ala-ag-luther-strange-appointed-to-sessionss-senate-seat (accessed on 29 August 2018).

Mixon, Franklin G., and J. Matthew Tyrone. 2004. The 'Home Grown' Presidency: Evidence on Localism in Presidential Voting, 1972–2000. *Applied Economics* 36: 1745–49. [CrossRef]

White, Halbert. 1980. A Heteroskedasticity-Consistent Covariance Matrix Estimator and a Direct Test for Heteroskedasticity. *Econometrica* 48: 817–38. [CrossRef]

MDPI

St. Alban-Anlage 66

4052 Basel

Switzerland

Tel. +41 61 683 77 34

Fax +41 61 302 89 18

www.mdpi.com

Economies Editorial Office

E-mail: economies@mdpi.com

www.mdpi.com/journal/economies

www.ingramcontent.com/pod-product-compliance
Lightning Source LLC
Chambersburg PA
CBHW051907210326
41597CB00033B/6059